STUDIES IN INTELLECTUAL HISTORY

General editor M. A. Stewart

Descartes' philosophy of science

Desmond M. Clarke

Descartes' philosophy of science

The Pennsylvania State University Press
University Park

Q
175
.C58

First published in the United States of America by
The Pennsylvania State University Press,
215 Wagner Building, University Park
Pennsylvania 16802

ISBN 0-271-00325-1

Library of Congress number 82-82082

Printed in Great Britain

To Nora

Contents

Studies in Intellectual History

This series has been inaugurated to attract some of the best new monograph work on the history of philosophy, and to redress the bias against historical scholarship in many other publishing series. It therefore fills a significant gap in current philosophy publishing.

There has been no shortage in the past of books purporting to discuss the work, or parts of the work, of individual philosophers and schools. In the English-speaking world, however, the long-standing tradition has been to assume, and sometimes explicitly to state, that the philosophical elements in their work can be studied and understood independently of the intellectual context of the works discussed. This has gone along with a complacent assumption that the way in which philosophical problems are conceived, and the methods which are available for dealing with them, have never been significantly different from what they are today, so that only the most superficial shifts in historical perspective are needed in order to engage dead philosophers in the still living debates of their successors. It is no part of the purpose of this series to stifle historical dialogue of this sort if a legitimate case can be made for conducting it; but at present, we are so far from understanding most of the authors who are accorded this treatment that it is premature to make the attempt.

For several years now, there has been a growing resistance in the literature to the narrowly combative and unhistorical study of the philosophers of the past which has been so characteristic of recent analytic philosophy. There is no historical insight to be gained from using one's sources simply for shooting practice, or from setting them up as representatives of simplified, stereotyped positions which closer reading would show them not to have held. A work of philosophy is not a timeless curiosity, but the product of a particular age, place and upbringing, and it reflects some of the interests characteristic of that environment. The important contextual links will vary according to the authors studied, but they may be philosophical or political or scientific or theological or literary; so it is of no surprise that some of the most interesting and most successful work currently being done on seventeenth- and eighteenth-century philosophy is interdisciplinary. To study works in the history of philosophy in detachment from those links is to cut them off from many of the sources both of their problems and of their concepts; the dead residue that is left, if studied in isolation, generates an inbred scholasticism which is not worth the historian's time or interest. For concepts change, and so does the meaning of recurrent phraseology, and the background of knowledge and belief that any writer assumes in his contemporaries. It can therefore be a major task to understand what an older writer's argument actually is, and understanding is the serious historian's first priority.

We are fortunate in being able to launch this series with two such excellent studies as those by Desmond Clarke on Descartes and by John Wright on Hume. The aims and achievements of both Descartes and Hume have been seriously misconceived by commentators working within an unhistorical tradition. Dr Clarke and Dr Wright have worked extensively on their respective primary sources, and been led to radical reinterpretations of their subjects which run strongly counter to prevailing orthodoxies. Some of their interpretations will no doubt be found controversial; if so, we shall look to the controversy to advance our understanding further. But what is beyond doubt is that their work resoundingly vindicates the new contextual approach to the history of philosophy, and belies the claims of those who still believe that no special preparation or training is needed to reach an accurate understanding and valid assessment of a historical text.

M. A. Stewart
December, 1981

Preface

I was first introduced to Cartesian science by reading the English translation of the *Dioptrics*, *Meteorology* and *Geometry* by Paul J. Olscamp, in a graduate course at the University of Notre Dame. There were enough issues raised by the text, despite the best efforts of the translator, to warrant a closer look at the original; and that in turn led to my attempt to suspend our standard interpretation of the *Discourse* and *Meditations* in favour of a possibly fresh approach to Descartes' science. My initial efforts were encouraged by Professor Ernan McMullin, to whom I am grateful for many helpful suggestions en route. And I was further encouraged to find that this approach to Descartes was not entirely novel; Gerd Buchdahl, among others, anticipated my strategy. I spent some time at the Department of History and Philosophy of Science in Cambridge in 1978 and Gerd Buchdahl, Mary Hesse, John Shuster and Stephen Gaukroger (perhaps unwittingly) provided the appropriate 'quantity of motion' to initiate writing this book. I also owe a word of thanks to colleagues in Paris, especially Pierre Costabel, J.-R. Armogathe, and J.-L. Marion, who facilitated my writing in numerous ways. It is certainly not a mere formality to acknowledge that none of those mentioned shares any responsibility for the negative features of the resulting interpretation of Descartes.

Some early versions of the issues discussed here were published in a variety of journals; most of this material has been significantly reworked for the present publication. However, it is appropriate to acknowledge these sources and to thank publishers and editors for permission to re-use earlier material:

the Philosophy of Science Association, for 'The ambiguous role of experience in Cartesian science', *PSA 1976*, edited by P. Asquith and R. N. Giere, pp. 151–64; the Editor of *Isis*, for 'The impact rules of Descartes' physics', *Isis*, **68** (1977), 55–66; the editor of *The Modern Schoolman*, for 'Descartes' use of "demonstration" and "deduction" ', *The Modern Schoolman*, **54** (1977), 333–44; and Franz Steiner Verlag, for 'The concept of experience in Descartes' theory of knowledge', *Studia Leibnitiana*, **8** (1976), 18–39.

Finally, I am glad to acknowledge the many improvements in the text which were suggested by the editor of Studies in Intellectual History, Dr M. A. Stewart.

A note on texts

With the exception of the *Conversation with Burman*, I have translated all Descartes quotations from the latest Adam and Tannery edition of the *Oeuvres* (Paris: Vrin, 1964–74). There were a number of reasons for this apparently quixotic procedure. Most of the scientific works and letters of Descartes were not available in English translation when I began writing; and among those which were translated, there were too many incomplete translations available to make simple references possible. Besides, in many cases my interpretation of texts would have required further changes in already published translations. So in the interests of simplifying references I have given the volume and page number only to the standard edition of Descartes. I have also adopted the changes in Descartes' correspondence which were proposed by the editors of volume V of the Adam and Tannery edition (1974). My translations of original texts are not guaranteed to be consistent, and there may be a few cases where the same Cartesian text is translated in slightly different ways.

Whenever the text is quoted in Latin or French, I have simply reproduced the text in the standard edition; and where the spelling or use of accents is not consistent, even in such words as '*expérience*', I have made no efforts to amend the original. I have quoted the *Conversation with Burman* from John Cottingham's English translation (Oxford, 1976), with minor changes in some places; I am grateful to Oxford University Press for permission to use this translation.

Desmond M. Clarke
September, 1981

Chronology of texts frequently cited

ONE

Introduction

René Descartes is, in many ways, a victim of his own success as a philosopher. He notoriously wrote a small number of readily accessible, brief, and apparently clear classics of perennial philosophical interest in which he proposed a standard of clarity and distinctness as a practicable criterion of truth in the sciences. Among these classics are the *Regulae* (1628, publ. 1701) and the *Discourse on Method* (1637). He also wrote a large volume of scientific correspondence and tentative essays in which he applied his methods to various problems inherited from tradition, or suggested by contemporaries, concerning a scientific account of nature.

It is not surprising, in retrospect, that the short classics were extensively discussed and eventually incorporated into a distinctive tradition of philosophical inquiry, and that they were considered – perhaps too hastily – to have realised the ideal of clarity and distinctness which they recommended. On the other hand, the scientific work of Descartes, although by far the major portion of his extant work, has gradually faded into the respectable, but infrequently visited, domain of the history of science. The net result of this historical development is that the philosophy of Descartes has come to be crystallised in standard solutions to the problems raised, and apparent answers provided, in his classic texts. This has given rise to major distortions in Cartesian interpretation, and in one case at least the standard interpretation is almost a caricature of the original; ironically, this is also the question to which he thought he had made his most original contribution, namely, the nature of scientific method.

In an attempt to dislodge the caricature from the history of philosophy, Jean Laporte wrote in 1945: 'if we wish to insist on characterising the philosophy of Descartes by a single name, then the description which would best fit his philosophy – without paradox – would be "empiricism", a comprehensive and radical empiricism'.[1] Laporte's bold description of Descartes as an empiricist underlined the need for a re-examination of Descartes' scientific method, and particularly of the relative functions of experiential and a priori procedures in his science. The almost canonical approach to this question has been to adopt Descartes' philosophy as a guide to what he thought he was doing in science; perhaps more narrowly, to read the *Meditations* as Descartes' major contribution to philosophical literature and to infer much of what he must have meant, or should have said if he were consistent, about scientific method from his first philosophy.[2]

The opposite approach is adopted here. I interpret the extant writings of Descartes as the output of a practising scientist who, somewhat unfortunately, wrote a few short and relatively unimportant philosophical essays. In other words, I read Descartes' scientific essays and his abundant scientific correspondence as the primary evidence of Cartesian scientific methodology, and then attempt to interpret the methodological essays, the *Regulae* and the *Discourse*, as consistently as possible with that evidence. There are a number of reasons which warrant this approach, apart from the fact that it seems sufficiently different from the standard approach to Descartes to make it worth exploring. These reasons are examined in §1 below. In the subsequent section, §2, I situate this approach and its anticipated results in the context of other interpretations of Cartesian methodology, and attempt to classify the variety of interpretations of Descartes' method in four rather rough categories. Within the scope of the categories listed, I hope to show that Descartes was both (i) reasonably consistent over time in his understanding of his own scientific method, and (ii) generally accurate in correctly reporting on the actual method he used in his scientific work.

§1   Descartes as a scientist

If Descartes' discussions with Burman can be trusted to provide an accurate indication of how he hoped readers would approach his work, then we have clear guidance in this text from the *Conversation*:

A point to note is that you should not devote so much effort to the *Meditations* and to metaphysical questions, or give them elaborate treatment in commentaries and the like. Still less should one do what some try to do, and dig more deeply into these questions than the author did: he has dealt with them quite deeply enough. It is sufficient to have grasped them once in a general way, and then to remember the conclusion. Otherwise, they draw the mind too far away from physical and observable things, and make it unfit to study them. Yet it is just these physical studies that it is most desirable for men to pursue, since they would yield abundant benefits for life. The author did follow up metaphysical questions fairly thoroughly in the *Meditations*, and established their certainty against the Sceptics and so on; so that everyone does not have to tackle the job for himself, or need to spend time and trouble meditating on these things. It is sufficient to know the first book of the *Principles*, since this includes those parts of Metaphysics which need to be known for Physics and so on. (Cottingham, pp. 30–31).

Not only should the *Meditations* be limited to a routine study; Descartes further confirms that his work in physics is of much greater value than anything else he has written:

[the author] confesses that the few thoughts that he had concerning the universe are a source of the greatest pleasure for him to look back on. He values them most highly, and would not wish to exchange them for any other thoughts he has had about any other topic. (Cottingham, p. 39).

The same demotion of metaphysics is commended, in similarly blunt language, in a letter to Elizabeth in 1643:

I can say with truth that the chief rule I have always observed in my studies, which I think has been the most useful to me in acquiring what knowledge I have, has been never to spend more than a few hours a day in the kind of thought which occupies the imagination, and only a few hours a year in thought which occupies the pure intellect. . . . I think that it is very necessary to have understood, once in a lifetime, the principles of metaphysics since it is by them that we come to the knowledge of God and of our soul. But I think also that it would be very harmful to occupy one's intellect frequently in meditating upon them, since this would impede it from devoting itself to the functions of the imagination and the senses. I think the best thing is to content oneself with keeping in one's memory and one's belief the conclusions which one has once drawn from them, and then to *devote the rest of one's study time to thoughts in which the intellect co-operates with the imagination and the senses.* (Descartes to Elizabeth, June 28, 1643: III, 692/695; my italics).

The fact that these 'guides' to study are given to two rather persistent questioners might imply that they are simply expressions of Descartes' impatience in coping with unending queries about the *Meditations.* However, they are also consistent both with Descartes' actual commitment of time to non-metaphysical studies, and with his often-repeated claim that the purpose of all his work is the construction of a pragmatically successful science.

Descartes' correspondence suggests that he devoted a considerable portion of his study time to scientific questions. It is true that he was also interested in metaphysical questions as early as 1629,[3] and that he planned to write a 'little treatise' on metaphysics that year; however, before this project was realised he interrupted his work to study anatomy, meteorology and chemistry. The metaphysical work was suspended as a result until it eventually emerged in summary in the *Discourse*, and in its final form in the *Meditations* and the *Principles*.

It is more than two months since one of my friends showed me a fairly complete description of it [a parhelion], and asked for my opinion about it. As a result I had to interrupt the work I had at hand to examine all the meteors in an orderly fashion, before I could be satisfied. However, I think I can give an explanation of it now and I have decided to write a little treatise which will contain the explanation of the colours in the rainbow . . .

I would like to begin studying anatomy . . .

I am now studying chemistry and anatomy together, and every day I learn something new which I cannot find in books.[4]

Once this kind of scientific work was initiated, the evidence of Descartes' correspondence between 1629 and 1637 suggests that he devoted almost all his time to scientific pursuits, some of which culminated in the *Optics, Geometry* and *Meteorology* of 1637. As is well known, *Le Monde* was also written during this period but was not published because of fears of Church interference following Galileo's experience on publishing his version of the heliocentric theory.[5]

Apart from the overwhelming evidence of the correspondence and the scientific essays that Descartes' primary interest was in physical science, Descartes also explicitly clarified the basic motivation for his work on a number of occasions. In a letter to Villebressieu, in 1631, he wrote:

Since mechanics is nothing other than the order which God has impressed on the face of his work (which we commonly call Nature), the author thought that it would be worthwhile to examine this great model, and to try to follow this example, rather than the rules and maxims which depend on the caprice of a few men of letters; their imaginary principles produce no fruit, for they agree neither with Nature nor with those who try to educate themselves. (I, 213–14.)

The rejection of the men of letters and their books in favour of direct observation of phenomena is reflected in the *Discourse*:

as soon as my age allowed me to relinquish the supervision of my teachers, I completely abandoned the study of letters. And, resolving not to look for any other science apart from what I could discover in myself, or indeed in the great book of the world . . . (VI, 9).[6]

At the same time, the clear objective was to subordinate scientific studies to pragmatic results:

I have decided to use the time remaining to me in life for nothing other than trying to acquire some knowledge of nature, from which one might derive some rules for medicine which would be more reliable than those we have had up to the present. (VI, 78).

A similar concern for worthwhile results in medicine emerges from a letter to the Marquis of Newcastle some years later: 'The conservation of health has always been the principal objective of my studies' (Oct. 1645: IV, 329).

If the major portion of Descartes' extant writing is concerned with scientific questions (in our current sense of the term 'science'), and if the author repeatedly enjoins his readers to consider his work in physics as his principal contribution to posterity, then it is at least not unreasonable to assume that we should read his work exactly as he proposed we ought: as a practising scientist who also concerned himself with methodological, theological and metaphysical questions. Descartes' own theory about how these various facets of his work fit together remains to be seen. What can hardly have escaped his seventeenth-century readers is that his methodological remarks and short essays were commentaries on the method he thought he followed in his scientific work. Again, a question remains as to whether or not Descartes was an accurate commentator on his own scientific method; but at least we ought to assume that he was attempting to provide such a commentary.

Even if the historical Descartes spent most of his time studying physical phenomena and regarded the results of his scientific work as his major contribution to knowledge, one still has considerable latitude in choosing a strategy for interpreting his scientific methodology. Two other factors should be mentioned at this point to support the strategy adopted here. The first of these considerations is that the portion of the *Regulae* which is extant is only about one-third of the originally planned manuscript, and that precisely that section (Book III) which was envisaged as a discussion of method in the physical sciences was never written. The *Discourse*, by contrast, was composed as an introduction to the three scientific essays of 1637,[7] and while the contingencies of its final editing suggest that it was not planned as a coherent or comprehensive discussion of scientific method, it cannot be reasonably understood as anything other than a discussion of the method Descartes thought he was using in science. Thus both essays can only be understood by reference to the method actually adopted by Descartes in his scientific work.

The other consideration which inclines towards the approach followed here is this: Descartes' two essays on method are unusually opaque. In fact, they are close to being unintelligible in isolation from the scientific work which they were intended to explicate. Thus we do not have available the luxury of constructing an independent interpretation of the methodological essays for later comparison with Cartesian science in operation.

In summary: because Descartes spent most of his time at scientific work, and thought of himself primarily as a practising scientist; because the methodological essays are almost unintelligible on their own, apart from a close reading of the scientific work they purport to clarify; and because the *Regulae* only discusses method in the physical sciences in an incidental way, while the *Discourse* is specifically a commentary on the accompanying scientific essays: it is preferable to interpret Descartes' scientific methodology as consistently as possible with the method actually adopted in his scientific work, rather than to extrapolate, from his philosophical essays, what he must have thought about scientific method. And for these reasons the consideration of the *Regulae* and the *Discourse* is left to the later sections of the book; the earlier sections attempt to explain the method used by Descartes both in his scientific essays and in his published correspondence.

§2   *Method and methodology*

It is not unusual in scientists' commentaries on the methodology of their own work that one finds a significant discrepancy between what they do in science and what they claim to do. When Newton writes in the General Scholium of the *Principia*: 'whatever is not deduced from the phenomena is to be called an hypothesis; and hypotheses, whether metaphysical or physical, whether of occult qualities or mechanical, have no place in experimental philosophy',[8] no-one takes him at his word. Whether he likes it or not, he does in fact rely on hypotheses in his physics.

One might reasonably anticipate a similar discrepancy in Descartes between the method he actually follows in science, and the method he says he has successfully followed and ought to follow in the pursuit of the truth about nature. In order to highlight the problems of interpretation which one encounters here it may be helpful to distinguish – somewhat artificially – between Descartes' scientific essays and his methodological comments on these essays. The latter include, obviously, the *Regulae* and the *Discourse*, but also many significant passages in the *Principles* and the correspondence where Descartes obliges us with some explanation of the method he claims to have adopted in physical science. This loose collection of disparate texts could be called Descartes' methodology. By contrast, Descartes also wrote abundantly on scientific topics without much reference to scientific method or the philosophical basis of his physics. One finds these texts, for example, in *Le Monde*, the *Dioptrics*, the *Meteorology*, the *Principles*, and in most of the first five volumes of the Adam and Tannery edition of the *Oeuvres*, devoted to Descartes' correspondence. For ease of reference this motley collection could be called, somewhat anachronistically, Descartes' science.

It is readily conceded that this kind of distinction is arbitrary and artificial, and that it holds the seeds of abuses in understanding Descartes' project. For Descartes moves with ease from philosophy or theology to dynamics or optics, and he mixes discussions of magnetism or blood circulation with apparently unwarranted claims about the efficacy of his scientific method. Despite these caveats it still seems at least tentatively acceptable to distinguish how Descartes actually proceeded in scientific work – i.e. the scientific work he claims to have done – from the interwoven efforts to clarify Cartesian method. Given some such distinction, the question arises as to whether Descartes' reported scientific practice corresponds to what he claims in his methodology. More specifically, to what extent is Cartesian method a priori or experimental, and to what extent does Cartesian methodology accurately reflect Descartes' scientific practice?

An extreme kind of apriorism in science would be the following. One might consider the first principles, axioms or primary postulates of a science as warranted by a purely intellectual intuition into their truth, or logically entailed by some other propositions which are so warranted; and one could consider the relation between these first principles and scientific explanations of specific phenomena as one of logical implication in such a way that the truth-value of the explanations is entirely decided, in a derivative fashion, by the intuitive warrant of the first principles. Such an understanding of scientific method, with an a priori justification of first principles and a logical deduction from them of particular explanations, will be called an 'a priori' method below.

If, on the contrary, one's scientific method leaves open the possibility of falsifying one's scientific explanations by experiential data, then such a method can be said to be 'a posteriori'. Evidently one's method can be a combination of both a priori and a posteriori elements, in the sense that one might anticipate the possibility of disconfirming experiential evidence for some hypotheses and at the same time maintain that one's basic principles are not open to experimental testing.

If one combines this distinction between a priori and a posteriori science with the distinction made above between Descartes' method and methodology, one has at least four categories in which to classify interpretations of Cartesian method. These categories reflect the claim that Descartes is either a priori or a posteriori, in both his method and methodology, or in one of these only.

The first interpretation of Cartesian method is to the effect that Descartes is predominantly a priori, both in science and in his methodological discussions of science. Thus John Randall writes:

> But he [Descartes] remained the mathematician interested in chains of proof, devoted to the Aristotelian ideal of a science like geometry that would prove why things must be as they are; and his system of physics remains independent of experience, save for incidental illustration . . .
> A mathematical physics could never be founded on trust in common experience; there must be substituted an abiding faith in reason, despite the obvious appearances of nature.[9]

The rationalist interpretation of Cartesian method has often been adopted in discussions of the *Discourse*, and in expositions of Descartes' contribution to the history of science.[10]

A somewhat more plausible reading of Descartes is to assume a discrepancy between his method and methodology, and to claim that the latter is a priori while the former is at least as a posteriori as that of any other scientist of the time. This suggests that Descartes proposed an unrealisable ideal of indubitable knowledge in science but that he falls short of this ideal in the execution of his plan to construct a comprehensive scientific account of nature.[11]

A slight variation on the previous interpretation is to consider the methodology of Descartes a priori in the sense already specified and to assume that Descartes tried to implement this view of science in, for example, the *Principles*. The first principles of physics are a priori, and this is consistent with the demands of the *Regulae* or the *Discourse*. However, once he tries to deduce the explanation of specific natural phenomena from these intuitively warranted principles the project weakens and he eventually has recourse to experientially warranted hypotheses. This amounts to claiming that Descartes' methodology is a priori, and that his scientific work is partly a priori, partly a posteriori.[12]

There are no proponents of the theory that Descartes'

methodology is a posteriori and that his actual scientific method is a priori.

The final one of the four options available is to read Descartes as if he were consistently a posteriori both in his method and in his methodology. Some commentators have gone half-way towards this position by conceding that there is a significant a posteriori dimension in both, but that this must be qualified with the strong a priori demands of the methodology and the apparently a priori or metaphysical elements in Cartesian science. The inconsistency in methodology could be located in the *Discourse* itself between Parts V and VI, or between the *Regulae* and later work, or even between the two methodological essays and his reflections on method in the *Principles*.[13] In each case one might interpret the former member of the pair as a priori and the latter as a posteriori. And corresponding to whichever methodological inconsistency one defends among those listed, Descartes may be considered to be practising two very distinct methods in science, one metaphysical and a priori, and the other experimental and hypothetical.[14]

It remains to be seen whether Descartes can be systematically read in a consistent manner by interpreting both his theory and practice of scientific method in a way which reflects a recognition on his part of the essential role of experiential procedures in the construction and testing of scientific hypotheses. This is the interpretation which is canvassed in the following pages.[15]
Some obvious qualifications of this thesis should be introduced at this early stage to offset standard objections which are familiar in Cartesian literature. The first qualification is that one cannot necessarily hope to find that Descartes is unambiguously single-minded, over a period of approximately thirty years, in openly defending the experiential character of physical science. Descartes is surely as entitled as any other author of the time to historical development in his ideas on scientific method, to lapses in consistency, and to variations in the rhetoric with which he self-assuredly propounds his insights. However even if all these qualifications are anticipated, one can still claim that there is no clear discrepancy between the scientific method actually used by Descartes and the method he claims, in his methodological

essays, to have used, and that both of these are significantly a posteriori to a degree which has not generally been acknowledged in the literature.

A second standard objection is that, as everyone knows, Descartes proposed mathematics as an ideal for physical science and that he tried to base all knowledge ultimately on the intuitive certainty of the *Cogito*. It is almost as if it is indubitably clear that Descartes hoped to deduce the whole of physics from the *Cogito* and that anyone who refuses to accept the obvious here is just playing with words. Allen Debus has summarised this aspect of the Cartesian project as follows:

> For Descartes nothing less would suffice than to discard completely all past knowledge and to begin anew, accepting as axiomatic only God and the reality of one's own existence (*Cogito, ergo sum*). The Deity for him was known through the mind – indeed, the truth of God known in this fashion was far more evident than anything seen through the eyes. From this foundation Descartes was prepared to deduce the entire universe and its laws. It was his belief that each step in this mathematically inspired method would be as certain as the proofs in Euclidean geometry.[16]

As against this deductivist account of Cartesian method I hope to argue that it is mistaken both in the general lines of the picture drawn and in the details about mathematics and deduction which are included.

One could hardly deny that the *Cogito* was a significant point in Descartes' philosophy, although it could scarcely have meant as much to him as it seems to mean to the innumerable commentators who have written philosophical explanations of its logic and of its significance for theory of knowledge. Likewise, Descartes notoriously applauds the certainty and reliability of mathematics *compared to the philosophy of the schools*, and he characteristically describes his own efforts at theory construction as a deductive project. It would be unjustifiable, however, in attempting to decipher what he meant by a 'mathematical' or 'deductive' science to transpose gratuitously on to Descartes' vocabulary the meanings which those terms have come to have in the twentieth century. Of course Descartes does claim that his scientific explanations are a priori, mathematical, deductively warranted, and based ultimately on the certainty of the *Cogito*; but it remains to be seen what he means by these claims. In other words, the author's usage of logical terms which are significant for understanding his method cannot be properly understood out of the context in which they were used. And this context includes the scientific work which these enigmatic terms were supposed to clarify.

Thus despite the apparent obviousness of the thesis that Descartes' project in science is essentially a mistaken attempt to establish physics deductively on an a priori foundation, and despite the fact that Descartes consistently describes his project as an a priori, deductive account of nature, I wish to argue that these words do not mean what they seem to mean and that Cartesian method is significantly a posteriori both in theory and in practice.

I approach this thesis by directly confronting the assumption that Descartes is fundamentally a rationalist in science and that he prefers not to rely on experiential evidence whenever he can avoid it, even in the study of physical nature. The apparent conflict between experience and reason is examined in Chapters 2 and 3. Chapter 2 is principally concerned with explicating Descartes' concept of experience, and with isolating two special connotations of the word *'expérience'* in Cartesian science, namely experiment, and ordinary experience.

Chapter 3 concentrates on a similar attempt to clarify what is meant by reason – at least in so far as it is preferentially contrasted with experience. Among the issues discussed here are: the role of innate ideas in science; Descartes' use of the word *'intuitus'* as an original concept in the *Regulae*; the role of reason in making inferences in science, and Descartes' use of such terms as *'demonstratio'*, *'deductio'*, or *'inductio'*; and finally the significance of Descartes' repeated claim that he prefers reason to experience to decide all matters of significance, even in the physical sciences. The clarification of *'expérience'* and of the function of reason in science suggests that the priority of reason over experience does not at all mean what it might otherwise seem to imply.

Chapter 4 examines the sense in which metaphysics provides a foundation for Cartesian science. Evidently, if Descartes attempts to deduce scientific explanations of physical phenomena from metaphysical axioms, then experimental work cannot be assigned a significant role in science, no matter how many references one finds to *expérience* in his writings. Here I argue that metaphysics does in fact provide a foundation for physics, in a number of senses, but that Descartes does not attempt nor claim to attempt to deduce physics logically from a metaphysical foundation.

Chapter 5 examines the Cartesian concept of scientific explanation. While the explanation of a given physical phenomenon must be a priori, that is, an explanation of an effect in terms of its efficient and material causes, it is still possible for such explanations to be framed hypothetically and confirmed a posteriori. There are metaphysical and methodological constraints on what Descartes is willing to accept as a possible explanation, for he is uncompromisingly reductionist in his intolerance of theoretical entities. The demand that explanations ultimately reduce to descriptions of contact action between small particles of matter is aligned with a significant Cartesian dependence on mechanical models as an essential component in any scientific explanation.

Even a tentative admission of hypotheses into one's account of nature unavoidably introduces problems about their confirmation and the degree of certainty one can hope to achieve in science. In Chapter 6 I argue that Descartes is exclusively concerned with certainty, rather than truth, in science; and that he assumes that the strategies he adopts for testing hypotheses are sufficient to establish them as certain, at least as 'morally certain'. The role of crucial experiments is discussed in detail with reference to Descartes' disagreement with William Harvey about the explanation of blood circulation (§19).

The discussion of the *Regulae* and the *Discourse* in Chapter 7 raises a serious question about the historical development of Descartes' ideas on method, for it looks as if the very structure of the discussion is designed to force consistency on Descartes whether it fits or not. Indeed, part of the argument to be proposed here is that Descartes did modify his ideas about scientific method. So why not put the *Regulae* and the *Discourse* discussions at the beginning where they seem to belong both chronologically and conceptually?

The main reason for this apparently cavalier attitude towards history is that already mentioned above, namely, that these two texts are unusually opaque even by Descartes' standards. What I wish to focus on here is the concept of science one finds in

Descartes' mature work. Once this has been expounded it can then be shown, without warping the texts, that the *Regulae* and *Discourse* are consistent with this interpretation. There are changes in emphasis, in style, and even in Descartes' preferred rhetoric between 1628 and, for example, 1644; but I hope to show that there is no major change from a priori deductivism to a compromise hypothetical account of science.

The method of analysis and synthesis which is proposed in the *Regulae* is examined in §21 in conjunction with the discovery of the sine law of refraction, and it is further explicated, in §22, by unravelling the structure of Descartes' discussion of the rainbow in the *Meteorology*. In §22 I distinguish between the method of discovery recommended in Part II of the *Discourse*, and the method proposed in Parts V and VI as alternative accounts of the hypothetical status of physical explanations.

Descartes is characterised, in the concluding survey, as a self-proclaimed champion of a new science who borrowed both the language and methods, and the associated confusions, of Aristotelian methodology. Certainty derived from reflection on ordinary experience is the dominant feature of Cartesian science. And in that sense Descartes is, throughout his career, consistently empiricist.

Notes

1   J. Laporte, *Le Rationalisme de Descartes*, p. 477.
2   One has only to consult Sebba's *Bibliographia Cartesiana* or the reviews of the Équipe Descartes in *Archives de philosophie* to recognise the imbalance in Descartes studies in the direction of the *Meditations*. Two recent examples in English are Margaret Wilson's *Descartes*, and Bernard Williams' *Descartes: The Project of Pure Enquiry*. Williams acknowledges the imbalance on pp. 30–1. A notable exception to this tendency is Stephen Gaukroger, ed., *Descartes: Philosophy, Mathematics and Physics*.
3   See the letters to Gibieuf, July 18, 1629 (I, 17); to Mersenne, April 15, 1630 (I, 136); to Mersenne, November 25, 1630 (I, 182) and again to Mersenne, April 20, 1637 (I, 350).

4   Descartes to Mersenne, October 8, 1629 (I, 23); Descartes to
    Mersenne, December 18, 1629 (I, 102); Descartes to Mersenne, April
    15, 1630 (I, 137).

5   Cf. Descartes' letters to Mersenne, November 1633, and February,
    1634, in which he explains his reluctance to publish the completed
    manuscript of *Le Monde* (I, 270 & 281).

6   Cf. also VI, 10: 'After having spent some years studying in this way
    in the book of the world'; and the *Regulae*, rule 5: 'That is the way all
    astrologers act who hope to be able to predict the results of heavenly
    motions without any knowledge of the heavens, and without ever
    observing their motions accurately... Likewise for those
    philosophers who neglect experience and think that the truth will
    arise from their own heads as Minerva did from that of Jupiter.'
    (X, 380).

7   It is an indication of the extent to which the *Discourse* has been taken
    out of context that Carl Boyer, in his *History of Analytic Geometry*,
    refers to the scientific essays as 'the other appendices to the *Discours
    de la Méthode*' (p. 95). In the standard edition of Descartes' works, the
    Discourse is 78 pages in length, while the so-called 'appendices'
    number 539 pages!

8   I. Newton, *Philosophiae Naturalis Principia Mathematica*, 3rd ed.,
    p. 530.

9   John Herman Randall, Jr, *The Career of Philosophy*, Vol. I, pp. 384,
    385. Cf. G. Rodis-Lewis, *Descartes et le rationalisme*, p. 15.

10 See for example Peter A. Schouls, 'Reason, method, and science in
    the philosophy of Descartes', *Australasian Journal of Philosophy*, **50**
    (1972), 30–9; Louis Chauvois, *Descartes: sa méthode et ses erreurs en
    physiologie*.

11 This interpretation is proposed by the following: P. Tannery,
    'Descartes physicien', *Revue de métaphysique et de morale*, **4** (1896),
    478–88; G. Milhaud, *Descartes savant*; Hyman Stock, *The Method of
    Descartes in the Natural Sciences*; Pierre Duhem, *The Aim and Structure
    of Physical Sciences*, trans. from 2nd edn by Philip P. Wiener, pp.
    43–46; Leon Roth, *Descartes' Discourse on Method*.

12 See for example, A. I. Sabra, *Theories of Light from Descartes to Newton*,
    pp. 17–45; J.-L. Allard, *Le Mathématisme de Descartes*, pp. 179-83; L. J.
    Beck, *The Method of Descartes: A Study of the Regulae*.

13 Proponents of this interpretation include Ernan McMullin,
    'Empiricism and the scientific revolution', in *Art, Science and History
    in the Renaissance*, ed. Charles S. Singleton, p. 351; J. Segond, *La
    Sagesse cartésienne et la doctrine de la science*, pp. 198–216; Izydora
    Dambska, 'Sur certains principes méthodologiques dans les
    "Principia Philosophiae" de Descartes', *Revue de métaphysique et de
    morale*, **62** (1957), 57–66; N. Kemp Smith, *New Studies in the
    Philosophy of Descartes*, pp. 51, 96-7.

14 The a priori part of Descartes' science, in this interpretation, consists
    in the more general and theoretical claims concerning the nature of
    matter and motion. E. McMullin puts it this way: 'It [i.e., Descartes'

philosophy of nature in the *Principles*] derives its warrant from its metaphysical starting point rather than from any specific appeal to experiment or even to everyday experiential concepts.' *New Scholasticism*, **43** (1969), p. 44.

15 This has already been proposed by a number of authors in studies of specific Cartesian essays, or in studies devoted to particular scientific questions. For example, Alan Gewirtz formulates his position in this way, in a study almost exclusively devoted to the *Regulae*: 'this paper will attempt to show that the view which finds a divorce between Descartes' practice and his doctrine of method, on the ground of the latter's exclusively mathematical and non-empirical character, is . . . invalid.' (A. Gewirtz, 'Experience and the non-mathematical in the Cartesian method', *Journal of the History of Ideas*, **2** (1941), 184.) With some qualification, H. Mougin, Gerd Buchdahl and E. Denissoff have proposed a similar interpretation of Descartes' science: H. Mougin, 'L'Esprit encyclopédique et la tradition philosophique française', *Pensée*, **5** (1945), 8–18, **6** (1946), 25–38 and **7** (1946), 65–74; Gerd Buchdahl, *Metaphysics and the Philosophy of Science*, pp. 78–180; Élie Denissoff, *Descartes: premier théoricien de la physique mathématique*; Ralph M. Blake, 'The role of experience in Descartes' theory of method,' in *Theories of Scientific Method*, ed. Edward Madden, pp. 75–103; J.-P. Weber, 'Sur une certaine "méthodologie officieuse" chez Descartes', *Revue de métaphysique et de morale*, **63** (1958), 246–50; Laurens Laudan, "The clock metaphor and probabilism', *Annals of Science*, **22** (1966), 73–104.

16 Allen G. Debus, *Man and Nature in the Renaissance*, p. 106.

TWO

Experience in Cartesian science

Descartes has consistently communicated the impression to his readers that he undervalues the significance of empirical evidence in science and that he is anxious to substitute 'rational arguments' in place of empirical research. This impression is not peculiar to contemporary readers; many of Descartes' contemporaries read his work in a similar way and some of them objected to his scientific method on precisely these grounds. Descartes however took exception to such criticism – as he did to most other criticism also. Surprisingly his defence in this case was not that his critics were mistaken about the importance of experience in science; instead, he agrees with their methodological suggestions about the role of experience but claims that they have seriously misunderstood his work. Thus, in reply to an unknown critic who charged him with a lack of experiential evidence in his science, Descartes replied:

What I find most strange is the conclusion of the critique you sent me, namely that what will prevent my principles from being accepted in the schools is that they are not sufficiently confirmed by *expérience*, and that I have not refuted the explanations of others. For I am surprised that, even though I have demonstrated, in particular, almost as many *expériences* as there are lines in my writings, and having explained in general in my *Principles* all the phenomena of nature I have explained by the same means all the *expériences* which could be done in respect of inanimate bodies, while by contrast none of these things has been properly explained by the commonly accepted philosophy; despite that, those who follow the accepted philosophy go on to accuse me of a lack of *expériences*. (IV, 224–5).

Those who are familiar with his scientific essays and

correspondence can at least sympathise with Descartes' almost peevish reply; there are, indeed, almost as many references to various kinds of *expérience* as there are lines in his writing.

On the other hand, Descartes' readers can be excused for taking the interpretation of his work which they normally adopt; he almost provocatively proclaims his thesis that we can know physical objects only through the agency of the intellect, and not by sense or imagination (see VII, 34). Besides, there is a whole cluster of apparently rationalist theses which provide the context in which the frequent references to experience occur. For example, sense-knowledge is said to be often unreliable; knowledge of any kind is established by a classical foundationalist strategy on innate ideas; physics is deduced from metaphysics; and so on. And where empirical evidence seems to run counter to Cartesian scientific convictions, the author is not slow to reject the former in a way which suggests that we should put our trust in reason rather than experience. For example, he wrote to Mersenne (February 9, 1639) that he was amused at an opponent's efforts to disconfirm the law of refraction by experiments because such efforts were hardly better than attempting 'to show, with a poorly constructed set-square, that the three angles of a triangle are not equal to two right angles' (II, 497). A more notorious example of a similar defence is when Descartes acknowledges that the impact rules of Part II of the *Principles* seem to contradict our experience of colliding bodies. His characteristic response to this problem is: 'the proofs of all the above [rules] are so certain that even if experience seemed to indicate the contrary, we would be obliged nevertheless to put more trust in our reason than in our senses' (IX-2, 93).

These contrasting reactions to critics of his use of experience at least indicate that Descartes' views on the relative significance of reason and experience in scientific knowledge are not clear. And the ambiguity involved here is at least partly a function of the ambiguity of the concepts 'experience' and 'reason' which are used both by critics in opposition and by Descartes in his own defence. In an effort to resolve this particular feature of Cartesian methodology, one needs to examine both of these concepts in turn, together with their usual Cartesian synonyms. The concept of experience is examined in this chapter, and the concept of reason is taken up in detail in Chapter 3. At the conclusion of

Chapter 3 various kinds of experience/reason conflict are examined in the light of the preceding discussion.

§3   *The term* 'expérience'

Descartes' concept of experience is not univocal, nor does he normally reserve any special term to discriminate between scientific experiments and any other empirical procedures which might be more generally classified as an experience. Instead he uses the word *'expérience'* in French and *'experientia'* or *'experimentum'* in Latin, and their corresponding verb forms *'expérimenter'* and *'experiri'*, in as many senses as we ordinarily use the words 'experience' or 'to experience' in English.[1] In a few cases he also uses *'épreuve'* (and *'éprouver'*) and *'sentiment'* (and *'sentir'*) with almost the same ambiguity of meaning as *'expérience'*. The Cartesian repertoire does not, however, include the word *'expériment'*.[2] Thus in the absence of clear linguistic distinctions, one must rely very much on the context to decide what Descartes means, in specific cases, by his use of *'expérience'* or its apparent synonyms. In the following pages I distinguish a number of clearly definable uses of the term *'expérience'*; those which are most relevant for Descartes' scientific methodology are taken up again for further clarification in §5. And to facilitate this conceptual analysis there is a brief discussion of the Cartesian theory of the subject of experience in §4.

In a variety of contexts Descartes refers to acts of awareness or consciousness of our own mental activity as *'expériences'*. For example, we experience acts of the will as being caused directly by ourselves: 'we experience the fact that they come directly from our soul' (XI, 342). We are equally conscious, in the case of ideas which do not derive from our wills, that they are not under our personal control.[3] Likewise we experience the freedom of the will to withhold assent to whatever is not clearly and distinctly perceived: 'for we experienced (*experiebamur*) the fact that we were free to refrain from believing anything which was not certain and understood clearly' (VIII-1, 20).[4]

Besides acts of the will, we are also aware of our own thinking. This kind of intellectual awareness likewise comes under the rubric of Cartesian experience. 'The mind, reflecting on itself, can experience the fact that it thinks' (VII, 358).[5] Since experience, in this sense, is an activity of the natural light of reason we can even experience the validity of an inference from *cogito* to *sum* (VII, 140). The French translation of this instance of Cartesian usage makes the experiential connotations of the original even more evident: 'il sent en lui-meme qu'il ne se peut pas faire qu'il pense, s'il n'existe' (XI-I, 110–11). 'Experience' as the introspection of the contents or operations of one's own mind naturally extends to the experience of innate ideas, such as the idea of the infinite (VII, 365), or the ideas of doubt, thought, etc. (X, 524).[6]

Not surprisingly, the term *'expérience'* is often used to refer to sensory experiences such as the sensation of pain or the intensity of a colour. Thus Descartes claims in the *Meteorology* that we only sense two variables in light – its intensity and its colour – and that these ought to be explained by the two variable motions of the particles of light. 'And as there can be no variation in these movements apart from the one I mentioned, so likewise we find no variation in experience, in our sensations (*sentimens*) of these movements other than that of colour' (VI, 334). The introduction of *'sentiment'* here matches the use of *'sentir'* in corresponding texts, such as the *Description of the Human Body*: 'One can hardly doubt that there is heat in the heart, for one can even feel it (*sentir*) with one's hand' (XI, 228).[7] The sensation of muscular action in the eyes which occurs in changing focus from distant to near objects is similarly known by experience (*Dioptrics*, VI, 108).

This kind of *expérience des sens* (IX-2, 5) is also said to be a form of thinking. In the Sixth Meditation Descartes reviews his work and wonders 'if, from the ideas I receive from this mode of thinking which I call sense (*isto cogitandi modo, quem sensum appello*), I could construct an indubitable proof of the existence of corporeal things' (VII, 74). While this may look like an inadvertent collapse of the distinction between thinking and sensing, it is quite consistent with other texts where Descartes classifies sensation among the varieties of thought (VII, 28), and describes feelings as 'confused ways of thinking' (VII, 81). Accordingly, even if it is false that I hear or feel heat,

it is certain that I seem to see and hear and feel warm. It cannot be false that this is the case; and this, properly speaking, is what is called sensation (*sentire*). Taken precisely in this way, sensing is nothing other than thinking.[8] (VII, 29).

The distinction between thinking and sensing is taken up again in §5.

Another Cartesian use of *'expérience'* corresponds to the non-specialist's use of the word 'test' in English.[9] What is characteristic about this sense of *'expérience'* is that it does not involve any reference to a scientific theory nor does it imply any of the careful control and concern for quantitative results that would be required in a scientific experiment. Rather, this kind of test is appropriate to describing the spontaneous reaction of a small child 'testing' his dinner to see if he likes the taste of it, or to testing a technique to see if it works. There is a clear example of this usage in the *Geometry* where the author invites his readers to check his proposals about signs by reference to experience (VI, 422). A similarly non-scientific example of testing is invoked in the Preface to the *Principles* where Descartes invites readers to test his claim that scientific explanations are deduced from first principles. The test in question consists in reading the book (IX-2, 11). And in three places in the *Dioptrics* the author recommends trial and error testing as the best way of combining appropriate lenses to produce a microscope (VI, 202, 209, 225), for in matters of technical expertise 'l'experience enseignera mieux que mes raisons' (VI, 202).[10]

We infrequently use the term 'experience' in English to refer to the act of observing an object or event when the observation can be used as a source of knowledge. Descartes occasionally uses the word *'observation'* in French or *'observatio'* in Latin to indicate this sense; more often, however, he uses the more general term *'expérience'* to refer to instances of unproblematic observations of physical phenomena which might be explained by his corpuscular theory or which might be used to confirm or disconfirm hypotheses. Thus he refers to astronomical observations (*observationes astronomicae*), and to the observation of the behaviour of magnets (*observations de l'aimant*).[11] Experience, in the sense of observation, shows that heavy bodies descend towards the centre of the earth (IX-2, 8); that we encounter rainbows in many different types of situation, including the spray from fountains (VI, 325); that the dilation of the heart is sufficient to explain the observed results in the movement of the heart and the condition of the blood (XI, 244). In one unusual case the word *'expérimenter'* is used in reference to observing the movement of heavy spheres in a rotating machine (XI, 18).

By contrast with all the previous uses of *'expérience'*, each of which involved a subject who undergoes the experiential event which is attributed to him, Descartes also uses the term to refer to the objective phenomena which scientific theories are designed to explain. This is especially clear when he writes of seeing an experience: 'i'en ay vû cet este dernier une experience fort manifeste' (VI, 351). In this case the experience was the corona about a lighted candle. The use of *'expérience'* to mean 'phenomenon' is underlined by the interchangeability of the two words both within a given text and between Latin and French versions of the same text. For example, Part III, article iv of the *Principles* has this title: 'De phaenomenis, sive experimentis; et quis eorum usus ad philosophandum' (VIII-1, 81). [12] Where the Latin version has *'phaenomenis'* on page 86 the corresponding French is *'l'expérience'* (IX-2, 110). One even finds cases where both the context and the translation suggest that *'expérience'* means something like objective phenomena, as when Descartes claims that his hypotheses agree with all the facts to be explained: 'cum omnibus naturae phaenomenis . . . consentiant' and 'cum experimentis consentiant' (VIII-1, 99). The French equivalent has: 's'accorde exactement avec toutes les experiences' and 'sont entierement conformes aux experiences' (IX-2, 123). [13]

Apart from the distinctions already indicated, two other nuances of Cartesian usage need to be introduced at this stage; both of these will later be found to have significant implications for one's understanding of Cartesian methodology. Relative to the distinctions already mentioned they can be understood as finer specifications of experience in the sense of observation; considering their significance for Descartes' science, they merit independent names. The first of these sub-categories of observation will be called 'ordinary experience'; while the second is normally called an experiment.

The principal linguistic indicators of 'ordinary experience' are the phrases *'experientia quotidiana'* (VIII-1, 63) and *'expérience vulgaire'* (III, 10, 34). [14] For example, Descartes appeals to ordinary experience to confirm the first law of nature in the *Principles* by observing what happens when one throws a stone up into the air. Another example of a simple fact known by experience to the untutored and unsophisticated man on the street is that we have the ability to learn new words in whatever language we already speak.[15] This kind of pre-theoretical experience is common to all men, 'experientia omnibus hominibus communi[s]' (VII, 580).

Accordingly, Picot distinguishes ordinary experience from experiments, in the introduction to the *Passions of the Soul*:

these experiences are of two kinds: one of them is easy and only presupposes that we reflect on those things which are spontaneously presented to our senses. The other kind of experience is more infrequent and more difficult, and cannot be had without some study and expense. (XI, 319).

In almost the same words Descartes commends the appropriateness of ordinary experience as a foundation for physical science. 'At the beginning it is better to use only those experiences which present themselves to the senses, and which we cannot be unaware of provided that we reflect even the slightest on them' (*Discourse*, VI, 63). By contrast with such readily available and simple experiences, progress in scientific theories demands that one rely on other observations which are such that 'the circumstances on which they depend are nearly always so special and so detailed that it is very difficult to notice them' (VI, 63).[16]

Those observations which were not common to all untutored observers of nature but which required skill and scientific knowledge to make are evidently experiments. Apart from infrequent references to '*expériences particulières*' Descartes does not reserve any special term for scientific experiments.[17] The context, however, makes it very clear in a great number of cases that '*expérience*' does refer to experiments, in the precise sense of an artificially arranged or contrived observation which is designed to test some implication of one's scientific theory. Descartes refers on many occasions to Mersenne's experiments on the flow of water through tubes, and in most cases the phrase used is '*faire une expérience*'.[18] Likewise he writes to Debeaune thanking him for making an exact measure of angles of refraction;[19] Descartes himself plans to do some 'fairly exact experiments' on metal.[20] The experimental character of some experiences is equally clear when he writes about experiments which are so easy to do that it is almost impossible to do them poorly;[21] or of experiments which are so '*belles*' that he includes a description of how to set them up;[22] or when they are so complicated that, as in the case of weighing air, there are many ways in which the experiment can go wrong and provide untrustworthy results.[23] Not surprisingly, the need for financial assistance to pay for experimental work is a constant theme of his correspondence. Thus he writes to Mersenne that he would 'need more money than the King of China if I were to undertake all the experiments which might be useful for discovering the truth' (III, 590).[24]

The variety of ways in which Descartes uses the term *'expérience'* or its synonyms and the ease with which he changes from one usage to another constitute a seductive trap for the translator or interpreter of his work. On the one hand, there is nothing surprising here for those who speak English, because the richness of Cartesian experience is reflected in a corresponding ambiguity in the English term 'experience'; however, the Cartesian concept is immersed in a context which, at least on first reading, provides ample opportunity for contrasting the reliability of experience vis-à-vis reason. The result of this contrast is that one tends to think that one knows what is meant by *'expérience'* – it is what the empiricists defended against the Cartesians!

The indications provided by Descartes' own word usage do not support this interpretation. For *'expérience'* can mean, among other things: intellectual awareness, test, observation, experiment, phenomenon, and ordinary experience. Presumably Descartes evaluates the cognitive value of these experiences in different ways, and the kind of evaluation he is likely to endorse is partly a function of his scientific theory of the subject of human experience.

§4   *The Cartesian subject of experience*

It is a well known feature of Descartes' philosophy that he adopted a dualist theory of mind and body and that the theory raised many more questions than it could have hoped to answer both for his readers and for his correspondents. There is enough evidence in the failure to develop the theory in detail and in his apparently conflicting versions of it to suggest that Descartes' discussion of dualism, or at least the substance language in which it was expressed, was an unfortunate incursion into the categories of classical Aristotelianism from which he could hardly have hoped to emerge unscathed.

However its merits are appraised, Descartes seems to have been fairly clear that dualism was a *theory*; i.e. that it was some kind of metaphysical construction designed to explain what were accepted, by its proponents, as facts to be explained. The knowledge of these facts to be explained is therefore logically prior to the theory devised to explain them. And if the theory turns out to be rather questionable or downright unintelligible, it remains that we still have the 'facts' which mistakenly justified its introduction in the first place. In reply to queries from readers Descartes adopted roughly this strategy: to defend, qualify and try to explain dualism, but at the same time to acknowledge that it is merely an hypothesis.[25]

Thus he argues, in the Sixth Meditation, that 'my essence consists in this alone, that I am a thinking thing' (VII, 78). The Preface to the *Meditations* clarifies the implications of the 'alone'; the author at least acknowledged that he needed an argument for his position:

what I meant was that I did not know clearly that anything belonged to my essence except that I was a thinking thing, or a being who had the faculty of thinking. But I will show in what follows how, from the fact that I do not know that anything else belongs to my essence, it follows that nothing else in fact does belong to it. (VII, 8).

The way in which Descartes shores up the argument in the Sixth Meditation – by showing that his clear and distinct perception of the nature of the soul is an adequate basis for objective claims about it – remains problematic.[26] For it remains unclear how one can argue from the fact that one has a clear and distinct idea of one's soul as complete and distinct from the body to the conclusion that it must be so in fact.[27]

Given the assumed substantial independence of the soul vis-à-vis the body, Descartes can hardly hope to re-establish anything more than a very problematic and accidental conjunction of mind and body in his discussion of the unity of man. The cluster of concepts which he had at his disposal to describe the metaphysical nature of man – immortal soul, substance, substantial form, essence, accidental or substantial unity – could not have resulted in any other outcome. This point seems to have been conceded, implicitly, in reply to queries from

Elizabeth. When pressed for clarification of the mind–body theory, Descartes claimed that he relied on three fundamental concepts which are so distinct that he can make no more progress in explanation than he had already made.

I consider that we have certain basic notions in us which are like the originals on the model of which we form all our other knowledge. There are only a very few such notions . . . As regards body in particular, we have only the notion of extension . . . and as regards the soul as such we have only the notion of thought . . . Finally, as regards soul and body together, we have only the notion of their union (III, 665).[28]

Descartes adds further that since these notions are basic (*primitives*), it would be folly to try to explain one concept in terms of another or to attempt to explain some phenomenon by reference to an inappropriate basic concept. This explanation seemed understandably inadequate to his correspondent who requested further enlightenment. In response Descartes claims that it is impossible to conceive of the union and distinction of mind and body at the same time:

It does not seem to me that the human mind is capable of conceiving distinctly and simultaneously the distinction and the union between body and soul, because to do so it is necessary to think of them as a single thing and at the same time to think of them as two distinct things; and this is absurd.[29]

This amounts to a candid admission that the traditional conceptual scheme within which Descartes was attempting to explain human experience is incoherent. It is interesting that Descartes' response to this kind of incoherence is to underline the theoretical character of the mind–body dichotomy and to revert to the incontrovertible facts of experience. In the *Conversation with Burman* the following question and reply are found:

How can the soul be affected by the body and vice versa, when their natures are completely different?
(R) This is very difficult to explain; but in this matter our experience is sufficient (*sufficit hic experientia*) since it is so clear on this point that it cannot be denied in any way; this is evident in the case of feelings, etc. (Cottingham, p. 28; adapted).

This reflects his earlier reply to Elizabeth, that 'those things which pertain to the union of soul and body are known only obscurely by the understanding alone or even by the intellect in conjunction with the imagination, but they can be known very clearly by the senses' (III, 691–2).[30]

In other words, even if the mind–body theory is defective or if it fails to explain matters as it should,[31] it remains certain that we have an indubitable experience of feeling pains, etc., which, for a dualist at least, can only be explained by mind–body interaction. If our indubitable experience of the unity of man fails to fit easily on to our theories, this is certainly no reason for doubting our experience. For the data of experience, in this instance, are more certain than the theoretical and somewhat incoherent explanation of the data which we rationally accept. In a somewhat similar context Descartes faced this problem of a lack of fit between theory and facts. The experience of free will seemed to conflict with his theory of God's conservation of man in existence and, by implication, of God's concurrence in man's free actions, including those which are morally evil. Descartes' response to this problem was, characteristically, that it would be absurd to doubt the clearly established facts of our experience because of theoretical difficulties in our explanation of these facts: 'It would be absurd to doubt something which we subjectively understand (*intime comprehendimus*) and which we experience in ourselves, because we do not understand something else which we know from its very nature to be incomprehensible' (VIII, 20). While the unity of mind and body is evidently not as incomprehensible as God's nature is, it is acknowledged to be sufficiently problematic to justify doubting the dualist theory rather than the unity of our experience if the two cannot be reconciled.

In the co-operation of mind and body towards the production of experience, each member of the pair has an indispensable function to perform. Descartes' understanding of mental acts will be taken up in the next chapter; for the present it will be enough to summarise his reasonably familiar mechanical theory of how information is transmitted to and processed by the brain in conjunction with our sense organs. The most explicit discussion of this topic is found in the *Dioptrics*, in the fourth and sixth discourses.

Sensation involves at least three distinguishable stages:

(*a*) A necessary condition for any sensation of a physical object is that there be some physical contact between the object in question or some emanation from the object, and the appropriate sensory organ of the human perceiver.

(b) The effect of this physical contact on the sensory organs is transmitted through the nervous system to the brain, and there is some kind of structural isomorphism between the effect on the perceiver's brain and the initial effect of the perceived object on the sensory organs. This should not be understood to imply that the brain-pattern is an image or picture of the external object or event – that suggestion is rejected by Descartes on a number of occasions.[32] The brain patterns are combined in the *sensus communis* and, in so far as they are representative of objects, events etc. outside the mind, they may even be called ideas. 'Light, sounds, odours, heat and all the other qualities of external objects can impress ideas on it [i.e. the brain] through the intermediary of the senses; the place where these ideas are received should be taken to be the common sense' (VI, 55).[33]

(c) The inexplicable unity of mind and body results in the appropriate brain activity causing the mind to have an idea or intellectual representation which corresponds to the condition of the brain triggered by the sensory organs. It is only at this stage of an act of awareness occurring in the mind that the subject of perception can, for the first time, be said to perceive anything. 'It is already agreed that it is the soul which senses (*qui sent*), and not the body' (VI, 109).[34]

Besides sensation, the 'bodily' dimension of man's nature influences both imagination and corporeal memory, both of which are functions of the brain.[35] The imagination is that part of the brain which performs the following functions:

(a) it can receive impressions from the common sense as the information centre of the brain, and from these impressions it can construct images of the objects which caused these impressions.

(b) It can function as the locus of creative imagination when the intellect – or rather, the human subject through the agency of his intellect – freely constructs new images from previously received ones. Adopting Descartes' own language, these images in the brain could be called constructed ideas.

(c) Finally, the imagination is the centre for triggering motor activity which results from either of the two kinds of image already mentioned. For this purpose the imagination is connected, through the nerves, to the various motor activating centres of the human body.[36]

Memory is also a function of the brain to the extent that the recall of prior conscious states depends on vestiges of the corresponding brain states being preserved in the brain. 'For the recollection of thoughts which the mind had during the time it was joined with the body, it is necessary that some traces of these thoughts be impressed in the brain; the mind then recalls these thoughts by turning towards or applying itself to these traces' (VII, 357). The *Conversation with Burman* qualifies this theory of memory, in the sense that Descartes distinguishes between the recall of universals which is a function of the intellectual memory, and the recall of particulars which is a function of corporeal memory.

The scientific theory of sensation, memory and imagination which is associated with the metaphysical theory of mind and body is on a par, as an hypothesis, with any other Cartesian hypothesis. A more precise estimate of how hypothetical he regards his scientific work remains to be developed in detail. If it can be assumed in the meantime that he does acknowledge its hypothetical character, then both his dualist theory and the scientific explanation of the cognitive functions of the body are hypothetical. What he adamantly refuses to classify as an hypothesis are the data of immediate sensory experience which imply a unity in man's nature that is not appropriately conceptualised in terms of the concepts of body or mind as distinct substances. Hence Descartes introduces a third basic concept, namely the concept of the union of body and mind, which is just as fundamental as either of the pair, 'mind' and 'body'.

For this reason it is a mistake to establish the mind and body as individual substances as the first tenet of Descartes' philosophy of man and to suggest, by implication, that he cannot possibly have a coherent theory of sensory experience. For he seems to be quite prepared to concede that the metaphysical theory is indeed incoherent, but that he cannot unfortunately think of a better alternative. Hence the assumed incoherence of Cartesian dualism is no argument against Descartes' admission of precisely those facts of experience which the theory was designed to explain, namely, our consciousness of sensory experiences.[37] It follows that Descartes is not necessarily committed to any implications of his dualist theory which would preclude the possibility of those experiences which his theory was meant to explain. More specifically, Descartes' theory of man's nature is no argument against the reliability or otherwise of sensory experience. If sensory experience is thought to be suspect, on occasion, then independent evidence must be introduced to support that thesis; and reason can evidently be invoked to decide when sensory experience may or may not be trusted.

This does not amount to claiming that Descartes fully appreciated the kinds of epistemological difficulties which were implicit in his version of dualism. He was rather closer to the scholastic tradition, and to recent neo-scholasticism, in maintaining both dualism and the thesis that 'there is nothing in the intellect which is not first in the senses'. When pressed for an explanation of how sensory experience can be converted to mental awareness, Descartes had nothing to offer. And it was only when he was pressed in this way that he realised more clearly how little he had to offer and how theoretical dualism was. Consequently, one cannot interpret the Cartesian estimate of the value of empirical evidence by first positing dualism and then working out its implications for a theory of knowledge. Descartes approached the question differently. He claimed: (i) that there are some facts of our experience which are indubitable evidence for believing in the unity of man's nature; and (ii) that dualism was an acceptable metaphysical and scientific theory of how these experiences arise. Once he acknowledges the incoherence of maintaining both dualism and the unity of man – even if only under pressure from correspondents – we are free to interpret his endorsement of experiential knowledge and his acceptance of empirical evidence in science at the expense of dualism, if necessary. For the experiential data of our own consciousness are both logically and epistemologically prior, for Descartes, to the theory which is proposed to explain them.

§5   *Experiments and ordinary experience*

As is clear from §3 above, Descartes refers to such disparate conditions of the subject as feeling pain, thinking about feeling pain, observing a thunderstorm or doing a scientific experiment as *'expériences'*. Among the variety of experiences to which he appeals two in particular are very significant for his scientific methodology: ordinary experience and scientific experiments. Since both of these are special cases of the wider category of observation, Descartes' concept of observation requires some analysis before attempting to clarify what is meant by 'ordinary experience' or 'experiment'.

Descartes distinguishes three levels or degrees of sensory experience. The physical interaction of the environment with a sensory subject, although not in any sense a conscious event, is the first level of sensation. However, when the human subject becomes aware of this purely physical and passively received stimulation as a result of the mind–body unity,[38] then the second level of sensory experience is reached. This is what Descartes refers to as a sensation; it is the condition of a subject who is at least non-reflectively conscious of feeling warm, or of seeing a colour, etc., and it might be described by someone else in the phrase: 'he is aware of red' or 'he has the experience of warmth'. A third level of experience is achieved when a subject, making inferences from present sensations of colour, magnitude, etc. and using his previous experience of judgments made in similar situations, reaches the point of having an idea of some extra-mental object. The condition of the subject of experience, at this stage, could be described by saying: 'he is thinking of a house' or 'he is observing the pendulum'.

Descartes reflects this tri-level distinction of sensory experience when he discusses the degrees of certainty which are appropriate to sensation, in the Sixth Replies to Objections:

In order to gauge correctly the degree of certainty of the senses we must distinguish three degrees, so to speak, of sensation. To the first pertains only that level of sensation by which the bodily organ is immediately affected by external objects, and this can be nothing more than the motion of the parts of that organ and the change of shape and position which results from that motion. The second level includes whatever immediately results in the mind from its union with the corporeal organ thus affected, and such are perceptions of sorrow, of pleasure, of thirst, . . . which are said, in the sixth Meditation, to arise from the union and virtual merging of the mind and body. The third level finally contains all those judgments which, on the occasion of movements of a corporeal organ, we have been accustomed to make from our early years about external objects. (VII, 436–7).

This text unfortunately confuses the issue by equating the third level of perception with perceptual judgments. However, if we distinguish between the experience or actual condition of a subject of experience, and the reports of his experience that such a subject is likely to make, we can throw some light on Descartes' concept of sensation and on the related concept of clear and distinct ideas.

If a person has a sensation of blue, he could have this sensation without adverting to the fact at all and he would still be said to have an experience of blue. If he is reflectively aware of his sensation he can use an intuition into his own mental state to report his experience. The report itself is a judgment, which might take this form: 'I seem to see something blue'. Since the only evidence which is relevant to the truth of this judgment is the person's own awareness of his mental state, and since Descartes never seriously doubts the capacity of intuition to provide indubitable evidence, we find such claims endorsed in the Second Meditation before he has 'proved' the existence of God and thereby validated the use of the senses as a means of acquiring knowledge of the external world. For example he writes: 'But I certainly seem to see, to hear, to feel heat. This cannot be false; this is what is properly meant by having a sensation (*sentire*). But understood in this precise sense, this is nothing other than thinking' (VII, 29).

The actual sensation of something cannot be false since no judgment is involved.[39] The reporting of one's sensation at the time of having these experiences is a judgment, however, and could be false. Reporting one's sensations involves remembering previous instances of similar sensations and correctly associating the new sensation with the word which is appropriate to the class of sensations to which it belongs. Descartes' claim is that it is possible to be certain about the intuitions of our own mental states which provide the evidence for these reports. This is a slip on his part, because he ignores the possibility that we may fail to identify a sensation correctly and misclassify it through a defect of memory, or we may report a sensation incorrectly because of a linguistic mistake.

When the Cartesian has sensations he has made little progress towards the interpretation of the data which are provided by his sensory organs. He can be said to have sensations of colour, of pain, of heat, etc., and this involves having ideas or being conscious in ways which are appropriate to the physical condition of his body at the time of having such sensations. It should be obvious that the subject of a sensation does not reflectively interpret the condition of his body nor is it necessary for him to work at initiating the appropriate mental counterpart of his physical condition. The mind and body are so united that the subject of sensations is automatically aware of thirst, of pain, etc. once his senses are stimulated in certain ways.

Observation is a further level of interpretation of the data of perceptual experience. Besides giving an objective reference to the source of one's experience, observation involves an implicit reliance on previous experience. In observing any object we synthesise a series of distinct sensations and interpret their origin on the basis of previous experience. This presupposes the distinction of subject and object, and assumes that we have enough concepts at our disposal to categorise the object of our observation. One cannot properly be said to observe a house without at least enough conceptual sophistication to distinguish, among the possible objects of one's perception, between houses and elephants. Thus, the condition of the Cartesian subject of experience (in the sense of 'observation') could be described by saying: 'he is observing a house' or 'he is observing a tree with fading leaves'.

From the point of view of the observer this experience is still short of an observational judgment to the effect that 'this tree has fading leaves'. For Descartes the construction of an idea which results from an observation is the work of the intellect, whereas the affirmation of a correspondence between the idea and the reality is a function of the will. A person reporting his observations might say: 'I observe a tree with fading leaves.' This report does not logically entail the truth of a proposition to the effect that the tree has fading leaves. It is merely a report of what is observed, not a claim that one's observation is true.

This understanding of observation allows Descartes the possibility of constructing ideas of objects without necessitating the affirmation of the judgments which they spontaneously tend to evoke. It is also consistent with the Cartesian theory of clear and distinct ideas because one may entertain a propositional idea and suspend affirmation or denial until the contents of the idea are checked against the criterion of clarity and distinctness. It is only after such a criterion has been applied and a decision reached that one should proceed to make a judgment.[40]

In summary, observation is thinking about an object in a specific manner as a result of the interaction of the object with one's sensory faculties. It is not merely a sensation, which is limited to having an idea of something extra-mental without any reference to its source. On the other hand an observation is not yet a judgment, because it does not necessarily involve an affirmation by the will of a correspondence between one's idea and its extramental counterpart. In an observation, a person constructs a mental idea of an object on the basis of his sensations and of his previous experience of similar situations. This step involves transcending the security of what is reported in such minimal claims as: 'I seem to see something blue' and thinking about one's sensations as caused by an object having properties corresponding to one's sensations. It is no longer just being aware of what is happening to oneself; it is thinking of an object, as such.

Observations, like sensations, cannot be false. They may be faulty, i.e. lacking clarity and distinctness. Descartes suggests this latter possibility as an explanation for why we make false observational judgments. Both the experience of making an observation and the spontaneous or critical judgments which tend to result from an observation are conflated by Descartes in the third level of sensation above.[41] To avoid confusion he should distinguish the actual experience of making an observation from the judgments which result from the experience, either the report of the observation or the knowledge claims such an observer is likely to make on the basis of his experience.

This is an important feature of the Cartesian attempt to explain the fallibility of sensory knowledge by contrast with 'reason', and this is discussed further in §9 below. The exact mistake we are likely to make in observations is the one made by Descartes himself in conflating observations and observational judgments. Observations may be faulty or misleading, but they are not judgments and have no truth-value. However we tend to make judgments uncritically as a result of observational experiences and we thereby camouflage one of the major sources of error in empirical knowledge. One of the functions of reason, in scientific method, is to oversee critically inferences from observation to observational judgment and thereby exploit the valid resources of sensory experience.

Among the kinds of observation which are important for physical science, Descartes distinguishes experiments and ordinary experience.

Experiments

While Descartes' experiments and his experimental technique may seem rather primitive to the contemporary scientist, many of the *expériences* on which he relies to warrant scientific claims were in fact scientific experiments. The concept of a scientific experiment is hardly capable of exact definition in terms of necessary and sufficient conditions.[42] Some of the following characteristics, however, are usually included in the concept of an experiment:

(*a*) The basic motive of experimental procedures in science is to establish the truth-value of some proposition or theory. Bunge distinguishes between the experimental method and an experimental approach to realising a scientific objective.[43] For example, an artisan might succeed in putting things together in an appropriate way by a trial and error approach which could be legitimately called 'experimental'. But the objective of such an exercise is to make something rather than to decide if a theory or proposition is true. The scientist, by contrast, is characteristically interested in specific experiments only as paradigms of universal claims whose truth-value is to be established. This is not to suggest that scientists do not engage in experimental procedures in the artisan's sense; the point is rather that whatever the scientist does or however he approaches his task, his basic motivation is a cognitive one rather than the production of an artifact.

(*b*) Besides the cognitional motivation, Claude Bernard mentions two other characteristics of scientific experiments which seem to reflect the Cartesian understanding of the term. One of these characteristics is the relation between one's technical operations and some hypothesis to be examined. 'I consider it therefore to be an absolute principle that experiments must always be devised in view of a preconceived idea, even if the idea is more or less vague, or more or less well defined.'[44] The qualification 'more or less' may be so wide as to make the suggestion unfalsifiable; however, Bernard's point is that some hypothesis, however vague, is presupposed in order to specify both what phenomenon is to be investigated and what question one wishes to ask about it. In cases where one's hypothesis is less vague, the 'preconceived idea' may specify precisely those variables of a physical system which one hopes to consider, and even what relations between the variables is subject to scrutiny.[45]

(c) With a reasonably specific working hypothesis and a question to answer, an experiment is further characterised by the control which the experimenter exercises over the physical system being examined. Thus C. Bernard: 'Observation is investigation of a natural phenomenon and an experiment is the investigation of a phenomenon altered (or modified) by the experimenter.'[46] The intervention of the experimenter into the condition of the phenomenon, and his attempt to control it, is normally aimed at isolating precisely those features of the phenomenon which he thinks are relevant to his work. It was the lack of such control, at least in Bernard's time, which made astronomical observations non-experimental despite their significance for science.

This last criterion of experiments is less easy to insist on, given the diversity of ways in which observations are made, even in astronomy. The idea underlying the demand for intervention and control is that, without any control, the scientist is passively observing whatever evidence is spontaneously presented by the natural occurrence of events. However it also seems that 'intervention and control' is too rigorous a criterion for cases where the observer conspires to put himself in a favourable position to observe whatever is expected to be relevant to his hypotheses. This less stringent criterion is reflected in P. Caws' description of an experiment: 'An experiment is only an artificial device for putting the observer in a favorable position with respect to nature – a contrivance to have things happen where they can be seen.'[47]

It is clear from Descartes' correspondence that he understands an experiment in this sense: an experiment presupposes some prior theory or hypothesis; its objective is cognitive, and it almost invariably involves the intervention of the observer into those features of natural phenomena which are less accessible than the features which are available for inspection by the non-scientist. This intervention normally implies controlling or modifying a phenomenon in such a way that observations can be made which are otherwise impossible. The theoretical presupposition of experiments is clear in the Cartesian contrast between trial and error testing, and scientific knowledge. For example, Descartes claims in the *Dioptrics* that the telescope was discovered by experimental manipulation of lenses without a theory to explain the result: 'To the shame of our sciences, this discovery, which is so useful and admirable, was initially made only by experimenting and by chance.' (VI, 81–82). The intervention and control over phenomena to be examined is likewise clear from Descartes' objections to experiments, which are discussed at the conclusion of this section.

Ordinary experience

Instead of experiments, Descartes favours what I have called ordinary experience, where ordinary experience is a type of observation. There is no way to distinguish sharply between ordinary experience and experiments; for example, to observe a pointer-reading on a measuring instrument and to notice that the clouds in the sky are (apparently) moving are both instances of observation. Descartes would presumably have classified only the second one of these as an ordinary experience. The basis of the distinction seems to be the relative certainty of knowledge-claims based on ordinary experience, and this in turn is a function of the simplicity of such experiences.

The ordinary-ness of Descartes' preferred observations depends on a lack of complexity both in the object of perception and in the activity of the subject who makes the observation. As regards the object of perception, ordinary experience is limited to those more obvious and universal phenomena which are given prior to any interference on our part with the natural occurrence of events. Non-ordinary observations, on the other hand, are such that 'the circumstances on which they depend are nearly always so special and so detailed that it is very difficult to notice them' (VI, 63);[48] the implication here is that they are either unreliable or unavailable. The simplicity of our observations as acts of a perceiving subject is determined by the few prerequisites which they presuppose. While it would be entirely implausible to suggest anticipations of the concept of theory-ladenness in Descartes' discussion, it does appear as if he distinguished between observations which can be made without a prior theory or training in a technique, and observations which can be made by the man of common sense. In general, then, an ordinary experience is an observation which can be made by the untutored and unskilled observer in the course of his acquaintance with those natural phenomena which are given independently of our interference with, or control over, their occurrence.

The question arises at this stage as to whether these distinctions among different kinds of experience help explain Descartes' theory of the priority of 'reason' over experience in constructing a scientific account of nature. Descartes seems to have two different objections to 'experience': one of them is a general objection to any knowledge-claim which is based on empirical evidence, and this objection is examined in §9. Apart from this general objection, Descartes also had special reasons to object to experimental evidence and to prefer, in its place, the evidence of ordinary experience.

As already indicated above, the Cartesian endorsement of ordinary experience is determined, in part, by the relative certainty of ordinary experience compared with experiments. Thus, in the early pages of the *Regulae* and the *Discourse*, Descartes contrasts the illusions of the learned with the simple certainties of the man on the street. 'Learned men may perhaps persuade themselves . . . that hardly any such [i.e. indubitable] knowledge exists . . . Nevertheless, I advise them that there is much more knowledge than they think' (X, 362). And in the first part of the *Discourse*: 'And so I thought that book learning . . . does not come as close to the truth as the simple reasoning which a man of good sense can naturally develop about those things which he experiences' (VI, 12–13). The certainty of such commonly known facts about the world is reflected in Descartes' rule that we should always begin an inquiry with the more simple and obvious truths before progressing to the obscure and uncertain. Among those who contravene this rule are those 'philosophers who neglect experience and think that the truth will emerge from their own heads as Minerva did from that of Jupiter' (X, 380).

By contrast with the reliable evidence of ordinary experience, scientific experiments are often so complicated that it is difficult to derive any conclusion with certainty from their results. Among the reasons for distrusting experiments Descartes mentions three:

(*a*) An experiment may be poorly executed. One often finds Descartes describing experimental techniques; for example in his correspondence with Mersenne, and Debeaune, he describes how to set up and conduct correctly experiments for measuring refractive indices, the polarity of magnets, the weight of air, etc.[49] His general criticism of inaccurate experiments is that people tend to get the results they expect, and if their theory is incorrect, they are inclined to perform faulty experiments to confirm them 'because those who have performed them have forced themselves to make them appear to agree with their theories' (VI, 73).[50]

(*b*) An experiment may not be repeated often enough to establish the results with certainty.[51]

(*c*) The correct results of an experiment may be incorrectly interpreted. The standard problem here is the presence of interfering factors in the experimental situation which are not taken into account by the theory or hypothesis being tested. For example, Descartes dismissed objections to his impact rules because collisions of the kind he describes in the rules involve such factors as elasticity, air resistance, etc. which are not considered by the rules.[52]

Descartes' general scepticism about reported experimental findings is summarised in a remark to Huygens: 'I have little trust in experiments which I have not performed myself' (III, 617).[53] For the source of Cartesian doubt about experiments is not their empirical character, but the fact that their relative complexity makes them more liable to errors and misinterpretations than the common experience of unscientific observers of nature.[54]

This assessment of the reliability of ordinary experience

compared with experimental evidence is consistent with the Cartesian understanding of a scientific explanation as a reduction of the complex and unintelligible to the simple and familiar. This is a point which is taken up for discussion in Chapter 5 below. For the moment it is enough to notice that the objections to experimental evidence are not in any way a result of denigrating empirical evidence in comparison with purely rational or a priori considerations; Descartes' choice – at least in so far as it has been discussed here – was between *two kinds of experiential evidence*.

In trying to situate Descartes' comments on the relative unreliability of sensory knowledge I have argued that *'expérience'* is an ambiguous concept, and that Cartesian dualism is not necessarily a decisive argument against an interpretation of the texts which would restore a significant place to empirical evidence in science. Dualism certainly complicates the issues involved here; however, it should also be recognised for what it is. It is a theory borrowed by Descartes from tradition to explain what he took to be an indubitable fact of our experience, namely the fact of our having sensory experiences. These experiences are logically prior to any theory which might be introduced to explain them. So that if the theory stumbles it does not follow that Descartes would question the reliability of precisely those kinds of experience which the theory was intended to explain.

However, Descartes evidently does have serious objections to at least some kinds of empirical evidence. I have distinguished two objections in this context. One is a general objection to any kind of observational evidence – this is discussed in the subsequent chapter. The other kind of objection results from Descartes' unfavourable contrast of experimental results with the evidence provided by ordinary experience. None of the three reasons for doubting experimental results implies any distrust of experiential evidence as such; what is at stake in this objection is a choice between two kinds of empirical evidence. With appropriate controls, even experiments can be seen to have a central place in science.

Notes

1 For an analysis of English usage, see J. M. Hinton, *Experiences: An Inquiry into Some Ambiguities.*

2 In a letter to Mersenne (Nov. 13, 1638), Debeaune uses the word *'expériment'* to refer to tests of Galileo's work (V, 527). The term *'expériment'* is also found as the French equivalent of the English 'experiment' in Randle Cotgrave's *A Dictionarie of the French and English Tongues.*

3 'experior illas non a mea voluntate nec proinde a me ipso pendere' (VII, 38); 'les mouvemens que nous n'experimentons point estre conduits par nostre volonté' (XI, 226).

4 Descartes frequently refers to our experience of freedom in withholding assent to propositions or judgments. See for example VI, 56, 57, 58, 59, 191, 377, 378; Descartes to Buitendijck (1643) (IV; 62); Descartes to Elizabeth, Nov. 3, 1645 (IV, 332–3); VIII-1, 6. In French the *'experimur'* of the last reference is translated as *'éprouver'* (IX-2, 27).

5 See VII, 427 (*experiri* and *experiamur*); VII, 440 (*experimur*); X, 419.

6 In sorting out Descartes' usage here it is not yet clear whether one should say that experience is a kind of intuition or vice versa. See for example J. Segond, *La Sagesse cartésienne et la doctrine de la science*, p. 209: 'C'est donc qu'à ses yeux [i.e. Descartes'] l'expérience est une sorte d'intuition'. L. J. Beck makes a similar point in *The Method of Descartes*, pp. 83–4: 'By "experience", in the context of Rule 2, it is clear that he means nothing more than the right intuitive use of the intellect.'

7 Similar uses of *'sentire'* occur in VII, 76, 79 and 80 where pain, various appetites resulting from the interaction of mind and body, and ideas of physical objects are said to be sensed.

8 Cf. *Description of the Human Body*: 'nostre ame . . . ne nous est connue que par cela seul qu'elle pense, c'est à dire, qu'elle entend, . . . & qu'elle sent, pource que toutes ces fonctions sont des especes de pensées' (XI, 224).

9 *'Expérience'* meaning 'test' is also found in the *Dictionnaire Universel*, p. 980: 'Expérience, essai, épreuve, considerés comme synonymes.' The second alternative proposed by the *Dictionnaire de l'Académie* (Paris, 1694) has the same meaning: 'Epreuve qui se fait à desein, ou par hazard.'

10 Cf. Descartes to Mersenne, June 19, 1639 (II, 560): 'But because those [lenses] which are made by chance never correspond to that theory [i.e. dioptrics], it is much easier to determine their power by experience than by reason.' See also Descartes to Ferrier, November 13, 1629 (I, 60) concerning the problems encountered in grinding

lenses: 'However the proportion between these movements can only be learned by practice; that is to say that even if you were an angel you would not be able to do it as well on the first attempt as on the second.'

11   Descartes to Hogelande, February 8, 1640 (III, 723); Descartes to Mersenne, December 25, 1639 (II, 636). The word 'observation' also seems to mean experiment as in: 'Thank you for your *observation* about the forces which are required to break different cylinders of the same size.' (Descartes to Mersenne, December 1638 (?): II, 465).

12   The French reflects this with: 'Des Phaenomenes ou experiences, & à quoy elles peuvent icy servir.'

13   Descartes also uses the word *'expérience'* to denote whatever characterises the person who travels widely and is familiar with a variety of cultures, lifestyles, etc. For example, he writes in the *Discourse* about 'studying in the book of the world and trying to acquire experience' (VI, 10). A letter to his brother Pierre confirms that he plans a journey to Italy, 'which should be very useful to familiarise myself with public affairs and to acquire some experience of the world (*expérience du monde*)' (I, 3).

14   On two occasions Descartes uses the term *'experience ordinaire'* but not in the sense in which I use it here. It occurs in the *Discourse* (VI, 51), in reference to the surgeon's experience of ligating veins, and in the *Meteorology* (VI, 335) it refers to the experiment of mixing primary colours to produce intermediate hues.

15   'Ainsi que l'expérience fait voir' (XI, 369).

16   Cf. Descartes to Mersenne, April 20, 1646 (IV, 392).

17   Cf. IX-2, 20; also Huygens to Descartes, January 25, 1642 (III, 779), where Huygens refers to Bacon's experiments as *'experiments particuliers'*.

18   See Descartes to Mersenne, Nov. 15, 1638 (II, 422); Descartes to Mersenne, January 9, 1639 (II, 489); to Huygens, February 18, 1643 (III, 617); to Mersenne, Sept. 15, 1640 (III, 176), 'ie dois faire moy mesme quelques expériences'.

19   'Thank you for your exact measurement of refractions' (April 30, 1639: II, 542). On February 20, 1639, he rejected apparent counter-evidence to Debeaune's experiments: 'I take little notice of anyone who says he has done experiments which show the contrary' (II, 521).

20   Descartes to Mersenne, April 15, 1630 (I, 141).

21   Descartes to Mersenne, April 30, 1639 (II, 530).

22   *Principles*, IX-2, 293.

23   Descartes to Mersenne, January 4, 1643 (III, 609).

24   Cf. IX-2, 17; XI, 232–3; Descartes to Picot, XI, 326; Descartes to Mersenne, January 4, 1643 (III, 610).

25   For recent work on Descartes' dualism, see A. Kenny, *Descartes: A Study of his Philosophy*, pp. 90–2; N. Malcolm, 'Descartes' proof that his essence is thinking,' in *Descartes: A Collection of Critical Essays*, ed. W. Doney, pp. 312–37; Richard Kennington, 'The "teaching of

nature" in Descartes' soul doctrine', *Review of Metaphysics*, **26** (1972), 86–117; B. Williams, *Descartes*, pp. 279–303; Margaret D. Wilson, *Descartes*, pp. 177–220; Michael Hooker (ed.) *Descartes: Critical and Interpretive Essays*, pp. 171–85 ('Descartes' denial of mind–body identity', M. Hooker), 186–96 ('Descartes' ''synthetic'' treatment of the Real distinction between mind and body', A. Donagan), 197–211 ('Cartesian dualism', M. D. Wilson), 212–22 ('Descartes' correspondence with Elizabeth: Concerning both the union and distinction of mind and body', R. Mattern), 223–33 ('Dualism in Descartes: the logical ground', F. Sommers).

26 See especially Margaret D. Wilson, *Descartes*, pp. 188–200.
27 The conceptual or logical character of Descartes' argument is clear from VII, 161, 162; whatever can be clearly and distinctly thought of as existing independently is created as a substance by God.
28 For a commentary on this passage see Charles Adam, 'Descartes: ses trois notions fondamentales', *Revue philosophique de la France et de l'étrangère*, **123** (1937), 1–14; N. Kemp Smith, *New Studies*, pp. 256–8; Ruth Mattern, 'Descartes's correspondence with Elizabeth', in M. Hooker, ed., *Descartes*, pp. 212–22.
29 Descartes to Elizabeth, June 28, 1643 (III, 693). Cf. IX-1, 213: 'These objections presuppose, among other things, the explanation of the union which exists between the soul and the body, and I have not yet dealt with that.'
30 Cf. Fourth Replies, VII, 228–9, where he refers to the 'close conjunction of the mind with the body, which we constantly experience through our senses'; and the Sixth Meditation, VII, 80, where the union of body and soul is taught indubitably by 'nature', i.e. it is communicated through the experience of mind–body duality.
31 Descartes goes so far as to say, on one occasion, that the ideas of the mind and body are the clearest ones he can think of, apart from the idea of God. 'However I am only offering my opinion in this matter . . . I am prepared to change it.' (Descartes to the Abbé of Launay, July 22, 1641: III, 421).
32 See VI, 109, 130, 131.
33 For Descartes' use of the term '*idée*' to refer to the patterns in the brain caused by sensations, see the *Treatise on Man*, trans. and ed. Thomas S. Hall, pp. 86–7, notes 135 and 136.
34 This coincides with the *Meditations*, where Descartes claims that sensing is a form of thinking: VII, 29.
35 'This *phantasia* should be thought of as a true part of the body', *Regulae*, X, 414. This is consistent with Descartes' anatomical experiments with a view to explaining the nature of the imagination. 'I am dissecting the heads of various animals at present to explain what the imagination, memory, etc. consist of.' (Descartes to Mersenne, November or December, 1632: I, 263).
36 See *Discourse*, VI, 55 for the role of imagination relative to the ideas of the *sensus communis*.

37   Descartes often alludes to the influence of physical disabilities on thinking; and the passions of the soul are facts of our experience which are logically prior to the mind–body union theory which is supposed to explain them. See VI, 62; VIII-1, 37; VII, 228; and J. Dreyfus-Le Foyer, 'Les conceptions médicales de Descartes', *Revue de métaphysique et de morale*, **44** (1937), 267–81.

38   The source of the stimulation, for the human perceiver, might be his own body. In that case, the sensation would be an idea, in the mind, of a condition of the perceiver's body in so far as this condition is transmitted through the nerves to the sensory centres of the brain. Another point should be noted, in this context, about Descartes' concept of sensation. It is not an act–object analysis of sensation in the sense that the mind has a picture of the condition of the brain. The mind and brain are so united that the human subject is conscious of what is transmitted to the brain. Thus, in the case of sensing colours, the mind does not have an idea of the motions of the nerves, etc. in the brain, nor even of something like a colour sense-datum, but the person is conscious of the colour itself.

39   Descartes claims that 'there can be no falsehood' in the first two levels of sensation (VII, 438). Cf. H. H. Price, *Thinking and Experience*, Ch. 3: 'Errors of recognition'.

40   Wittgenstein's understanding of a proposition as a picture which is neither true nor false until projected onto reality is close to the Cartesian concept of a propositional idea which has no truth-value. See L. Wittgenstein, *Notebooks, 1914–16*, ed. G. H. von Wright and G. E. M. Anscombe, pp. 8 and 33: 'The proposition *only says something in so far* as it is *a picture*! . . . Can one negate *a picture*? No. And in this lies the difference between picture and proposition. The picture can serve as a proposition. But in that case something gets added to it which brings it about that now it *says* something. In short: I can only deny that the picture is right, but the *picture* I cannot deny.' Cf. *Tractatus Logico-Philosophicus*, trans. D. F. Pears and B. F. McGuinness, 2.1511; 3.11.

41   In discussing the mistake of identifying observational judgments with pure sensations, Descartes suggests that this error is due to the ease with which we compare present sensations with previous ones and our facility, acquired by experience, in moving from the level of sensation to perceptual judgment by inference.'In these matters we reason and judge so quickly from habit, or rather we remember judgments we formerly made about similar things, that we fail to distinguish these operations [i.e. observational judgments] from simple sense perception' (VII, 438). Descartes makes a similar mistake himself in not distinguishing between sensation and observation on the one hand, and on the other, judgments based on them.

42   For the concept of an experiment in science see the following: Claude Bernard, *Introduction à l'étude de la médecine expérimentale*, pp. 11–47; Marx Wartofsky, *Conceptual Foundations of Scientific Thought*,

pp. 190–204; Leonard K. Nash, *The Nature of the Natural Sciences*, pp. 43–9, 138–69, 256–64; Ernest Nagel, *The Structure of Science*, pp. 81–90; Mario Bunge, *Scientific Research II: The Search for Truth*, pp. 251–89; Peter Caws, *The Philosophy of Science*, p. 52; Pierre Duhem, *The Aim and Structure of Physical Science*, pp. 144–64, 180–218.

43 M. Bunge, *Scientific Research II*, p. 260.

44 C. Bernard, *Introduction*, p. 42.

45 In this connection, P. Duhem distinguishes between experiments of testing and experiments of application (*The Aim and Structure of Physical Theory*, pp. 183–4). Thus, if one has a specific hypothesis to the effect that $x = f(y)$, one might either test to see if it is true or, assuming its truth, apply the hypothesis to a new case to determine the values of relevant variables (experiments of application).

46 C. Bernard, *Introduction*, p. 29.

47 P. Caws, *The Philosophy of Science*, p. 52. Cf. M. Bunge, *op. cit.*, p. 251: 'By definition, *experiment* is the kind of scientific experience in which some *change* is *deliberately* provoked, and its outcome observed, recorded and interpreted with a cognitive aim.' Marx Wartofsky, *op. cit.*, p. 190: 'Experiment, then, is observation controlled by the framework of scientific hypothesis.'

48 Cf. Descartes to Mersenne, April 20, 1646 (IV, 391).

49 See the fragment of a letter, 1630–8 (IV, 688–9), where Descartes criticises the technique of an experiment to weigh a vaporised liquid, and another criticism of an experiment to test the velocity of falling bodies; Descartes to Mersenne, February 9, 1639 (II, 497–8), for a criticism of an experiment to refute his theory of optical refraction, and again to Mersenne, January 4, 1643 (III, 609), for a discussion of possible mistakes in an experiment to weigh air. Likewise, Descartes offers advice on correctly performing an experiment about projectiles (Descartes to Mersenne, May 15, 1634: I, 293).

50 An example of this is found in Maurolicus' measurement of the angle of elevation of the primary and secondary bows of the rainbow. Descartes commented: 'That indicates the little trust one should place in observations which are not accompanied by the correct explanation' (VI, 340).

51 Cf. Descartes to Mersenne, January 29, 1640: 'instead of three observations, I would like a thousand, before I could trust them entirely, because the slightest thing makes them vary' (III, 7); Descartes to the Marquis of Newcastle, November 23, 1646 (IV, 571–2), where Descartes suggests that his correspondent has not done enough experiments to explain the nature of quicksilver.

52 This is discussed in greater detail in Appendix 2 below. In discussing the problem of how many strikes of a small hammer are equivalent to one strike of a larger one, Descartes writes to Mersenne, June 11, 1640: 'there are so many factors to take into account in such calculations, and they match our experience so poorly and matter so little, that it seems best for me not to talk about them at all' (III, 80). See also Descartes to Mersenne, November 13,

1629, apropos of the law of falling bodies: 'However, as regards the interference from the air which you wish me to take into consideration, I claim that it is impossible to cope with it and it does not fall within the scope of science; for if it is warm, or cold, or dry, or humid, or clear, or cloudy, or a thousand other circumstances – they can all change the air resistance' (I, 73); see also Descartes to Cavendish, May 15, 1646, (IV, 416–17).

53   Huygens seems to have been an exception to this general sceptical attitude of Descartes, for Descartes writes about him to Golius, April 16, 1635 (I, 315); 'if it is possible for it to succeed at all, he [Huygens] will find a way to do it sooner than anyone else'. Cf. Descartes to Mersenne, March 11, 1640 (III, 38): 'Nevertheless, it is an experimental matter to determine if this difference is observable, and I doubt very much those experiments which I have not done myself.'

54   Compare P. Duhem, *The Aim and Structure of Physical Theory*, p. 163: 'an experiment in physics does not have the immediate certainty, relatively easy to check, that ordinary, non-scientific testimony has'.

THREE

Reason in Cartesian science

Descartes provides the casual reader of his work with many explicit indications of his preference for reason, rather than experience, in deciding the truth-value of scientific knowledge claims. Besides these explicit texts he also avails himself of a rather characteristic cluster of ideas which normally imply allegiance to a rationalist tradition in philosophy. Any attempt to reinterpret the role of reason in Cartesian science must take account of both explicit and apparently implicit indications of the supremacy of reason. Thus, if one understands 'reason' as a general term to refer to cognitive faculties which are in some sense independent of experience, the clarification of the role of reason is equivalent to answering the following question: are Cartesian references to experience genuine tests of hypotheses or are they merely illustrations of intuitively warranted first principles?[1] In other words, does reason independently provide the fundamental explanatory concepts, the first principles or laws and perhaps even the general structure of what counts as an explanation for Descartes, while experience functions only at the point where scientific theory is applied to physical reality? What does reason, independent of experience, contribute to Cartesian science?

Two issues immediately come to mind in this context: innate ideas and the role of axioms in Cartesian science. The first of these is traditionally classified as a question about the understanding, rather than about reason; however, the understanding/reason distinction will be ignored here in favour of a discussion of what intellectual faculties, independent of experiential evidence, can be shown to contribute to Cartesian science. The initial evidence of Descartes' terminology suggests that scientific knowledge is independent of experience in three respects: (i) we have certain innate ideas or simple natures which constitute the basic explanatory conceptual framework of science; (ii) we know some scientific laws or axioms a priori; and (iii) scientific inferences or deductions are guided by reason rather than experience. In §§ 6–8 I examine the implications of each of these for the more general thesis that Cartesian science is fundamentally rationalist, and I argue that it is possible to interpret Descartes' remarks about innate ideas, axioms and deduction without compromising the role of experience in science.

In §9 I explain a further sense (in addition to those mentioned in §5) in which Descartes has reservations about the importance of experiential evidence for science; and it is precisely this type of legitimate reservation which he describes as a preference for reason rather than experience.

§6　*Innate ideas*

Descartes notoriously claims that some of our ideas are innate and he supports the theory, in the *Regulae*, that science must be based on simple natures which are known by intuition. The almost incidental reference, in the Third Meditation, to the astronomical concept of the sun as an innate idea helps to reinforce the suspicion that he is fundamentally committed to some kind of innateness theory even if it emerges in incidental rather than in explicit formulations.[2] From the point of view of scientific methodology, then, one question which must be faced sooner rather than later is: in what sense does Descartes think that some, or all, of our scientific ideas are independent of experience?

It is somewhat easier to say what Descartes does not mean by his innateness theory. He does not mean – as Jacques de Rives had claimed – that before any learning begins there are 'actual notions, species and ideas concerning God implanted by nature . . . in the human mind' (VIII-2, 365). To this suggestion he replied in the *Notes Against a Programme* that he considered such a theory 'patently absurd and false'. More explicitly:

I never wrote or thought that these ideas are actual, or that they are species in some unknown way distinct from the faculty of thinking; in fact, more than anyone else I am opposed to that empty class of scholastic entities, so that I can hardly restrain myself from laughing when I see the amount of evidence which [our opponent] . . . has collected to prove that infants in the womb do not have an actual idea of God, as though he could spectacularly refute me by this means. (VIII-2, 366).

This point is ambiguously reiterated in the *Conversation with Burman*, where the author claims that we have no evidence to believe that the child has an *actual* idea of God.

It would be rash to maintain that, since we have no evidence relevant to the point. It does not, however, seem probable that this is so. For in infancy the mind is so swamped inside the body that the only thoughts it has are those which result from the way the body is affected. (Cottingham, p. 8).

This could be interpreted, as it is by Cottingham, as leaving room for actual innate ideas in the child, with the suggestion that the child is so taken up with more mundane concerns that he fails to notice his innate ideas. However one might just as easily understand this text (if it accurately reports Descartes) as not taking sides at all on the issue of whether innate ideas are actual or potential. Even if a child has potential ideas – however that might be further explicated – Descartes' point is this: the principal difference between the adult and the child is that the trained and methodic thinking of the adult can make his innate ideas explicit, whereas the mind of the child is submerged in other overriding and more immediate concerns.[3] This is also consistent with the Annotations to the *Principles*, where the actuality of innate ideas is again·rejected:

I do not understand that they [innate ideas] are always actually depicted in some part of our mind, in the way in which many verses are contained in a book of Virgil. (XI, 655).

If Descartes does not mean that an infant has actual ideas (such as the idea of God) in his mind at birth, what can he mean over and above the suggestion that man is born with a capacity to acquire ideas? This seems to be all he is claiming when he says: 'I never wrote or believed that the mind needs ideas in the sense of something different from its faculty of thinking' (VIII-2, 357).

One consistent feature of his theory, which is part of the innateness hypothesis, is that ideas are irreducible to the sensory stimuli which cause them or to the brain-states which accompany them. Descartes perhaps should not have felt any need to underline this feature of his theory, given his blatant adoption of dualism. However there was still room for ambiguity in his theory of ideas, precisely to the extent that he thought of ideas as caused by sensory stimulation, and also because he sometimes referred to the resulting brain-patterns as ideas.[4] Once he accepts the inexplicable causal relationship between sensory stimulation and the occurrence of appropriate ideas in the mind, Descartes may wish to clarify the special status of these ideas vis-à-vis their causes; and to do this he calls all ideas in the mind innate.

The argument for this position is as follows:

whoever correctly notices how far our senses can extend, and what precisely can reach our faculty of thinking through the senses, should admit that the ideas of things, in the way in which we form these ideas in our thought, are never presented to us by the senses. So much so that there is nothing in our ideas which is not innate to the mind or the faculty of thinking, apart from those circumstances which pertain to experience. (VIII-2, 358).

The argument can be summarised as follows. It is clear that there are specifiable conditions under which an idea is provoked in the human mind by extra-mental stimuli. Yet, what is transmitted from the external stimulus is nothing more than a physical disturbance of the nerves and eventually of the *sensus communis*. Mental entities, such as ideas, are different in their nature from the physical patterns in the brain which accompany them. Hence, even those ideas which are provoked by and correlated with extra-mental stimuli are innate in the sense of being irreducible to the type of reality which triggers them in the mind:

nothing reaches our minds through the organs of sense from external objects, except certain corporeal motions . . . [ideas] have no similarity to corporeal motions . . . hence it follows that the ideas of those motions and figures are innate in us (VIII-2, 359).[5]

This irreducibility meaning of 'innate' will be designated in what follows as 'innate$_1$'. For Descartes, the innateness$_1$ of ideas follows from a series of considerations concerning the immateriality of the mind, the universality of concepts as opposed to images, and the perfection of concepts relative to the imperfect instantiations of them which are encountered in physical reality. What is significant about innateness$_1$ is: (i) that it applies indiscriminately to all ideas, and (ii) that it is not a specifically Cartesian thesis, but represents Descartes' attempt to draw a distinction between the conceptual and the non-conceptual orders which is consistent with dualism.

Among our ideas, all of which are innate$_1$, Descartes further distinguishes those which are innate, acquired or constructed.[6] The sub-division of ideas which are said to be innate in this narrower sense will be called innate$_2$. Descartes provides no more than a few hints of what he means by 'innate' in this second sense of the term.

There are three categories of innate$_1$ ideas:

(*a*) those ideas which arise in the mind as a result of extra-mental stimuli (i.e. acquired ideas);

(*b*) those ideas which are constructed as a result of combining simple ideas. This process may or may not require the use of the imagination and memory, depending on the kinds of ideas to be combined. These are called constructed ideas.

(*c*) those ideas which are found in the intellect, and which do not belong to either of the two categories already listed. These ideas are innate$_2$.

This distinction is found, among other places, in the *Notes Against a Programme*:

when I noticed that I had certain thoughts which were derived, not from external objects or any determination of my will, but solely from the faculty of thinking which I possess, I called the ideas or notions which are the forms of those thoughts 'innate' in order to distinguish them from those which are acquired or constructed (VIII-2, 357–8).[7]

To further explain the provenance of these innate$_2$ ideas which are not actually present in the mind from birth, Descartes has recourse to the idea of a potential existence which can be actualised by the intellect's own activities. Of course, the notion of a potency to have ideas is not much clearer than the idea of being innate. Descartes explains that just as a piece of wax has a potency to have different images imprinted on it, the human mind has a potency to have different ideas and in that sense may be said to have innate ideas.[8] However, innate ideas in this explanation are not really distinct from the mind itself to the extent that the capacity to have ideas belongs to the definition of the human mind. Descartes seems to corroborate this conclusion:

ideas which do not come to us from anything else but our own faculty of thinking . . . are therefore innate in us with that faculty, that is to say, always existing in us in potency. For to be in a given faculty is not to be in act, but only in potency, since the term 'faculty' designates nothing else but a potency (VIII-2, 361).

Hence, to posit the existence of innate ideas is to claim 'only that we have in ourselves the faculty of eliciting ideas' (VII, 189). This clarification is vague enough to apply to all ideas in so far as they are innate₁; for we have a capacity or potency to acquire any of the three categories of ideas listed above, and that would make them all equally innate.

In a number of other texts, however, one finds the suggestion that innate₂ ideas result from a native disposition or propensity of the human mind to conceive of a particular class of ideas among the many which are possible, and to realise this capacity independently of any extra-mental agency. Thus, in the *Notes Against a Programme*, the innateness of ideas is said to be similar to the innateness of a disease for the contraction of which one has a natural propensity. Ideas are innate

in the same sense in which we say that generosity is innate in certain families and in others certain diseases such as gout . . . not that the infants of these families thereby suffer from these diseases in their mother's womb, but that they are born with a certain disposition or faculty to contract these diseases (VIII-2, 358).

This dispositional analysis of innateness involves more than the simple possibility of having certain ideas. It implies something actually present in the human mind which tends to give rise to innate₂ ideas once certain conditions are fulfilled.

An attempt to clarify this sense of potency brings Descartes to compare innate₂ ideas in the child to the condition of an adult who habitually has many ideas which he is not thinking about at any given time.[9] For example, a person who has exercised his intellectual faculties for some time has had experience of making judgments, of denying propositions, of pondering decisions, etc., and therefore can be said to have innate ideas of truth, doubt, and certainty. This amounts to implying that the exercise of one's cognitive faculties is alone sufficient to produce in the reflective mind the concepts of truth, doubt, etc. These ideas are innate₂ in the sense that they are not derived from any sensory experience; at the same time, the mind is not necessarily aware of them at all times in an explicit manner. The propensity to generate these ideas spontaneously in the mind by reflecting on our intellectual activities is what Descartes means by claiming that we have innate₂ ideas.

The discussion thus far indicates that Descartes uses the word 'innate' to characterise two rather different features of ideas. All ideas are innate₁, and this is a metaphysical thesis about the irreducibility of (intellectual) ideas to the physical stimulations and brain-states which often cause their occurrence in the mind. Among innate₁ ideas some are even more independent of experience in so far as the mind can come to have these ideas by reflection on its own intellectual activities or by inferences from these reflections. It is in this sense that the idea of truth, of doubt or of thought is acquired, as is the idea of the soul.[10] Even the idea of God is innate₂ only in the sense that I can come to have the idea of a perfect being by reflection on my own imperfection:

God, in creating me, put this idea in me as an artisan's mark is impressed on his work. Nor is it necessary that that mark be something distinct from the work itself. For from the mere fact that he created me it is very plausible that I am created in some sense in his image and likeness, and that likeness, *in which the idea of God is contained*, can be perceived by me by means of the same faculty by which I perceive myself (VII, 51; my italics).

Whether or not it is plausible, this suggestion is at least reasonably clear. We are not born with the idea of God, except in exactly the same sense in which we are born with the idea of ourselves;[11] by reflection on our mental faculties we can generate the idea of a thinking being, as Descartes does in the *Meditations*. And by suitable qualification of this idea, we can generate the idea of God. What we cannot do is to simply perceive God in the sense in which we can perceive heat or cold or physical objects. Descartes' 'innate₂' is his way of signalling the special epistemological status of some such ideas.[12]

If matters had been left at this point one might regard the innateness hypothesis as an interesting philosophical distinction rather than as an epistemological theory. However, Descartes complicates the situation by claiming that, besides ideas, some axioms and common notions are also innate;[13] and by distinguishing between ideas which involve judgments and those which do not, he can further claim that all innately known axioms are true.[14] Even more puzzling is the repeated suggestion, in the *Regulae*, that the basic explanatory concepts of science can only be known by 'pure intuition'. In other words, it seems as if innateness is much more pervasive and significant for Descartes than the above account allows.

The innate characteristics of axioms or common notions can best be discussed in the next section. Before taking up that question, the peculiar status of 'simple natures' in the *Regulae* must first be broached with the question in mind: in what sense are these simple natures innate, and what might Descartes mean by an 'intuition' of such simple natures?

Simple natures

The word 'innate' does not occur at all in the *Regulae*; however among the simple natures which are proposed as foundational, some are known 'by a certain light which is in us' (X, 383),[15] and this is sufficiently close to 'innate' to warrant further examination. For the present the principal question which arises is the extent to which this 'certain light' operates to reveal more innate ideas than were listed above, and especially in what sense the *intuitus* of the *Regulae* seems to bring all ideas within the revelatory scope of the natural light of reason.

The interpretation of the *Regulae* and the *Discourse* is problematic, for the reasons outlined in Chapter 1 above. Since the *Regulae* is obviously incomplete, and the *Discourse* is apparently a reworking of earlier draft material, it is unlikely that one can simply read the texts as they stand and know what Descartes means. Despite these caveats, it is necessary to anticipate later discussion and say something at this stage about the role of simple natures in science and their possible relation with innate ideas.

The discussion of simple natures occurs in Book I of the *Regulae* which was originally understood as a general summary of a method which is claimed to be appropriate for any scientific enterprise. In other words, the discussion in Book I cannot be specific to either mathematics or physics or metaphysics, but must remain at such a general level that whatever is proposed there is applicable, with appropriate qualifications, to any discipline of a scientific nature (meaning: productive of knowledge which is certain). The lack of specificity at this stage of the discussion is very obvious in the case of simple natures; for 'simple natures' is apparently a role characterisation of whatever may be accepted as unanalysable in any science. This suggestion is corroborated by Descartes' distinction between those elements which are simple in themselves and those which are simple in relation to the human inquirer. He is only concerned, in rule 12, with the latter, i.e. those elements of a science which are simple *quoad nos*.

We say . . . that it is necessary to consider each thing in different ways when we are talking about it either in relation to our knowledge or in so far as it exists on its own . . . Since we are only considering things at this point in so far as they are perceived by the understanding, we apply the term 'simple' only to those which are so clearly and distinctly known that the mind cannot further distinguish them into more distinctly known parts. (X, 418).[16]

Simple natures are further defined by reference to their role in explanations. They may be ideas of purely intellectual operations such as doubting or thinking, ideas of material objects, or even ideas which apply to matter and spirit indiscriminately.

Secondly, we say that those things which are said to be simple in relation to our understanding are either purely intellectual, or purely material, or common (X, 419).

Simple natures may even include rules of inference, which are also classified as common notions (X, 419). What is common to all the simple natures, whether they are concepts or propositions, is that they are so clear to the inquirer that he regards them as incapable of further analysis. Descartes provides no effective criteria for recognising when one has reached the limits of possible analysis. What he does claim, more modestly and reasonably, is that at any stage in a scientific investigation there are some concepts or propositions in terms of which others are analysed or warranted, and that they themselves are not subject to further analysis or questioning.

That there are any simple natures at all or that the concept of a simple nature is explanatory, is an acknowledged hypothetical claim on Descartes' part which can only be confirmed by evaluating the success of the method proposed in the *Regulae*. In an infrequently noticed comment on his own procedures in analysing scientific method Descartes consciously refers to the saving-the-phenomena tradition in astronomy. Simple natures are proposed by analogy with the imaginary circles or epicycles of astronomers; no more reality is claimed for simple natures than is required to give an explanatory account of the structure of human, scientific knowledge:

> Here, as in earlier cases, some assumptions must be made which may not be accepted by everyone; however it makes little difference if they are only accepted as being no more true than those imaginary circles by which astronomers describe phenomena, as long as, with their help, we can distinguish what knowledge about any matter can be true or false (X, 417).

The simple natures theory, as a methodological hypothesis, may be assessed at a later stage; for present purposes the only question at issue is whether all simple natures are known only by intellectual intuition, i.e. whether simple natures are (whatever they are) necessarily innate$_2$.

If one prescinds for the moment from the status of propositional simple natures or axioms and concentrates only on simple natures which are non-propositional concepts, the evidence in the *Regulae* is consistent with Descartes' usual distinction between innate$_2$ and acquired ideas. Simple natures of a conceptual character are acquired either through sensory experience or by pure intuition.[17] When simple natures are distinguished into purely intellectual, material or common as three types, the purely intellectual ones can be known 'by a certain innate light' (X, 419), while the common simples can be known 'either by the pure intellect or by the same faculty understanding the images of material objects' (X, 419–20). It seems almost redundant for Descartes to have to add that the material simples can be known in the way in which acquired ideas of any physical object or event are known – namely, through the joint co-operation of sensory experience and understanding.

There are other clear indications in the text of the *Regulae* that the author assumes that the theory about simple natures does not imply some kind of exclusively non-experiential access to the explanatory concepts which are appropriate for a physical science:

(*a*) In rule 12, Descartes recommends that a simple idea of a material body can best be had by producing a distinct image of the object in the imagination; 'and in order to do this more satisfactorily, the object itself which the idea represents should be exhibited to the external senses' (X, 417).

(*b*) As long as someone follows the proposed method there is only one way in which he can fail to achieve the kind of certain knowledge which is appropriate to a science: 'every time he applies his mind to understanding something, he will either discover it right away, or he will notice that it depends on some experience (*ab aliquo experimento*) which is not within his power' (X, 400). If Cartesian science were based exclusively on innate ideas and deductive inferences, there could be no unavoidable obstacles in a lack of '*experimenta*'.

(*c*) In rule 14 one finds a text, almost in the spirit of Hume, to the effect that many basic concepts cannot be acquired by those who lack the relevant sensory faculties. Thus, the ideas of the primary colours cannot be acquired by those who are blind from birth.

If anyone is blind from birth, there is no hope that we could ever get him, by whatever arguments, to perceive the true ideas of colours which we have drawn from our senses. If however he has perceived at least the primary colours a number of times, without having ever seen the intermediate or mixed hues, it may happen that he could construct images of these intermediate colours, which he has not seen, by a kind of deduction from those he has seen. (X, 438).

(*d*) Finally, in the general summary of Book I in rule 12, Descartes enlists the aid of all four faculties of knowing at each stage of constructing a scientific theory:

Finally, it is necessary to avail oneself of all the help which the understanding, the imagination, sense and memory give, for distinctly understanding simple propositions; for appropriately comparing what is being sought with what is already known, in order to recognise them; and for finding those things which ought to be compared with one another; so that no kind of human effort is left untapped. (X, 410).

These texts indicate that there are no additions to Descartes' innateness hypothesis in the theory of simple natures. Precisely those ideas which are elsewhere said to be innate₂, such as the ideas of doubt or ignorance, are also recognised in the *Regulae* as innate₂, or as being purely intellectual (X, 419). On the other hand those ideas which are elsewhere thought to result from our sensory experience are likewise classified as material simple natures in the *Regulae*, and are acquired as usual though sensory experience. What seems to be troublesome here is the suggestion that all simple natures are acquired by the operation of the 'pure *intuitus*', despite their sensory origins. However this is nothing more than the familiar Cartesian thesis that all ideas are innate₁, i.e. that it is only in the understanding and not in the senses that one has ideas of any kind and that these ideas are irreducible to their sensory causes.

The scope and operations of this Cartesian *intuitus*, especially for the identification of axioms or common notions, is taken up in the next section.

§7   *Axioms and* intuitus

There is a well-known Cartesian thesis familiar to readers of the *Meditations* that *intellectual* understanding is the only kind possible. For example, the piece of wax discussed in the second Meditation was understood only by an *'inspectio mentis'* (VII, 31).[18] This is consistent with Descartes' innateness₁ theory: conceptual understanding is attributable only to the intellectual faculties, and the inspection or perception of the mind is a usefully vague way of referring to this thesis. I wish to argue that the use of *intuitus* in the *Regulae* is an earlier version of the same thesis.

The relative infrequency of the term *'intuitus'* in other parts of Descartes' work only serves to highlight the importance of the concept in the *Regulae*.[19] Some indication of what Descartes means by *intuitus* can be gleaned both from the suggested contrasts with other cognitive procedures, and from the way in which it functions in relation to simple natures and logical inferences.

Intuitus is contrasted with both deduction and induction as one of the only two reliable operations which result in scientific knowledge.[20] It is a form of intellectual seeing, and the metaphorical basis of the term is clear in Descartes' use of visual perception as a model for *intuitus* (X, 400, 454); *intuitus* is a kind of seeing with the mind's eye (X, 425, 427). By contrast with inferences which normally presuppose examining relations between a whole series of propositions, *intuitus* is restricted to understanding individual propositions (X, 369, 370, 389, 407, 408, 425), or to seeing the necessary connection between two propositions (X, 369, 370, 389, 407, 425, 459, 460). An *intuitus* is not a judgment (X, 420) and hence it has no truth-value (X, 432).

This is consistent with Descartes' standard theory that a judgment presupposes an act of the will and that *intuitus* is a stage of understanding which is prior to affirmation or negation. It is not surprising then when *intuitus* is equated with clear and distinct perception (X, 366, 400, 407).

When the time comes for an explicit definition Descartes warns that he is using words in a novel sense:

> Furthermore, so that no one will be disturbed by this new usage of the word [*intuitus*] and of other words also, which I will be constrained in the following pages to modify from their customary usage, I give notice here that I am usually not thinking at all of the way in which these terms have been used in recent years in the schools, for it would be very difficult to use the same words and to mean something very different by them. Instead I note the Latin meaning of each term, so that whenever appropriate words are lacking I exploit those which seem closest in meaning to what I wish to say (X, 369).[21]

The attempt to provide an explicit definition of the Cartesian sense of the term *'intuitus'* is found in rule 3, a few lines before the passage just quoted:

> By *'intuitus'* I do not mean the fluctuating evidence of the senses, nor the deceptive judgment of imagination when engaged in incorrect composition; rather I mean the understanding of a pure and attentive mind which is so simple and distinct that there is no room for doubt in what we understand. Or what amounts to the same thing, the indubitable understanding of a pure and attentive mind which derives from the light of reason alone, and which is more certain even than deduction . . . Thus everyone can intellectually understand that he exists, that he thinks (X, 368).

Descartes could be understood in this text to be either (*a*) denying the relevance of sense and imagination to *intuitus*, or (*b*) denying that one can define the term by reference to the characteristic functions or normal operation of the senses and the imagination. I argue in Chapter 7 that he is not proposing option (*a*); one clear piece of evidence may suffice for the present to justify adopting the second option. The discussion of optical refraction in Rule 8 includes the suggestion that a natural power is intelligible by means of an *intuitus mentis*. The subsequent rule clarifies this when it explains that such an *intuitus mentis* is available when we reflect on the experience of ordinary physical bodies moving in space.[22] This is further corroborated by a letter to Mersenne in 1638. Descartes had assumed in the *Dioptrics* that the refraction of light could be understood by analogy with tennis balls hitting a solid object and being deflected or refracted. In defence of this approach he wrote to Mersenne: 'What I claim to have demonstrated about refraction depends . . . only on my assumption that light is an action or a power which follows the same laws as local motion' (II, 142–3). Thus what was called an *intuitus mentis* in the *Regulae* is, in more mundane terms, a reflection on what happens when physical bodies undergo local motion. Even for Descartes, such an understanding presupposes an experiential familiarity with what is being reflected on.

Descartes' use of expressions such as *'intuitus purus'* (X, 440) admittedly has unfortunate connotations for the contemporary reader, connotations of a kind of direct, non-empirical inspection of the essence of rather suspect ontological simples. It should be understood rather as a term to refer to the intellectual dimension of human understanding which Descartes wishes to regard as an unanalysable datum of our experience. The unanalysable character of understanding is communicated by contrasting it with the discursive nature of inferences and, on the other hand, by means of the analogy with seeing. It is directed towards simple natures (X, 379); it provides a paradigm of certainty (X, 366, 389, 400); in fact, it is nothing more than an early formulation of the theory of clear and distinct perception. It reappears in the *Discourse* where Descartes claims that 'our imagination and our senses could never assure us of anything, if our understanding (*entendement*) did not intervene' (VI, 37).[23] And it found its most notorious expression in the *Meditations* in the wax example: 'I cannot understand what this wax is by using my imagination; I can only understand it (*quid sit . . . percipere*) by using my mind' (VII, 31). It is almost as if Descartes said: the intellect is the faculty of understanding, and the most simple or primitive act of understanding of the intellect is what I wish to call an *intuitus*. Since it is the most basic act of intellectual understanding it is not analysable into component parts and, a fortiori, it is not definable by reference to sense or imagination.

This basic intellectual act of understanding is exploited by Descartes for understanding concepts, but also for grasping conceptual relations between concepts or inferential relations between propositions. It is in this sense that one understands (*intueri*) that one thinks or exists (X, 368). The function of *intuitus* in understanding propositions is best discussed by reference to an example, such as the claim that 'matter is extended' is necessarily true.

Rule 12 explains the necessary connection between simple natures as follows:

we say that the conjunction of two simple natures . . . is necessary when one of them is so implied in the concept of the other in some integral way that we cannot conceive of either one distinctly if we think of them as separated; in this way, figure is conjoined with extension . . . because it is impossible to conceive of a figure which lacks extension (X, 421).

This rather vague explanation of the necessary conjunction of simple natures is applied to matter and extension in rule 14:

Let us look at the words: 'a body has extension', where we understand that 'extension' means something different from body. Despite this [difference in meaning] we do not form two distinct ideas in our imagination, one of the body and the other of its extension, but only one idea: of an extended body. And there is no distinction from the point of view of the object in saying: 'the body is extended' or 'what is extended is extended'. This is characteristic of those entities which exist only in another being and can never be thought of without a subject. (X, 444).

This text implies that 'matter' and 'extension' are not intensionally synonymous and therefore that the proposition that matter is extended is not analytically true.[24] A similar type of argument is given in the *Principles* (Part I, lx–lxiv) where Descartes develops the distinction between real identity and conceptual identity. In this terminology the concepts of matter and extension are not identical but there is no distinction in reality between their referents. And this is decided by recourse to the imagination! Since Descartes apparently does not wish to claim that 'matter is extended' is analytic, it could at best be classified as a synthetic a priori proposition. And then the question of how one justifies such a priori claims becomes more acute than before.

This is another case where *intuitus* or understanding is too accommodating to the complexity of the situation. Descartes sometimes refers to what he calls axioms or common notions, such as 'ex nihilo nihil fit' or 'impossibile est idem simul esse et non esse',[25] and it is not clear whether 'matter is extended' is equivalent to such axioms from the point of view of their justification. In fact, Descartes is not even sure what to think about the axioms themselves, and his ambivalence in this regard is another indication that he thinks of the act of understanding as more basic and important than any axiom, no matter how obvious.

Descartes apparently conceded a significant role to axioms in a letter to Plempius (Dec. 20, 1637). His correspondent had read the *Meteorology* and *Dioptrics* and had misunderstood the hypothetical status of the general assumptions about matter and motion which initiate those essays. In reply Descartes wrote:

The things which I say in the first chapters about the nature of light . . . are not my principles, as you seem to object, but rather the conclusions which are proved by everything that comes later. . . . The principles or premisses from which I derive these conclusions are only the axioms on which geometers base their demonstrations; for instance, 'the whole is greater than the part' . . . but they are not abstracted from all sensible matter as they are by geometers, but applied to various experiences which are known by means of the senses and are indubitable. (I, 476).

This suggests that the axioms are much more useful than they might appear to be when they are considered abstractly. They could also function as rules of inference or, in the language of the material mode, as a priori truths which could be known in advance and with certainty and then applied to various disciplines, including physics.

Despite this suggestion there are no examples of Descartes appealing to such axioms in the construction and elaboration of his physical theory. He certainly does construct more or less a priori arguments – that matter is extended, and divisible, and that empty space is impossible, is an obvious example of such a priori reasoning. But even in cases such as that one he does not appeal to abstract axioms to make his point. And this coincides with his attitude when he wrote to Clerselier, in 1646, that such axioms are 'of very slight importance and make us no wiser' (IV, 444). The apparent inconsistency in Descartes' evaluation of the worth of axioms is explained by the fact that *intuitus* is fundamental to the justification of both axioms and other a priori truths. Therefore, the axioms have no special status in science if that implies that they are more certain than other necessary truths which could be seen to be true by the exercise of *intuitus*. The impression given by the letter to Plempius is that the mind must somehow establish the truth of axioms in the abstract and then apply them to various physical or mathematical problems; once it is acknowledged that the axioms themselves are justified by *intuitus* it is a relatively short step to admitting that, as abstract or formal truths, they play no significant role in physical science. Whatever we can prove by using axioms we can just as easily prove by directly invoking the use of *intuitus*.

Thus *intuitus* can function both to understand basic concepts, and to understand the necessary connection between concepts, where the necessity of the connection provides unimpeachable evidence for the truth of judgments which report such necessary relations. Descartes assigns a third role to *intuitus* in the *Regulae*, that is, 'seeing' the logical relations between propositions. Once this is discussed it will then be possible to face the question of Descartes' comparative evaluation of the roles of reason and experience in scientific knowledge.

§8   *Reason and inference*

One might anticipate of Descartes a respectful and rationalist deference towards formal logic, even if he contributes little himself towards the development of the discipline. What one finds instead is a reasonably consistent rejection of formal logic as being of any significance for the discovery of truth in the sciences.

This attitude to logic is evident as early as the *Regulae*:

But perhaps some will be surprised that at this point where we are looking for a means of making ourselves more secure in deducing one truth from others, we omit any mention of the rules of the Dialecticians, by which they think human reason can be regulated. They prescribe certain forms of discourse which result in such necessary conclusions that the mind (*ratio*) which trusts these forms can reach certainty merely as a result of the forms, even if it fails to give attentive and clear consideration to an inference. (X, 405–6)

The forms of the syllogism do not help us in any way to perceive the truth about things. (X, 440).

The inadequacy of dialectic or syllogistic logic is reaffirmed in the *Discourse*:

in logic, its syllogisms and most of its other rules serve to explain to others the things one already knows – and even, in the art of Lull, to speak with apparent authority about things of which one is ignorant – rather than to learn them. (VI, 17).

In clarifying this text for Burman Descartes softens the criticism by claiming that his objections should be understood as directed at dialectic rather than at logic:

This [objection] really applies not so much to Logic, which provides demonstrative proofs on all subjects, but to Dialectic, which teaches us how to hold forth on all subjects. In this way it undermines good sense, rather than builds on it. For in diverting our attention and making us digress into the stock arguments and headings, which are irrelevant to the matter under discussion, it diverts us from the actual nature of the thing itself. (Cottingham, p. 46; adapted).

Descartes certainly found dialectic unacceptable because it camouflaged one's ignorance in such a sophisticated way that one could appear learned. However he also had two other objections to any kind of formal logic; these are important for his theory of science, and he must retain them if he hopes to be consistent. The two objections are: (i) that syllogistic logic does not help one discover anything new in the sciences but only provides a standardised form in which what is already known can be demonstratively expressed; and (ii) that the logical forms of the syllogism are not themselves self-evident or self-justifying.

The first point is more relevant to an examination of the Cartesian logic of discovery which is taken up below;[26] the second criticism of logic is implicit in the theory of reason or *intuitus* which Descartes defended as early as the *Regulae*. No more than the axioms discussed above, syllogistic forms are not transcendentally delivered with guarantees of validity. The mechanical use of forms of inference is clearly unjustified because if such forms can validate inferences then they must themselves be validated by reference to something else. And this something else is *intuitus*. So why should we settle for something less than the natural light of reason when formal logic presupposes the use of reason to validate its canonical forms? In fact, Descartes' point is rather stronger; the natural light of reason needs to be exercised to keep it in peak form and formal logic both cramps its versatility and diminishes its creativity in so far as it restricts its use to a mechanical application of rules. Any given inference is not valid, for Descartes, because it conforms to some rule; on the contrary, it can be seen to be valid or invalid only by recourse to *intuitus*. And the rules of formal logic, in turn, can be seen to be valid by induction from the particular cases of valid inferences which they model.[27]

In place of the fossilised forms of the logicians he was criticising, what is Descartes proposing to substitute for the working scientist? The one-word reply, *intuitus*, explains almost nothing to the extent that it denotes an unanalysable act of the human understanding. What one needs to explain the Cartesian alternative to formal logic is to look more closely at the kinds of inference which Descartes is willing to endorse as scientifically fruitful. An examination of the texts shows a surprising degree of flexibility here and an almost calculated ignoring of the distinction between inductive and deductive arguments. Any inference is acceptable, whether inductive or deductive, on condition that it is the best available access to the truth.

Among the terms used to denote inferential procedures one finds the following: *'illatio'*, *'inferre'*, *'deducere'* and *'deductio'*, *'demonstrare'* and *'demonstratio'*, *'inductio'* and *'probare'*, in Latin; and in French, *'inférer'*, *'déduire'*, *'prouver'*, *'démontrer'* and *'démonstration'*, *'dénombrer'* and *'dénombrement'*.[28] In attempting to sort out some of the ambiguities implicit in this repertoire one needs to distinguish two factors which determine Descartes' choice of terms on different occasions. The first one is what may be called the logical characteristics of an inference – the most obvious distinction here being between an induction and a deduction. The second factor which is more or less implicit in some contexts is the function of a given inference. For example, one could use a deductive argument to prove a theorem in geometry, to apply a moral principle to a specific set of circumstances, or to draw out some of the implications of adopting a given physical theory. In the case of scientific inferences, the basic functional distinction among types of inference is the difference between explanation and justification or, in Descartes' language, between explanation and proof.

The evidence of the texts suggests that it is seriously misleading to translate Cartesian terms into what might seem to be their contemporary English equivalents. Not only is a *deductio* sometimes not a proof but an explanation; it may also be what we would call an induction. To establish this point it is necessary to examine some texts in detail because the conclusions drawn here will be put to use in the next chapter in discussing the alleged logical relationship between metaphysical foundations and physical hypotheses.

Taking the second factor mentioned above as a starting point, it is clear that Descartes was aware of such a distinction and that he chose to use the word *'démontrer'* to mean either 'explain' or 'prove'. For example he claims in the *Discourse* that it is legitimate to propose hypotheses and then validate them by reference to their implied consequences. This is not circular: 'since experience makes most of these effects very certain, the causes from which I deduce (*déduire*) them serve less to prove them than to explain them (*expliquer*); but on the contrary, it is the causes which are proved by the effects' (VI, 76). This clarification was still somewhat enigmatic for readers of the *Discourse* and it is further explained in a letter to Morin, July 13, 1638: 'there is a big difference between proving and explaining. I should add that the word *'démontrer'* can be used to signify either, at least if it is used according to common usage and not in the technical philosophical sense' (II, 198). This is consistent with Cartesian practice; one finds the words *'demonstratio'*, *'démontrer'*, *'expliquer'* and even *'déduire'* or *'deducere'* used interchangeably to denote what we would classify as an explanation.[29] So that at least in the case of so-called demonstrations or deductions, it is not clear from the choice of terminology alone whether we are being offered a proof or justification of some hypothesis, or the explanation of known physical phenomena by reference to an hypothesis.

Even if this point is easily conceded it may still appear that, whether some inference is an explanation or a proof, it must be a deductive argument in the contemporary sense of that term, and that Descartes at least claims such logical rigour for whatever he is willing to endorse as scientifically viable. Again the texts are more ambiguous than may appear on first reading; even the *Regulae* includes inductive arguments among those classified as a *deductio*.

The *Regulae* reduces the sources of human knowledge to two, namely, experience and deduction. Since some kinds of experience are liable to error, scientific knowledge must rely on *intuitus* (a specific kind of experience) or deduction. This contrasting pair, *intuitus* and deduction, is mentioned six times in the *Regulae* together with a very significant variation in rule 3, *intuitus* and induction.[30] Since there are only two ways of acquiring scientific knowledge it follows that any inference which is acceptable to Descartes must be understood in terms of *intuitus* or as a deduction.

One of the objections already mentioned against formal logic was that it did not help the researcher discover anything new; it merely provided a technique for expressing what one already knows. If Cartesian deductions, by contrast, are meant to go beyond what is implicit in one's premisses then they cannot hope to be valid deductions in our sense of the term. It is most improbable that Descartes was aware of the problem he was dealing with here. He had no qualms in relying on a variety of supplementary propositions, many of them implicit, in the course of his type of deduction. The situation is further complicated by the fact that Descartes recognised the anomalous character of some scientific inferences and accordingly introduced the terms 'induction' or 'enumeration' to indicate their special status. This suggests that, at least within the terminology of the *Regulae*, almost all acceptable or reliable inferences are deductions (in the Cartesian sense, to be determined) and that some scientific deductions are special enough to merit the title 'induction' or 'enumeration'.[31]

This interpretation is corroborated by the few examples of scientific inference which appear in the *Regulae*. Rule 12 suggests a three-stage approach to discovering the nature of magnetism, and these suggestions are repeated in rule 13. Step 1 involves a diligent collection of whatever is experimentally known about magnets (X, 427); alternatively, one could become acquainted with the results of Gilbert's work and arrange these findings in a series which provides an adequate enumeration (*sufficienti enumeratione*) for the task at hand (X, 431–2). Step 2: from the evidence collected one should deduce (*deducere*) which combination of simple natures could explain the experimental findings. Where rule 12 uses '*deducere*' rule 13 substitutes '*inferre*'. Step 3: Once a workable hypothesis has been 'deduced' the scientist must acknowledge that he knows the nature of magnetism in so far as it can be known on the basis of the experimental evidence available to him (X, 427, 432).[32]

A sufficient enumeration or induction of empirically known facts, which is the starting point for this deduction, does not mean that one has all the information which could possibly be relevant for one's inquiry. Descartes more sensibly says that a sufficient enumeration involves some kind of choice on the part of the scientist of what information he thinks is relevant, and hence all physical theories are hypothetical, because there may be other factors which would require a change in theory and are either ignored or unknown:

> It should be noticed, besides, that by a sufficient enumeration or induction I merely understand one from which the truth can more certainly be concluded than from any other method of proof apart from a simple *intuitus* . . . it often happens that if one had to consider everything which was relevant to a proposed issue, one thing at a time, the life of any one individual would not be long enough (X, 389, 390–91).

There is another example of scientific reasoning in the discussion of the anaclastic; briefly, the following steps are involved in the discovery of the anaclastic:

(*a*) the correlation between the angle of incidence and the angle of refraction depends on changes in these angles in different media;
(*b*) this in turn presupposes some understanding of how light penetrates a medium, which implies that the nature of the light itself must be understood;
(*c*) to understand the characteristic way in which light acts, one must first understand natural powers in general because light is a natural power; the concept of a natural power is therefore the most primitive or basic concept in this investigation, i.e. it is the appropriate simple nature for explaining the optical phenomenon in question.
(*d*) if the nature of the action of light cannot be directly understood as a natural power, then one should enumerate as many other natural powers as one can so that the nature of illumination can at least be understood by analogy;
(*e*) once this step is reached, the inquirer is in a position to retrace the steps already taken and eventually discover the anaclastic.

Evidently this kind of inference includes some unlikely candidates for our understanding of deduction. The enumeration or induction over instances of natural powers which are understood from different contexts is an argument from analogy. And the step-by-step analysis of the problem could hardly be classified as a deductive procedure in our modern logical sense of the term. Yet both are acknowledged components, even in the *Regulae*, of Cartesian scientific inferences and such inferences must be analysable in terms of Descartes' pair, *intuitus* and deduction/induction.

One might be tempted to suggest here that *intuitus* could explain each step of such scientific inferences and that these examples throw no light on what Descartes means by 'deduction'. However, it is clear that *intuitus* can only discover or justify inferential moves from one proposition to another (X, 389, 407). As soon as an inference involves a series of more than two propositions, the conclusion one arrives at is no longer guaranteed merely by *intuitus*.

We can distinguish between the *intuitus* of the mind and certain deduction in this way: we conceive of some kind of movement or succession in the latter [deduction] but not in the former. And besides, the kind of present evidence which is necessary in the case of *intuitus* is not required in deduction, for deduction derives its certainty in a sense from memory. (X, 370).

Whatever else they might be, the discussions of magnetism and optics in the *Regulae* are paradigms of Cartesian deductions.

Therefore, in addition to the explanation/justification ambiguity in the Cartesian use of such words as 'deduction', there is a further ambiguity with respect to the logical character of the inferential procedures which they denote. 'Deduction' is a general term to refer to any inference which is reliable, no matter what its precise logical character in the contemporary sense of that phrase. *Intuitus* is the act of understanding, among other things, the evidentiary connections between propositions. Some inferences can be explained entirely in terms of *intuitus* and these approximate to what has traditionally been called immediate inferences.[33] Even here some qualification is necessary because Aristotelian immediate inferences were limited by the canonical forms in which arguments had to be expressed. If we must give Descartes the same term 'immediate inference', it evidently needs to be understood in a wider sense. Any inference from p to q without intermediate steps is a Cartesian immediate inference.

Apart from such unmediated inferences, other kinds of deduction presuppose that the understanding can traverse a number of steps before arriving at a conclusion and this kind of procedure involves the use of memory.[34] This explains why Descartes should confuse us in using apparently one concept to denote rather different logical steps. In its primary sense, induction involves a systematic consideration of all the members of a series, without specifying what these are. This is sometimes the textbook sense of examining many instances of the same phenomenon to generalise inductively about a class or kind, and this is one sense of Cartesian induction. However, the inquirer may just as likely be required to consider a series of propositions – in the course of an inference – and Descartes sees enough similarity between this procedure and induction over members of a class to warrant calling both ambiguously 'induction'. Since scientific inferences are characteristically long, complex reasoning processes involving the use of models, hypotheses, experimental evidence, etc. it is consistent both with the common usage of the day and with Descartes' own reflections on logic to call such inferences 'inductions'. So that scientific inductions in this more general sense of a complex reasoning process normally includes an induction over empirical findings as one of its constituent elements.

Neither of these kinds of induction is reducible to *intuitus*. Since all scientific knowledge is ultimately explicable either in terms of *intuitus* or deduction, it follows that Cartesian inductions are a species of deduction. This terminology will only surprise those who have not examined standard examples of what Descartes proposes as paradigms of his method at work in physical science.

This rather uninformative interpretation of Cartesian deduction – in the sense that it fails to define what would not count as a deduction, apart from immediate inferences – is consistent with Descartes' general attitude towards the natural light of reason and its alleged capacities. The innateness of ideas does not preclude a relevant empirical input in appropriate cases; *intuitus* does not preclude reflection on ordinary experience or experiments. And now deduction in physical science is consistent with the use of models and analogies, the collection of empirical evidence, etc. Despite these concessions, Descartes claims that reason is more reliable than experience.

§9 *Experience versus reason*

In Chapter 2 I have examined Descartes' understanding of the concept *'expérience'* and clarified some of the kinds of experience which he considers to be important in physical science; I suggested, in §5, that the notorious Cartesian criticism of empirical evidence involves at least two different issues, one of which was the preference for ordinary experience over experimental evidence even in situations where it might seem to us that the latter is both available and more reliable. The other issue was a general objection to any kind of empirical evidence when compared with the deliverances of 'reason'.

In §§6–8 of this chapter I have outlined a corresponding analysis of the concept 'reason'. In the light of the discussion to this point one may now raise the question: what could Descartes possibly mean by his repeated indications that he prefers reason to experience, or that experience is unreliable, or that only reason can be trusted to secure an indubitable access to the truth?

Two texts explain clearly what Descartes means; the first one is from the Replies to the sixth set of objections to the *Meditations*. It was urged against Descartes that the senses *are* reliable, and that mistakes which arise from trusting the senses are not corrected by recourse to the understanding but by reference to other empirically based knowledge. In reply Descartes explained his position thus:

when we say that the certitude of the intellect is much greater than the certitude of the senses, that simply means that those judgments which we make in mature years as a result of some new evidence are more certain than those we made in our infancy, without any critical reflection. And this is obviously the case. (VII, 438).

Descartes goes on to explain, against his critic, that one could not possibly correct an erroneous judgment based on the visual perception of an apparently bent stick in water by reference to tactual evidence alone. For one must also have a reason for preferring the tactual evidence to the visual evidence, and this can only be provided by 'reason' (VII, 439).

The final article of Part I of the *Principles* repeats the same contrast between sense and reason: those who wish to be considered true philosophers 'should put their trust less in the senses, that is in the ill-considered judgments of infancy, than in their mature reason' (in French: ' . . . than in his reason, when he is in a condition to guide it well'; IX-2, 62) (VIII-1, 39). As in the previous text, Descartes is not contrasting the senses with reason at all, at least in the way in which we normally use these terms.

Instead the proposed choice is between two kinds of judgment, *both of which are equally and unavoidably based on empirical evidence*. The first kind represents the spontaneous, uncritical[35] judgments we tend to make on the basis of our initial experience, and although such judgments evidently involve the understanding and the will, Descartes calls them 'sense'. The other kind – the more rational or reasonable judgment – is equally based on sensory evidence, at least in the sense that a judgment is made only after one has had a sensory experience or made an observation in the usual way. However this kind of judgment has the advantage of consulting more empirical evidence, and of being coupled with an explanation – perhaps even the correct explanation – of the phenomenon observed.

There are no decisive texts at all available where Descartes suggests that we ought to prefer reason to experience in any other sense. There are examples, discussed in §5 above, where he has reasons for doubting experiments; and there are all the well-known cases where he is reluctant to trust uncritically those judgments which are based on sensory data. But these texts do not justify our imposing on Descartes precisely the thesis which he claims to refute in the *Meditations*, namely that we must be suspicious of the validity of any kind of empirical evidence as such.[36] Once the Cartesian theory of our cognitive faculties is taken into account it seems that there is no way in which he could not say that all knowledge results from the understanding, whether or not this understanding, in turn, presupposes an empirical input. On this latter point he is often bluntly explicit: For example, in a letter to Mersenne, August 6, 1640, he wrote: 'That is a question of fact, which cannot be determined by reason' (III, 147).

A more nuanced picture of the precise balance between experience and reason in Cartesian science can only be sketched after examining the role of hypotheses in science, and the relationship between physics and metaphysics. These questions are taken up in the following chapters. Pending further investigation of the texts, at least this tentative conclusion may be drawn: that Descartes' word usage is considerably less clear and distinct than a casual reading of the texts might suggest, and that one should seriously question an interpretation of Cartesian texts which attributes to Descartes a position which is scarcely reasonable for an active, working scientist. Thus, whatever else the priority of reason over experience might mean, it most probably does not mean that one approaches the explanation of physical phenomena without a careful examination of all the relevant empirical evidence available, or that one might justifiably substitute rational arguments for observations and experiments. Descartes' practice of scientific investigations and his ample correspondence clearly show that he presupposes – as something almost too obvious to mention – that research in the physical sciences must begin with empirical evidence.

When he claims that reason must be trusted rather than experience, he may mean:

(*a*) that experimental evidence is inferior to reflection on ordinary experience; or
(*b*) that experimental evidence is not trustworthy when it is not considered in conjunction with the correct '*raison*', i.e. theory; or
(*c*) that uncritical judgments based on any kind of observational evidence are inferior to the critical judgments of maturity, where these critical empirical judgments are called *reason*.

But pure reason, i.e. the use of intellectual faculties without any sensory input, is useless for a science of physical nature.

Notes

1 This was the interpretation adopted by L. Liard, in *Descartes*, p. 122.
2 See Cottingham, *Conversation with Burman*, pp. xxxiii–xxxiv for this position.
3 Cf. *Principles*, VIII-1, 35–6, which is consistent with this interpretation.
4 See VII, 160–1; *Discourse*, VI, 55.
5 The order of these three sentences has been changed, from the original text, to better represent the argument. A similar argument for the innateness of ideas, based on the disparity between the data of our senses and the intellectual character of ideas is found in Descartes to Mersenne, July 22, 1641 (III, 418).
6 Cf. Gilson, *Discours*, pp. 327–30.

7 The same distinction is found in the *Meditations* (VII, 37–8), and the Annotations to the *Principles* (XI, 655). The letter to Voetius, (VIII-2, 166–7), makes it clear that the mind is not explicitly aware of these innate ideas prior to some kind of intellectual activity, and that they are known without any experiential contribution ('absque ullo sensuum experimento').

8 This analogy is found in the Annotations to the *Principles*, where innate ideas are said to exist in the mind 'potentia duntaxat'; (XI, 655).

9 This analogy is suggested in a letter to an unknown correspondent, dated August 1641: 'The child has no less an idea of God, of himself and of all those truths which are said to be known *per se*, than adults have when they do not attend to them' (III, 424).

10 'Those [ideas] are purely intellectual which are known to the intellect by a certain innate light and without any assistance from corporeal imagination; for it is certain that there are some such ideas, nor can one imagine any corporeal image which would represent to us what knowledge is, or doubt, or ignorance . . . and similar things' (X, 419).

11 'It [the idea of God] must be innate in me, in the same way in which the idea of myself is innate' (VII, 51).

12 A good indication of how we ought to interpret Descartes is found in his immediate followers in France, at least those who claimed to be agreeing with him. For example, Pierre-Sylvain Régis (1632–1707) defends the suggestion that 'all our ideas come to us through sensation . . . Thus, the idea of God comes through sensation . . . When I say that the ideas of God, of the soul and of the body are innate, I do not mean that they are independent of the body; I mean to say only that these ideas are always in the soul explicitly or implicitly' (*L'Usage de la raison et de la foy, ou l'accord de la foy et de la raison* (Paris, 1704), pp. 21, 27).

13 See VIII-2, 357, 358 and 359; the *Conversation with Burman* (Cottingham), p. 3.

14 VIII-1, 9.

15 Cf. the translation by Jean-Luc Marion, in *Règles utiles et claires pour le direction de l'esprit en la recherche de la vérité*, p. 19: 'Il faut remarquer deuxièmement qu'il n'y a que bien peu de natures pures et simples, qu'il soit permis de regarder d'abord et par elles-mêmes, . . . soit dans les expériences mêmes, soit par une certaine lumière mise en nous.'

16 The same distinction between simple in itself and *quoad nos* is drawn in the *Recherche de la vérité*, X, 504–5. The simplicity *quoad nos* is reflected in the *Regulae* in X, 420 and 422.

17 X, 383. 'It should be noted, secondly, that there are few pure and simple natures which we can intuit initially and absolutely, independently of all others, either in various actual experiences or through some innate light in us.' Descartes lists the sources of human knowledge as experience or deduction, and the sources of

scientific knowledge as *intuitus* and deduction. Hence *intuitus* must be a special kind of reliable experience. When, in X, 389, he contrasts experience and *intuitus*, one can assume that by 'experimentis' he means some kind of sensory experience which would not qualify as 'an innate light of the mind'.

18 See also *ibid.*, 'mentis inspectio' (VII, 32).
19 There are thirty-three references to *intuitus* in the *Regulae*, and a further thirty-three forms of the verb *'intueri'*, in the relatively short space of a text of 109 pages.
20 X, 366, 368, 369, 370, 372, 400, 425.
21 See the texts collected by J. L. Marion, in *Règles*, pp. 119–26, which illustrate some of the senses in which 'intuitus' was used in the schools. 'Descartes se situe donc face à une position précise, constante et repérable, qui comprend la sensation elle-même comme, dans certains cas au moins, dépositaire de l'*intuitus*. Il récuse donc une thèse historiquement constatable' (pp. 121–2).
22 X, 402.
23 Cf. *Discourse*, VI, 39: 'We should never allow ourselves to be persuaded of anything except by the evidence of reason. And one should note that I say "of reason", and not [the evidence] of our imagination or of our senses.'
24 Descartes is not always consistent in this regard. Thus he wrote to Mersenne, September 30, 1640, that 'an atom can never be conceived distinctly, since the very meaning of the word involves a contradiction' (III, 191). This should be understood as an exaggeration rather than a change in theory. He returns to the same theme in writing to More, February 5, 1649, where he does not claim that the meanings of words can establish the same thesis: 'in the same way I say that it involves a contradiction that there should be any atoms which are understood as extended and also indivisible' (V, 273).
25 See *Le Monde*, XI, 47; *Principles*, IX-2, 35; VIII-1, 23; *Conversation with Burman* (Cottingham), p. 34.
26 Cf. Gerd Buchdahl, 'Descartes' anticipation of a "logic of scientific discovery" ', in *Scientific Change*, ed. A. C. Crombie, pp. 399–417.
27 This is also consistent with Descartes' thesis that we normally proceed from our knowledge of individual instances to general knowledge claims. See the *Conversation with Burman*, p. 4; VII, 140–1; IX-1, 205–6.
28 There is some indication of either flexibility in word usage or change in understanding, reflected in a change of terminology, in the fact that neither 'induction' nor 'deduction' occurs in the *Discourse* at all, although they had been used five times and nineteen times, respectively, in the *Regulae*.
29 There is a more detailed discussion of deduction and demonstration, together with examples from Cartesian texts, in Appendix 1.
30 X, 366, 369, 370, 373, 400, 425 and 368. I follow the recent French translation of the Crapulli edition of the *Regulae* in not translating 'intuitus' as intuition and in preserving the variant reading, 'induc-

tion', in rule 3. See *Règles*, trans. Jean-Luc Marion.

31   The 'almost' here is inserted to cover those cases of immediate inference, mentioned below, which can be adequately accounted for in
terms of *intuitus* alone.

32   Compare the hypothetical approach to explaining magnetism in the
Principles, Part IV, articles cxxxiii–cxxxix.

33   Cf. *Regulae*, X, 389 and 407: 'All the propositions which we have
derived immediately from others, on condition that the inference
was evident, have been to that extent reduced to a genuine *intuitus*';
'we have said that the simple deduction of one thing from another is
made by an *intuitus*'.

34   Cf. *Regulae*, X, 370, 389, 408, where Descartes links the fallibility of
deductions with their assumed dependence on memory. In a letter
(to the Marquis of Newcastle), in March or April, 1648, he wrote:
'whatever knowledge we have or acquire by the use of reason is as
dark as the principles from which it is derived and is infected with
the uncertainty we find in all our reasonings' (V, 137).

35   In Latin, 'absque ulla consideratione' (VII, 438); 'judicia incon-
siderata' (VIII-1, 39).

36   Cf. *Principles*, VIII-1, 17.

FOUR

Metaphysics and physics

By the time Descartes published the *Discourse* in 1637 one might assume that he had clarified how the various disciplines with which he was familiar should be related. Granted he was critical at this stage of how the specialists in various disciplines had pursued their work and he apparently had rather definite ideas as to how their mistakes should be remedied. But he also assumed that, at least with respect to the relationship between philosophy and physics, these two rejuvenated disciplines should continue to interact in much the same way as the scholastic tradition had demanded.

This is especially clear from the first two parts of the *Discourse* where he is reflecting on the body of learning he rejects and on his recommended method for discovering their appropriate replacements. Traditional philosophy, in his estimation, is so riddled with incompatible theories that most of it must be worthless; and he can say the same of most other disciplines too. In spite of this, Descartes still assumed that philosophy must provide some kind of foundation for all the other sciences:

I will say nothing about Philosophy except that, seeing that it has been cultivated by the most excellent thinkers who have lived for many centuries, and that despite this one finds nothing in it which is not in dispute and therefore doubtful, I did not presume to find anything better there than others. And considering how many different opinions about the same subject one can find there, which are defended by learned people, although not more than one of them could ever be true, I looked upon everything which was only plausible almost as if it were false. Then, as regards the other sciences, *in so far as they borrow their principles from Philosophy,* I decided that nothing solid could be built on foundations which were so weak. (VI, 8–9; my italics).

The same assumption comes through clearly in Part II, in which Descartes proposes four rules to improve the reliability both of philosophy and of the other sciences:

But having noticed that their principles [i.e. those of sciences other than algebra] should all be borrowed from Philosophy, in which I still had found nothing certain, I thought that I should try to establish some principles there before all else. (VI, 21–22).

This is a constant theme in Cartesian writing. The language in which it is expressed changes slightly from one context to another; in most cases not only is philosophy said to provide a foundation for other sciences or to lend them its principles, but the other sciences are said to be deduced from metaphysics or to be demonstrated from philosophical principles. This thesis raises doubts about the significance of experiential evidence in Cartesian science, at least with respect to its first principles or basic laws. For if Descartes means what he seems to say, then the principal warrant for the laws of nature derives, a priori, from the metaphysical principles from which they were deduced; the references to experience which occur in the enunciation of the laws must be taken as mere illustrations of how the laws apply to experience rather than as an a posteriori justification. If this is the case then Cartesian science is significantly a priori; if it assigns any role to experience for testing or corroborating hypotheses, it can only be at a much later stage of theory construction when the laws of nature are applied to the explanation of specific natural phenomena.

I wish to re-examine the extent to which the basic assumptions of Cartesian physics are in fact derived from a metaphysical basis by Descartes, and also to clarify the sense in which Descartes claims to have justified them in this fashion. The evidence from the texts shows that Descartes did not have a clear, exclusively logical relation in mind when he repeatedly suggested that physics is deducible from metaphysics.[1] In attempting to clarify Descartes' position I briefly investigate the Cartesian distinction between physics and metaphysics in §10. The subsequent section reviews the various ways in which Descartes describes the dependence of physics on metaphysics and suggests a number of logical models to which his rather loose language may approximate. Finally, in §12, I take a detailed look at the way in which Descartes actually warrants the fundamental principles of his physics in *Le Monde* and the *Principles*. By superimposing the logical models proposed in §11 on to Descartes' actual procedure as described in §12, one finds that physics depends on metaphysics in many ways, none of which is equivalent to a simple logical deduction of physics from metaphysics. It is nevertheless consistent with the loose understanding of 'deduction' proposed in §8 above to describe this multifaceted relationship as a deduction.

§10   *The Cartesian distinction between physics and metaphysics*

It is not easy to draw a sharp line of demarcation between physics and metaphysics, either in Descartes or in contemporary physics.[2] Nor does one need such a sharp distinction to investigate the issue at hand. Descartes assumed that it was possible to distinguish adequately between metaphysics and physics, and even to distinguish within the latter between the more basic assumptions of physics and the articulation of these assumptions or principles in the explanation of specific natural phenomena. It was some such set of distinctions which was implicit in the metaphorical description of his scientific project as a tree of knowledge. This metaphor occurs in the Preface to the French edition of the *Principles*:

Thus Philosophy as a whole is like a tree whose roots are metaphysics, whose trunk is physics, and whose branches are all the other sciences. These reduce to three principal ones, viz. medicine, mechanics and morals (IX-2, 14).

This rather vague division of disciplines is clarified to some extent in the text of the *Principles*, Part II of which contains certain general laws or principles which Descartes claims are applicable to, and sufficient to explain, all physical phenomena. The tree metaphor also suggests the organic unity of the *Principles*, and this unity is explicated by Descartes as a deductive connection between the roots, the trunk and the branches. If one could assume that there are no issues involved in how one models the trunk–branch distinction on to the text of the *Principles*, or at least that whatever problems arise with the distinction are independent of the issue currently under consideration, then one can concentrate on deciphering the tree metaphor with respect to two issues: (*a*) the distinction between metaphysics and physics, represented as roots and trunk, and (*b*) the connection between metaphysics and physics represented as a deductive relation or, in the language of the metaphor, as a singularly dependent relationship analogous to the root–trunk connection.

Descartes variously characterises metaphysics in terms of the object of inquiry, the kind of evidence which is appropriate to verifying metaphysical claims, or by reference to its foundational role vis-à-vis other kinds of knowledge. The last of these – metaphysics as a search for first principles – seems to be the most basic criterion; in fact, all three criteria are interdependent. Thus the Preface to the *Principles* explains that philosophy must begin with 'the investigation of these first causes, i.e. of the principles' (IX-2, 2) and must 'seek out the first causes and the true principles from which an explanation may be deduced for all that we are capable of knowing' (*ibid.*, 5).

The use of the term 'principle' here is subject to the usual ambiguity between a principle as a thing and a principle as a proposition. This is especially clear when Descartes inquires about the nature 'de la cause ou du Principe' (IX-2, 8) which makes objects appear as if they were forced by gravity towards the earth's surface. Is the cause in question a natural phenomenon, such as a gravitational force, or a principle which describes the operation of such a force and thereby provides a starting point for a scientific explanation? Descartes attempts to clarify this ambiguity in a letter to Clerselier in 1646, but his very clarification is compromised by the same ambiguity again:

I will only add that the word 'principle' can be understood in several senses. It is one thing to look for *a common notion* so clear and so general that it can serve as a principle to prove the existence of all the beings, the *Entia*, to be discovered later; and another to look for a *being* whose existence is known to us better than that of any others, so that it can serve as a *principle* to discover them (IV, 444: italics in original).

In the very next paragraph he gives two examples, but both of them are propositions:

In the first sense, it can be said that 'the same thing cannot both be and not be at the same time' is a principle . . . In the second sense, the first principle is *that our soul exists*, because there is nothing whose existence is better known to us.

The slip in Descartes' exposition is understandable and does not undermine the point he is making. One sense of 'principle' refers to propositions which are guaranteed as certain; the other meaning of the term applies to things the knowledge of which is basic for understanding anything else. In the latter sense, knowledge of the existence of the soul is basic for Descartes and hence the soul is a principle. However, any knowledge claim about such thing-principles will be expressed in propositions, and such propositions also function for Descartes as principles of knowledge although they may not be self-evident. What the two kinds of proposition – i.e. self-evident common notions and knowledge claims about thing-principles – have in common is that they function as basic assumptions in the 'deductive' construction of science. This ambiguity in the term 'principle' will be put to use later in deciphering the arguments in favour of laws of nature in Part II of the *Principles*.

In the object sense of 'principle' Descartes invariably describes metaphysics as the study of God and the separated soul, i.e. of 'immaterial or metaphysical things' (IX-2, 10).[3] This suggests that the metaphysical nature of this study is a function of the immateriality of the objects of inquiry; however, since the study of God and the soul functions in the Cartesian project as a basis for the reliability of all knowledge claims, the study of God and the soul is equally metaphysical in so far as it provides the first principles – in the sense of propositions – of knowledge. The dual metaphysical status of such a study emerges in the Preface to the *Principles*, Part I of which is said to be concerned with 'metaphysics, which contains the principles of knowledge, amongst which is the explanation of the principal attributes of God, of the immateriality of our souls, and of all the clear and simple notions which are in us' (IX-2, 14).[4]

Metaphysics then for Descartes comprises the first principles of knowledge, i.e. those truths which must be known as a condition for the possibility of knowing anything else – and these include the study of God and the separated soul – and those axioms or primary notions which are known by the natural light of reason independently of experience. These principles are logically prior to all others which we are capable of knowing without the aid of divine revelation; they are known by the natural light of reason without any experiential input as evidence;[5] and they function as the foundations of all other knowledge claims. For ease of reference they can be classified here as metaphysical principles, or M-principles.

Apart from these fundamental principles which are assumed in any knowledge claim, Descartes needs some other principles about the nature of matter to launch him on an explanation of such diverse phenomena as rain, magnetism, optical refraction, the circulation of the blood, etc. Thus, while the M-principles function in one sense as the foundations of physics, they are just as much the foundations of mathematics or of morals; what is needed are other principles which are specific to physics and these will be called physical principles, or P-principles.

The following list does not claim to be exhaustive, but it does include a representative sample of the basic assumptions about matter and motion which Descartes explicitly introduces as first principles of physics:

P1: The essence of matter is extension. (Therefore matter is indefinitely divisible, space is identical with matter, etc.).[6]
P2: There are three basic types of material particles, and these are characterised by their geometrical properties and by their quantity of movement (IX-2, 128–9).
P3: The principle of inertia: 'Everything in so far as it is simple and undivided always remains in the same condition as long as it can and it is never changed except by external causes.' (VIII-1, 62).
P4: The principle of rectilinear motion: 'No piece of matter, considered on its own, tends to continue its movement in a curved line but only in a straight line' (VIII-1, 63).
P5: The principle of conservation of the quantity of motion: 'When a moving body encounters another, if it has less force to continue in a straight line than the other body has to resist it, then it is deflected somewhere else and, while it retains its motion, it loses only the determination of its motion; if however it has a greater force, then it moves the other body with itself and it loses as much of its own motion as it transfers to the other body.' (VIII-1, 65).

Using these five P-principles as a study sample and assuming the rough working model of metaphysics outlined above, the question at issue can now be formulated more precisely: in what sense does Descartes claim to deduce these P-principles logically from M-principles, and to what extent does he succeed in actually carrying out such a project?

§11 *Physics derived from metaphysics*

P. Costabel has argued that Descartes' views on the relationship between physics and metaphysics vary between a tentative and relatively unclear version in early correspondence and, on the other hand, an apparently clear and more rigid view in the *Meditations* and the *Principles*.[7] It is perhaps more likely that the apparent rigidity and relative unclarity are found both in private correspondence and in Descartes' public theory. To introduce a discussion of this issue it may be useful to examine texts from different published works and from different periods in Descartes' life; the variety of ways in which the metaphysics–physics relation is expressed provides strong evidence for thinking that the textual indications alone do not clearly favour a unique interpretation of the relationship in question.

As early as 1630 Descartes suggests that his projected physics would depend, in some sense, on a metaphysical foundation. He wrote to Mersenne that year (April 15), apropos of metaphysics:

It is there that I have tried to begin my studies; and I can tell you that I would not have been able to discover the foundations of physics if I had not looked for them in this direction. (I, 144).

The *Discourse* returns to this theme, in the texts quoted above, with the suggestion that the other sciences borrow (*empruntent*) their principles from philosophy (VI, 8–9; 21–22); there is also a rather different suggestion, in Part VI, that the first principles of physics are all so self-evident that Descartes could provide a demonstration for them if requested (VI, 68). However he does not indicate if the demonstration in question might involve a logical derivation of the principles from some more general or metaphysical principles, or by some other means.

There is an interesting twist in the language of demonstrating the first principles of physics at the beginning of the *Meteorology*, where Descartes writes:

It is true that, since the knowledge of these things depends on general principles of Nature which, as I realise, have not yet been well explained (*expliqués*), I must use some assumptions at the beginning, as I have done in the *Dioptrics*. However, I will try to make them so simple and easy that you will find no difficulty in believing them, even though I have not yet demonstrated (*demontrées*) them. (VI, 233).

While this text may initially suggest that explanation and demonstration are two distinct procedures, it may also be interpreted consistently with the discussion in §8 above: in that case, to explain the principles is equivalent to demonstrating them.

The deductive unity of science is evident from Descartes' repeated assertion that if some implications of physical principles are false, then the whole of physics is untenable. This view of the unity of science is found, for example, in a letter to Mersenne in 1639 (February 9):

I do indeed wish that one should consider that, if what I have written on this matter [blood circulation], or on refraction, or on any other topic which I have dealt with in more than three lines of what I have published turns out to be false, then the rest of my Philosophy is worthless. (II, 501).[8]

Although this implies a significant interdependency between general principles and specific applications of them it hardly enlightens us much as to the logical character of the relation involved.

In correspondence with Regius in 1640 Descartes explained that the existence of God merely makes scientific knowledge possible, in so far as science presupposes judgments which are certain.[9] In that sense he can claim that 'the *Meditations* contain all the foundations of my physics' (III, 298). The Synopsis of the *Meditations* reviews plausible reasons for doubt, 'at least as long as we have no other foundations (*fundamenta*) of science than those we have had up to the present' (VII, 12). The very next page, however, suggests that the proof of the soul's immortality depends on physics: 'the premisses from which the immortality of the soul may be concluded depend on the explanation of the whole of physics (*ex totius Physicae explicatione dependent*)' (VII, 13). The concept of interdependence which operates here comes close to the idea that physics and philosophy, in the Cartesian project, stand or fall together and that arguments made in one area presuppose either concepts or arguments used in another.

The first Meditation returns to the image of foundations for knowledge to examine plausible reasons for doubting those 'principles on which everything I previously believed rested' (VII, 18). The principles at issue here include the *senses*. In other words, Descartes is concerned with the reliability of our cognitive faculties and these faculties are counted among the principles or foundations of knowledge. Hence the certitude of all knowledge claims depends on (*pendere*) our certitude of God's existence. (VII, 69).[10]

The publication of the *Principles* in 1644 provided an ideal opportunity for clarifying the sense in which physics allegedly depends on metaphysics. As explained in a letter to Chanut, Part I of the *Principles* is a summary of the *Meditations*;[11] true to form what one finds there is another expression of Descartes' standard account of the way in which our cognitive faculties are warranted, and this account contains the 'praecipua cognitionis humanae principia' (VIII-1, 39). These primary principles are equivalent to Descartes' theory of knowledge. Just as one imagines that the ambivalence about foundations is resolved, however, we encounter another suggestion that physical explanations should be deduced from our knowledge of God:

Indeed, since God alone is the true cause of all that is or could be, it is evident that the best way of philosophising for us to follow would be to try to deduce the explanation of things created by God from our knowledge of God himself, and thereby to acquire the most perfect science, which is knowledge of effects through their causes. (VIII-1, 14).

This proposal is promptly qualified by the acknowledgement that God is infinite and therefore beyond the capacities of our intellectual faculties. So that the best approach might be to assume that God is the efficient cause of everything and then use the natural light of reason to discover what little God has deigned to make known to us about his nature by examining physical phenomena (VIII-1, 15–16).

The Preface to the French edition of 1647 is more forthcoming on this particular question than the Latin edition, at least in so far as it attempts to explain what is meant by a principle:

it is on these [principles] that the knowledge of other things depends, in such a way that the former can be known without the latter but not, reciprocally, the latter without the former; and besides one must attempt to deduce (*déduire*) from these principles the knowledge of whatever depends on them in such a way that there is nothing, in the whole series of deductions which results from them, which is not very obvious. (IX-2, 2).

There is also an endorsing reference, in the Preface, to the sages of the past who searched for 'first causes and true principles from which one could deduce (*déduire*) the explanation of everything which one is capable of knowing' (IX-2, 5). Descartes emulates their achievements by articulating his own principles 'concerning immaterial or metaphysical things, from which I deduce (*déduits*) very clearly the principles of corporeal or physical things' (IX-2, 10). Hence those who fail to acknowledge the Cartesian liaison between metaphysics and physics are chided for their mistakes; for example, Regius apparently agreed with Descartes' physics, but he mistakenly 'denied some truths of metaphysics on which the whole of physics ought to rest (*estre appuyée*)' (IX-2, 19).

Descartes returns once again to the theme in a letter to Clerselier in 1646 which has already been quoted in part above. Not only are there two kinds of principle, and at least one of them – the axioms or common notions – relatively uninformative, but Descartes concedes furthermore that we tend to expect too much from principles of any description:

I also add that it is not a condition one should impose on a first principle, that it should be such that all the other propositions could be reduced to or proven by it. It is enough that it could serve to discover some other [propositions], and that there is no other principle on which it depends nor which one could more easily discover than it. For it may be the case that there is no principle in the world to which alone all things could be reduced (IV, 444–5).

These texts indicate clearly that Descartes hoped to guarantee the reliability of our cognitive faculties and, at least in that sense, to provide foundations for physics. They also imply an ideal of scientific knowledge in which the metaphysical underpinnings would be deductively related to the explanations of diverse physical phenomena. And the precise way in which this deductive connection might be understood remains as vague as ever, despite the number and variety of ways in which Descartes mentions it.

To focus attention on this question it may be helpful to introduce some abstract logical models and then compare the models with the texts in which Descartes claims to deduce physics from metaphysics. Let p be any one of the five P-principles already identified. I assume that Descartes relies on a finite number of basic metaphysical propositions as the 'foundation' for physics; let $\mathscr{M}$ be the conjunction of such relevant M-principles. It is not clear whether there is any Cartesian distinction between metaphysical propositions and other propositions which are warranted exclusively by a purely intellectual intuition. If there is such a distinction in Descartes, then let $\mathscr{I}$ be the conjunction of a finite number of such relevant propositions. Finally, let $\mathscr{E}$ be the conjunction of a finite number of relevant, empirically warranted propositions. Using these symbols and standard Polish notation, the following models may approximate to the Cartesian 'deduction' of physics from metaphysics:

L1: Lp
L2: $LC\mathscr{M}p$
L3: $LCK\mathscr{M}\mathscr{I}p$
L4: $LCK\mathscr{M}\mathscr{E}p$
L5: $MK\mathscr{M}p$
L6: $LCKK\mathscr{M}\mathscr{E}\mathscr{I}p$

The question: what does Descartes mean by the deduction of physics from metaphysics, can now be transformed into the following – which of the logical models, L1–L6, if any, represents Descartes' procedure when he apparently deduces physics from a metaphysical foundation?

§12   Le Monde *and the* Principles

Le Monde

Descartes' first systematic account of physical nature opens with various examples of perception which are exploited to cast doubt on the thesis that we perceive external objects and events in such a way that our perceptions correspond to their primary qualities. The sceptical attitude generated here is put to use in the subsequent discussion of our experience of light.

The most obvious feature of the discussion in Chapter 2 is that the author proceeds hypothetically. He cannot claim to *know* that there are no such entities as 'the form of fire' or 'the quality of heat' (IX, 7); therefore he relies on the principle of not postulating unnecessary entities in our attempts to explain natural phenomena. 'For my part, since I fear to be mistaken if I suppose there is anything more [in the wood] than what I recognise must necessarily be in it, I am satisfied to think of the movement of its parts' (XI, 7). The assumption of a violent motion of its small particles appears to be enough to explain 'all the same changes which one experiences when it burns' (XI, 8), without postulating forms or qualities. The particles-in-motion hypothesis must explain not only what happens to the wood when it burns, but also our experience of heat and light while the wood is burning. If the hypothesis can explain these experiences as well then 'it will not be necessary that there is any other quality in it, and we can say that it is this movement alone which, by virtue of the different effects it produces, is sometimes called heat and sometimes light' (XI, 9).

Not surprisingly, Descartes tries to explain our experience of heat as an effect of small particles from burning objects impinging on our skin. And this theory is partly confirmed, he thinks, by experience: 'Some experiences even favour this opinion' (XI, 10). There is no hint anywhere in the treatise up to this point that we are discussing anything more than an hypothesis which has been formulated within the framework of a theory of small particles of matter in motion. As regards light, 'one could indeed likewise think that the same movement which is in the flame would suffice for us to perceive it' (XI, 10).

Chapter 3 begins with a long list of changes which have been observed in natural phenomena; it concludes that the particle nature of matter and the diversity of motions in matter are both known beyond doubt ('je connois evidemment', p. 11) because they are necessary to explain these observed phenomena. These two features of matter are enough 'to explain the cause of all the changes which occur in the world and of all the variations which appear on earth' (XI, 12). A new explanatory concept emerges later in the chapter – it is not only the speed of moving particles but also their size which helps explain why we experience them differently, such as our sensation of the wind or of burning (XI, 15). The specific description of the size and speed of the particles which explain any given sensation is a matter of conjecture ('on le peut conjecturer', XI, 16).

Chapter 4 involves a discussion of the non-existence of a vacuum in nature. Descartes wishes to establish the thesis that matter circulates in constant motion in the universe and that as soon as one part of matter moves to a new place, some other parts of matter come to fill the empty place. The examples he quotes in support of the thesis that there is no vacuum in nature do not suffice to prove it conclusively:

On the other hand, I do not wish to assume for all that that there is no vacuum at all in nature; I would be afraid that my discussion would become too long if I undertook to explain in what sense there is a vacuum in nature. And the experiences of which I spoke are not enough to prove it, although they do suffice to show that the places where we perceive (*sentons*) nothing are filled with the same matter and, to say the least, contain as much of this matter as those which are occupied by bodies which we perceive (XI, 20–21).

Again we find a typical Cartesian combination of speculative hypotheses and reliable sensory experiences combined to corroborate a proposal which might be translated as: assume that there is no vacuum in nature, for this assumption is consistent with various cited experiences. Then we can incorporate this new assumption into the general picture of physical nature on which the explanation of light depends. 'It only remains now to consider what these other bodies are [which are mingled with the air]; and after that I hope it will not be difficult to understand what the nature of light may be' (XI, 23).

Descartes next introduces his theory of three kinds of elements or basic types of matter. To some extent this theory is derived from 'les philosophes', and Descartes understands his procedure at this point as nothing more than 'following their opinion' (XI, 23). There is one major source of disagreement, however, between Descartes and those he follows; while many philosophers include secondary properties such as 'heat, cold, humidity and dryness' (XI, 25) as characteristics of the basic elements, Descartes wishes to describe the latter exclusively by reference to their 'motion, size, shape and the arrangement of their parts' (XI, 26). At the same time it is significant that the description of the three kinds of matter is introduced by such phrases as 'je crois', 'j'imagine', 'je me persuade' and so on; and the final paragraph of this chapter excuses the author from introducing more evidence to make his 'opinions more probable' (XI, 31), by changing from an explanation of this world to the articulation of a model universe which presumably matches it.

The construction of a model world is initiated in Chapter 6 by first postulating matter in space and attributing nothing to this matter except what 'everyone can know as perfectly as possible' (XI, 33). In other words, matter has no forms or scholastic qualities, nor anything 'in the nature of which one could say there is something which is not evidently known by everyone' (XI, 33); 'it contains nothing which is not so perfectly known to the reader that you could not even pretend not to know it' (XI, 35). This phrase re-occurs in the *Discourse*, part v. It is important to notice that it is first used in *Le Monde* as an indication of the conceptual limitations within which Descartes hopes to construct a viable explanation of light. One need not postulate metaphysical or unintelligible properties in matter; one need only think of it as having very simple properties which are such that no one could genuinely claim not to understand them very well, such as shape, size and motion. The only hint of the later Cartesian thesis that matter is extension occurs towards the end of the chapter:

But they [philosophers] should not find it strange if I assume that the quantity of the matter which I described does not differ any more from its substance than number differs from numbered things, and if I conceive of its extension, or its property of occupying space, not as an accident but as its true form and essence. (XI, 36).

The proposed justification for each of these conceptions was not explicitly metaphysical, but simply that they were very easy ways of understanding matter!

Once matter is created by God and is assumed to have the simple properties which Descartes attributes to it, the laws which God has imposed on nature are such that, of their own accord,[12] they will disentangle and structure matter to produce a world which contains not only light, but all the other things which appear in the real world (XI, 34–5). So far there is no suggestion of a metaphysical derivation of any basic assumptions of Cartesian physics; perhaps God's creating the laws of nature as he did will provide an instance of the theory standardly attributed to Descartes.

Descartes' discussion of God's agency in creating and conserving the universe is often understood as if God were constantly at work in the universe after its creation in such a way that whatever happens there can be attributed to his causal agency. This interpretation fails to take account of the scholastic view of God's actions which Descartes is simply repeating. If one can stretch human language to speak about God's point of view then – from that perspective – there is no real distinction between creation and conservation. God's actions are eternal or non-temporal, and it makes no sense to think of God first creating the universe and then conserving it. It is one and the same atemporal act on God's part to create/conserve the universe. From our perspective within time we view the atemporal action of God as being temporally implemented. So the fact that the universe continues in existence from one moment to the next is obviously attributable to God; but it cannot be meaningfully attributed to him as if he were acting from one moment to the next. Descartes assumes that his readers are familiar with this kind of temporal/atemporal talk about God; and he relies on such a distinction to explain the autonomy of the universe vis-à-vis God, before introducing the three laws of nature in chapter 7 of *Le Monde*:

For from this alone, that he [God] continues to conserve it [matter] in this way, it follows necessarily that there should be some changes in its parts, and since these cannot, it seems to me, be properly attributed to the action of God – for he does not change at all – I attribute them to Nature; and the rules according to which these changes occur I call the laws of Nature. (XI, 37).

God's immutability and the obvious changes in nature are compatible:

If God conserves them [parts of matter] at a later time in the same way as he created them, he does not conserve them in the same state; that is to say that God is always acting in the same way, and hence always producing the same substantial effect, and yet we find many diversities in the effect [of God's action] in the way of accidents. (XI, 37–8).

It seems as if Descartes is just now at the point of deriving some interesting conclusions about the way in which changes occur in nature in response to God's immutability. Instead we are suddenly stopped short with the following reversal to a hypothetical account:

But without involving myself any further with these metaphysical speculations, I will put down two or three of the principal rules according to which one must think (*il faut penser*) God makes the nature of this new world operate and which suffice, I believe, to inform you of all the others. (XI, 38).

The earlier discussion about God's immutability does no work, so far, in explaining the rules which follow. Descartes was anxious to show that God creates/conserves the universe without this involving any change in God; that the universe is endowed with certain principles from the beginning which explain how it can autonomously generate the diversity of physical phenomena we observe; but when the time comes to justify Descartes' choice of principles, the anticipated metaphysical justification is replaced with: I will propose those laws according to which one must think God makes nature operate. It remains to be seen in what sense one must accept the laws which follow. They may be necessary because they follow logically from other propositions which are considered to be necessarily true; or they may be necessary if one is to succeed in explaining what needs explanation, and in that case the necessity would be equivalent to an a posteriori justification.

The first rule or law is the following:

That every piece of matter, individually considered, continues always in the same state, as long as contact with others does not force it to change. (XI, 38).

Descartes argues for this principle by claiming that it has always been accepted in the ancient world, with one exception: philosophers assumed that a change in shape or size or a change from rest presupposed some causal action, but they did not include a change in speed as equally in need of causal explanation. Since Descartes' concept of motion – in so far as he explains it here – classifies motion and rest on equal terms with other qualities of bodies such as shape or size, he is merely extrapolating a general principle already accepted by all to the case of motion. 'If it [a part of matter] has once begun to move, it will continue forever with an equal force, until other bodies stop it or retard it' (XI, 38).

The next rule is introduced as an hypothesis and, together with the first rule, is said to be consistent with many *expériences*.

I assume as a second rule:[13] that when one body pushes another, it could not give it any movement unless it lost an equal amount itself; nor could it take some motion from it, unless its own motion increased by the same amount. This rule, together with the previous one, agrees very well with all those experiences (XI, 41).

There follow two pages of empirical evidence which becomes readily intelligible if the two laws are accepted. In each case we find the argument: if we assume these rules, then the observational facts we are already acquainted with can be easily explained.[14]

The hypothetico-deductive argument is suddenly interrupted by an entirely different kind of argument on page 43 in favour of the first two rules of nature. This passage is important enough to be translated and quoted in full:

But even if everything which our senses have experienced in the real world appeared manifestly to contradict what is contained in these two rules, the reason which taught them to me seems so strong that I would not cease to feel obliged to assume them in the new world which I am describing. For what more firm and solid foundation could one find on which to establish a truth, as long as one can choose at will, than to pick the very stability and immutability of God?

But is it the case that these two rules follow clearly from this alone, that God is immutable and, acting always in the same way, he always produces the same effect? Because *if we assume* that he put a certain quantity of motions in all of matter in general from the first moment he created it, one must grant that he always conserves as much [motion] in matter – or else not believe that he always acts in the same way. And *if we also assume* that, from the beginning, the various parts of matter in which these movements are unequally distributed began to conserve them or to transfer them from one to another, according as they had the force to do so; one must necessarily think that he makes them continue to do the same thing. And that is what is contained in these two rules (XI, 43; my italics).

Descartes had quite self-consciously refrained from this kind of metaphysical consideration on page 38; by page 43 he has already forgotten his self-imposed restraints, but only in describing a new model universe. It seems clear that the first sentence above is a counterfactual; Descartes does not think that empirical evidence is at odds with the rules, for he has just discussed many examples which confirm his rules empirically. The point seems to be: even if empirical evidence *seemed* to contradict the rules, we should still accept them and then look for some way to explain away the apparent discrepancies. What then follows is a tentative effort to derive the first two rules from the immutability of God's actions and various assumptions about matter ('supposant . . .', XI, 43).

Before considering the status of this supplementary

metaphysical argument, it is useful to introduce Descartes' third rule:

That when a body moves . . . each of its parts individually always tends to continue its motion in a straight line. (XI, 43–4).

Again this rule is followed by empirical confirmation with references to turning wheels and swinging a stone in a sling. As in the previous case, the empirical confirmation is followed by a metaphysical explanation:

This rule is built (*appuyée*) on the same foundation as the other two, and depends only on the fact that God conserves everything by means of a continuous action and, consequently, that he does not conserve it as it may have been at some previous time but precisely as it is at the same moment as he conserves it. And is it not true that, of all motions, only the straight line motion is simple and such that all of its nature is comprised in one instant? (XI, 44–5).

God's action is one of conserving everything as it exists at any given instant; and circular motion cannot be specified by reference to one instant. Hence God conserves motion in so far as it is linear, and non-linear motion can only be explained by reference to other interfering causes.

There is an interesting comparison on the next page of *Le Monde* between the scholastic theory of God's involvement as a primary cause in human actions and Descartes' theory of God's causal involvement with the motion of physical bodies:

Hence according to this rule one must say that God alone is the author of all the motions in the world, in so far as they exist, and in so far as they are straight; but it is the various dispositions of matter which make them irregular and curved. Just as theologians teach us that God is also the author of all our actions, in so far as they exist and in so far as they contain some measure of goodness, but it is the various dispositions of our wills which can make them evil. (XI, 46–7).

In an obvious reference to what later came to be written as the impact rules of Part II of the *Principles*, Descartes says that he will refrain from introducing any other more specific rules than the three already discussed. In retrospect the rules are said to have been *explained* (not proved), and those laws which he decides not to discuss are not 'assumed', despite the fact that they apparently follow infallibly from eternal truths or laws of nature: 'outre les trois loix que j'ai expliquées, je n'en veux point supposer d'autres' (XI, 47).

Without anticipating the evidence available in the *Principles*, it is already clear from *Le Monde* that there are no signs of an unambiguous attempt on Descartes' part to deduce physics logically from metaphysics in the sense of L2. P1 does not appear as such, although it is included among the assumptions about matter which were adopted in the early chapters of the book. The equivalent of P2 is introduced as an empirical hypothesis. P3, P4 and P5 are each initially warranted by empirical evidence, and then further corroborated by a metaphysical argument whose precise function is unclear. And in the case of P3, in particular, the metaphysical argument seemed innocuously like an extension of the principle of sufficient reason to include local motion. The ambiguity of the physics–metaphysics relation remains after reading *Le Monde* carefully.

The Principles

Part I of the *Principles* is concerned with the 'main principles of human knowledge' (VIII-1, 39), namely the limits and relative certainty of our cognitive faculties. The title of Part II indicates that it will be concerned with 'the principles of material things'. As in the case of *Le Monde*, Descartes is again attempting to supply explanations of a great variety of physical phenomena merely in terms of small particles of matter in motion. And to introduce the reader to his project he returns to the question about the essence of matter and the impossibility of a vacuum in articles iv–xx.

I suggested above that P1 is not proposed as an analytic proposition in the *Regulae*; the discussion of 'the essence of matter is extension' in the *Principles* supports this interpretation. Here Descartes conceives of extension as the defining or characteristic property of material substances. This is not equivalent to saying that matter has no other scientifically interesting properties, nor does it imply that all other properties of matter can be explained by reduction to a geometrical account of the extension of material bodies. What it does mean, for Descartes, is that being spatially extended is a necessary and sufficient condition of materiality; this is obviously a conceptual analysis rather than an attempt to construct an adequate physical theory.

The thesis that matter is defined by extension is supported by imaginatively stripping other qualities from matter, as in the wax example in the *Meditations,* and finding that one cannot conceive of a piece of matter which has no extension. The intuitive certainty of the conclusion, presumably endorsed by the natural light of reason, is sufficient warrant to establish P1 as one of the most certain first principles of physics. This account of P1, however, camouflages a number of different roles it plays in the Cartesian system. In one sense, P1 is a metaphysical proposition. Descartes' traditional understanding of substance and accidents is such that, since extension is an accident, it must inhere in a substance. One cannot conceive of extension without there being something which is extended. This metaphysical reading of P1 would justify its removal from the list of P-principles to take its rightful place among the M-principles. Such a reclassification would underline the negligible effects of P1 on Cartesian physics, for one could read the *Principles'* physical explanations without P1 with no loss of explanatory power, just as one could read Cartesian physics without discussing God's existence. Reclassifying P1 would also resolve another problem in Cartesian physics about density. If matter is not identical with extension but rather metaphysically defined by this property, then one could consistently introduce a concept of density; and Descartes acknowledges the need for such a concept on a number of occasions.[15]

However, although P1 metaphysically understood is idling in Cartesian physics, it also functions as a methodological assumption about how physics should be constructed. It is a summary statement, not only of the exclusion of scholastic forms from science, but also of a commitment to providing mechanical explanations of many of the other qualities which material bodies can be known to have, such as colour, magnetism, inertia, etc. As a programmatic statement of policy rather than a statement of fact or a metaphysical premise, P1 remains to be confirmed or disconfirmed by its relative success in shaping a successful physics, just as Descartes was willing to grant that his method in general was open to such experiential testing.[16]

P2 is an assumption, based on empirical evidence, which is taken for granted in the context of the *Principles.* There is a greater awareness here of the hypothetical status of the assumption than in *Le Monde,* and this emerges clearly in a key text in Part III, article xlvi:

But we cannot determine by reason alone how large these particles of matter are, how fast they move, and what circles they move in; for they could have been determined in innumerable different ways by God, and experience alone must teach us which of these ways he chose in preference to others. And therefore we are free to assume anything we wish about them, on condition that whatever follows from our assumption agrees with experience. (VIII-1, 100–101).

We might legitimately consider that Descartes' choice of hypotheses would have benefited enormously from taking a closer look at the options open to God; but we could hardly fault him for this very clear statement of the hypothetical and empirical status of P2.

The introduction of the three laws of nature in the *Principles* involves an interesting mix of conceptual analysis, empirical corroboration and metaphysical explanation. The explanation of the motion of parts of matter involves a specification of two kinds of cause: the first of which is 'universal and primary, which is the general cause of all the movements in the world,' and the second one is the particular cause which explains 'how the individual parts of matter acquire motion which they previously lacked' (VIII-1, 61). The primary cause is God and the secondary causes are the laws of nature, P3–P5.

Descartes thinks that it is obvious that God is the first cause: 'As regards the general cause, it seems (*videtur*) clear to me that it is none other than God . . .'. The French text reflects the uncertainty of the 'videtur' with: 'il me semble que . . .' (IX-2, 83). As in the discussion in *Le Monde*, God's causality is operative here by means of his 'ordinary concurrence', 'per solum suum concursum ordinarium' (VIII-1, 61). This reflects Descartes' scholastic assumption that there is no need for further activity on God's part, in addition to a single act of creation/conservation, to conserve matter in motion in the universe. Furthermore, it is a perfection in God that he is not only immutable in himself but always acts in a way which is most constant and immutable. Hence we should *assume* (*supponere debeamus*) no changes in nature except those which experience or divine revelation teach us. The conclusion to be drawn is only that we should *assume* that the quantity of motion initially impressed on matter at creation is conserved:

Hence it follows that it is most consistent with reason for us to think that

God . . . always conserves the same quantity of motion in matter. (VIII-1, 61–62).

It is these assumptions about the unchanging character of God's effects in nature which provide a basis of some kind for the laws of nature.

Descartes introduces the first law, P3, as follows:

And from this same divine immutability some rules or laws of nature can be known (*cognosci possunt*) which are the secondary or particular causes of the diverse motions which we notice in individual bodies. (VIII-1, 62).

The French edition translates 'cognosci possunt' as: 'nous pouvons parvenir à la connaissance' (IX-2, 84). In neither case is there any reference to a deduction. The justification of P3 is identical with the one found in *Le Monde*. Two arguments are proffered, one an extension of the principle of causality to the case of motion, and the other a patently empirical corroboration. 'Et vero quotidiana experientia, in iis quae projiciuntur, regulam nostram omnino confirmat'; 'Nous voyons tous les jours la preuve de cette première règle' (VIII-1, 63; IX-2, 85).

The role of God's immutability as a further argument in respect of the first law is ambiguous between the two senses of 'principle' discussed above in §10. In fact, the concept of a law is ambiguous in the same respect. Descartes talks about two causes of motion, the primary cause (God) and the secondary causes (laws). Evidently, the latter are not propositions. In this context, the term 'law' must refer to the actual regularities in nature which the propositions in Part II of the *Principles* describe. Correspondingly, 'cognosci possunt' could mean: (i) that we could discover the law or could be initially disposed to accept such an hypothesis because of our prior acceptance of God's immutability; and it could also mean, (ii) that we can establish the truth of the law, i.e. confirm it, by reference to God's immutability. However, it could also just as easily mean something rather different: namely that God's immutability, i.e. the property of God and not a proposition about it, is the cause of the natural condition which the first law of nature describes. The third interpretation is supported by article xxxix where one reads:

the cause of this [i.e. second] rule is the same as that of the former one, namely the immutability and simplicity of the action (*operationis*) by means of which God conserves motion in matter. (VIII-1, 63).[17]

This interpretation would be equivalent to saying: the explanation of the conservation of motion in the universe is God's immutability, but our belief in the latter does not necessarily constitute an independent confirmation of the laws of nature.

Again in the case of P4, God's immutability plays at least an explanatory role vis-à-vis the second law of nature. For the reference to God's immutability is followed, as in *Le Monde*, by an analysis of the motion of a body at any given instant of time. Since God conserves motion exactly as it is at any given instant, and since the motion of a body can only be specified in an instant as linear, God's immutability can be seen to explain why moving bodies tend to move in a straight line. 'And this is confirmed by experience' (VIII-1, 64).[18]

The third law of nature, P5, is introduced in article xl. The two subsequent articles begin with: 'Demonstratur . . . prior pars hujus legis' and 'demonstratur . . . pars altera' (VIII-1, 65, 66). The marginal titles both use the word 'probatio'; however, whereas in each case the French translation retains the connotation of proof in the article titles with the term 'la preuve', the first sentence in each considerably weakens the impact of 'demonstratur' with: 'On connaîtra encore mieux la vérité de la première partie' and 'on connaîtra mieux ainsi la vérité de l'autre partie' (IX-2, 87). The proposed proof of the first part consists of a conceptual analysis, with a distinction between the motion of a body and the determination of its motion.[19] The proof of the second part of P5 again relies on God's immutability. Since God's action in creating the universe is identical with his conserving what is created, it is obvious (*perspicuum est*) that whatever quantity of motion he initially impressed on matter is somehow conserved.

Descartes continues the discussion by determining how these laws operate in specific cases of collisions between two perfectly hard bodies. The Latin original speaks of 'determining' (*determinare*) the results in each case – roughly equivalent to 'calculating'; whereas the French translates this as 'deduce' (*déduire*: IX-2, 89). For those who think that Descartes' three laws have been deduced a priori from metaphysical considerations and that the impact rules are deducible, in turn, from the laws, it may seem as if the counter-experiential character of the latter is decisive evidence against the laws and, more importantly, against Descartes' methodological procedure at this point in his physics. However the impact rules are not as embarrassing for Descartes as they might initially appear, nor are they simply deduced from the laws. A more detailed discussion of the significance of the impact rules for Descartes' scientific methodology is provided in Appendix 2.

Having examined the way in which Descartes introduces P1–P5 both in *Le Monde* and in the *Principles*, we may return to the question posed at the outset: to what extent do the logical models, L1-L6, accurately represent Descartes' efforts to provide P1-P5 with a metaphysical foundation?

P1 ought to be reclassified as a metaphysical principle; more accurately, it should be acknowledged as an interesting example of the frontier between physics and metaphysics where an apparently metaphysical dispute has significant implications both conceptually and methodologically for the kind of physics which Descartes is interested in constructing. Granting the ambiguity in P1 as metaphysical and methodological, Descartes would presumably classify its justification within the terms of L1 and L2. In Kantian terminology, P1 is a synthetic a priori proposition which Descartes does not adequately recognise as relative to a given conceptual framework.[20]

P2 is obviously an empirical proposition for Descartes, and is hypothetical. This is not to suggest that the way in which Descartes approaches the classification of the parts of matter is not significantly influenced by the categories of prior philosophers of nature; however, even if Descartes can be convicted of insufficient and untrustworthy observation, and of undue restriction within classical categories, he at least does not understand P2 as being anything other than an apparently successful, empirically based, hypothesis.

What then of P3, P4 and P5? Should they be understood as paradigms of an L2-type procedure in Cartesian science? There are two good arguments for not thinking that Descartes construes P3–P5 as being logically deduced from M-principles. The first argument depends on Descartes' estimation of the relative immunity to error of physics and metaphysics; the second argument relies on exploiting the looseness of the Cartesian use of 'demonstrate' and 'deduce' to interpret the texts examined in this section.

Descartes concedes – even if only reluctantly – that his physics is capable of being fundamentally mistaken. If physics were logically deduced from metaphysics then, by contraposition, the refutation of his physics would imply a similar fate for the metaphysics. This option Descartes wants to avoid. Therefore, his relative willingness to concede the possibility of error in physics vis-à-vis metaphysics can only be accommodated by loosening the supposed deductive connection between them.

What is at stake here is not just minor challenges to a scientific theory which could be accommodated by appropriate changes in detail but a basic challenge to the conceptual and methodological assumptions of his entire scientific project. I assume that there was no scientific alternative available at the time which could have provided that kind of challenge; Descartes thought a fundamental challenge might derive instead from divine revelation – or from the Church's teaching about revelation to the extent that it is accepted on faith. Now one might, of course, understand Descartes' remarks about the church and revelation as mere lip-service to the establishment; but this fails to do justice to the evidence available from his correspondence and other writings, which point rather to a traditional understanding of the priority of revelation over reason. More realistically, perhaps, Descartes is playing both sides on this issue by claiming that science and religion cannot conflict but, if they do, that science must give way to the certainties of divine revelation.

Descartes writes that philosophy (which, in this broad sense of the term, includes physical science) cannot conflict with revelation: 'As regards theology, since one truth cannot conflict with another, it would be impious to fear that truths discovered by philosophy might conflict with those of the faith' (VII, 581). The truths of revelation are beyond the scope of rational criticism: 'the truths of revelation . . . are above my intelligence, and I would not dare submit them to the feebleness of my reasoning' (VI, 8). Since Descartes believed that divine revelation ought to be accepted without criticism, in the event of a real or apparent clash between the two the indications of faith are to be adopted:

those things which are revealed by God are to be believed as the most certain of all. And although the light of reason, no matter how clear and evident, might appear to suggest something else to us, we should put our faith in the divine authority rather than in our own judgment. (VIII-1, 39).[21]

And the final chapter of the *Principles* reaffirms this orthodox view: 'Mindful of my feebleness I affirm nothing; but I submit all these things both to the authority of the Catholic Church and to the judgment of wise men.' (VIII-1, 329 and IX-2, 325).

Descartes' theory about the priority of revelation over reason as a source of truth must be understood as conceding a real possibility that his physics and philosophy are mistaken in a fundamental way. If physics and metaphysics are tied together by logical deduction, then in the unlikely event of fundamental error the two would fall together. On the other hand, Descartes had two reasons for giving preferential treatment to metaphysics over physics: (i) the arguments supporting metaphysical claims are less liable to error than the experiential evidence which is relied on in physics; and (ii) Descartes needs his theory of knowledge intact in order to explain the possibility of error in physics. This should imply a slackening of the supposedly deductive connection between metaphysics and physics and, in the event of a challenge to the latter, it would imply that the source of error is most likely to lie in the foundations of physics, i.e. in the P-principles. This is part of what Descartes means by metaphysics providing a foundation for physics. For, apart from any other possible relation between them, the texts cited in §11 above clearly involve the thesis that metaphysics as a theory of knowledge establishes the possibility of scientific knowledge both in physics and in mathematics.

The second argument in favour of relaxing the supposed logical tie between metaphysics and physics depends on the overlapping senses of such words as 'demonstration', 'proof', 'explanation' and 'deduction' which were discussed above in Chapter 3.[22] Given the peculiar Cartesian use of these terms, there is no good reason to assume that the term 'demonstrate' must mean 'prove' in every context, or even that the term 'deduce' must mean 'derive by logical entailment'. For Descartes, an acceptable explanation of a physical phenomenon which appropriately relates propositions about causes with propositions about effects is called a deduction, whatever its precise logical character. Admittedly, the evidence in the texts of *Le Monde* and the *Principles* is not decisive in this case. However, it seems more than a coincidence that when Descartes reviews his discussion of P3–P5 in both contexts, he refers to the explanation rather than to the proof of the rules:

But I content myself with informing you that, apart from the three laws which I have explained (*expliquées*), I do not wish to assume (*supposer*) any others. (XI, 47).

And since one can explain all natural phenomena in this way, as can be seen from what follows, I do not think that one should accept any other principles in physics, nor that one should hope for others, apart from those that have been explained (*expliqués*) here. (IX-2, 102).[23]

Moreover it is obvious in the case of *Le Monde* that each of the three rules or laws of nature was introduced as an assumption; yet despite being consciously adopted as hypotheses they were still said to have been based on God's immutability. And in the *Principles*, although the laws are demonstrated by God's immutability they are also confirmed by ordinary experience. The empirical confirmation of the laws is reiterated at the end of the *Principles* where P3–P5 are said to be 'confirmed by everyday experiences which are certain' (VIII-1, 323).[24] If the laws are logically entailed by a priori metaphysical propositions, then it would be inconsistent to continue calling them hypotheses, and it would be redundant to remind the reader frequently that they are confirmed by ordinary experience.

Besides the kind of direct experiential corroboration which is appealed to in discussing each law, Descartes also argues for the adoption of the P-principles in a variety of other ways. Among such extra warranting arguments he mentions: (i) the simplicity of the principles (VIII-1, 102; XI, 201); (ii) the conceptual clarity and intuitive reasonableness of the principles (VIII-1, 102); (iii) the fact that they are few in number (VI, 239; XI, 7–8, 328); (iv) that their implications agree with experience (VIII-1, 99, 101); and (v) that they explain many phenomena which were not considered at the time of initially formulating the principles (IX-2, 122; Descartes to Morin, July 13, 1638: II, 199). One could hardly ask for a more explicit statement than this of the hypothetical status of the P-principles and of their empirical confirmation by their explanatory success. Of course such an empirical confirmation is logically compatible with attempting to derive the P-principles, by strict implication, from the M-principles. Where the evidence already points away from this interpretation, however,

Descartes' discussion of the empirical confirmation of the P-principles further corroborates the interpretation already suggested.

Thus, with the exception of P1 which oscillates between metaphysics and methodology, and P2 which is almost exclusively confirmed by empirical evidence, P3–P5 are confirmed by a variety of kinds of argument which are only partly explicated by L4, L5 and L6, in each case substituting some less rigorous deductive link for strict implication. The least plausible interpretation, in the light of the evidence, is L2.

In rejecting L1 or L2 as plausible models of Descartes' understanding of the relation between physics and metaphysics the burden of the argument rests on two points:

(*a*) Descartes does not in fact succeed in logically deducing any P-principle from metaphysics, with the exception of P1, and he should not be understood to be attempting the impossible if he can be excused from such folly.

(*b*) An examination of Descartes' language indicates that 'deduce' and 'demonstrate' do not mean what they may now appear to mean to the modern reader, nor does Descartes' discussion of the confirmation of the P-principles coincide with a strictly logical deduction of P-principles from M-principles.

Instead we should understand Cartesian metaphysics as providing a foundation for physics in a much richer and more ambiguous sense: metaphysics establishes the possibility of physical science as a type of knowledge which is certain; metaphysical considerations provide knowledge of the first cause which explains the operation of secondary causes of motion; metaphysical or methodological arguments determine what kinds of entity are admissible as explanatory in physics, and what kinds of arguments are probative. To some extent it is even true that the integration of appropriate P-principles with already established M-principles helps corroborate the P-principles. In this complex sense, physics is demonstrated by metaphysics or physics is deduced from metaphysics. But we may continue to describe the foundational role of metaphysics in this way only on condition that we recognise that we are speaking Descartes' language and not our own.

Notes

1   Among recent authors who understand Descartes as if he deduces the basic laws of physics from metaphysics are A. Kenny, in *Descartes: A Study of his Philosophy*, pp. 206, 213; E. McMullin, 'Philosophies of nature', *New Scholasticism*, 63 (1969), 44; E. J. Aiton, *The Vortex Theory of Planetary Motions*, p. 4. Bernard Williams comes close to the position I defend, but does not go far enough in his *Descartes*, p. 268: 'There is room for a suggestion (it cannot be stronger than that) that Descartes did not regard his basic laws of nature, or all of them, either as intrinsically self-evident, or as derivable by entirely logical reasoning from self-evident metaphysical premises.'

2   For the interconnectedness of basic physics and metaphysics, see for example, J. W. N. Watkins, 'Metaphysics and the advance of science', *British Journal for the Philosophy of Science*, 26 (1975), 91–121; N. Maxwell, 'The rationality of scientific discovery', *Philosophy of Science*, 41 (1974), 123–53, 247–95; L. Sklar, 'Inertia, gravitation and metaphysics', *Philosophy of Science*, 43 (1976), 1–23; G. Buchdahl, *Metaphysics and the Philosophy of Science*, Ch. 1.

3   Cf. Descartes to Mersenne, Nov. 25, 1630, where he mentions a 'little treatise of metaphysics . . . the main points of which are to prove the existence of God and of our souls when they are separated from the body' (I, 182); Descartes to Mersenne, March, 1636 (I, 339); Letter of Introduction to the *Meditations* (VII, 1).

4   For common notions and eternal truths, see above §7; *Principles*, IX-2, 35; VIII-1, 23; *Le Monde*, XI, 47; *Conversation with Burman*, Cottingham, p. 34.

5   Descartes does concede that we acquire the concepts we use in metaphysical discussions through experience, *Conversation with Burman*, p. 3.

6   See *Principles*, Part I, liii and Part II, iv–xii; in a letter to More, February 5, 1649, Descartes wrote: 'Moreover, I do not agree with what you very kindly concede, namely that the rest of my opinions could stand even if what I have written about the extension of matter were refuted. For it is one of the most important and, in my opinion, the most certain foundations of my physics' (V, 275).

7   P. Costabel, 'Physique et métaphysique chez Descartes', in E. G. Forbes, ed., *Human Implications of Scientific Advance*, pp. 268–77.

8   See Descartes to Mersenne, November 1633 (I, 271); Descartes to Beeckman, August 22, 1634 (I, 308).

9   Descartes to Regius, May 24, 1640 (III, 64–5); and Nancy Maull, 'Cartesian optics and the geometrization of nature', *Review of*

Metaphysics, **32** (1978), p. 271: 'But the striking thing about the celebrated *cogito* is that it has virtually no function in the foundation of science.'

10   The letter to Father Dinet which follows the seventh set of objections returns to the standard formula of deducing physics from metaphysics: 'For all the principles of the Philosophy which I am proposing are contained in these few Meditations which I published; in the *Dioptrics* and *Meteorology* I have deduced (*deduxi*) many particular things from them, which indicate what kind of reasoning process I use.' (VII, 602).

11   Descartes to Chanut, February 26, 1649 (V, 291).

12   Descartes talks about God establishing the laws of nature (*établir*) at XI, 34, and of imposing them on nature (*imposer*) at XI, 36. Once nature is created as Descartes imagines in this model, it is independent of further interventions by God in evolving into the state of nature we observe in the real world: 'les parties de ce Chaos se démélent d'elles-mesmes' (XI, 34), 'la Nature seule pourra déméler' (XI, 36).

13   Notice that the second rule here corresponds to the third law of nature in the *Principles* (P5), and the third rule is equivalent to the second law of nature (P4).

14   'ayant supposé la precedente' (XI, 41); 'supposant cette Regle, il n'y a point du tout . . . de difficulté' (XI, 42).

15   See Appendix 2.

16   For the hypothetical character of his method and its need for confirmation, see the *Regulae*, X, 371, 404, and 417; Descartes to Mersenne, April, 1637 (I, 349); Descartes to Vatier, February 22, 1638 (I, 560); and Descartes to Mersenne, December, 1637 (I, 478).

17   In French: 'Cette regle . . . depend de ce que Dieu est immuable' (IX-2, 86).

18   In French: 'Et nous en sommes assurez par l'experience' (IX-2, 86).

19   See Appendix 2 for further discussion of this distinction.

20   Cf. Wilfrid Sellars, 'Is there a synthetic *a priori*?' in *Science, Perception, and Reality*, pp. 298–320.

21   Despite the clear indications that revelation and reason cannot conflict, there is an interesting change in translating from Latin to French in this passage in VIII-1, 16. The original had: 'the natural light is to be believed as long as nothing contrary has been revealed by God', where the translation has simply: 'we should be assured that . . . whatever we have once seen clearly and distinctly to belong to the nature of things has the perfection of truth' (IX-2, 37). Perhaps the failure to qualify the reliability of reason in the second version is as much a sign of Descartes' confidence in reason as a possible indication of a change of opinion. Cf. Descartes to (Hogelande), August 1638 (II, 347–8); and Descartes to Mersenne, December 1640 (III, 274); *Conversation with Burman*, Cottingham, pp. 33, 46–7.

22   The ambiguity about 'demonstration' was not peculiar to Descartes. See Ernan McMullin, 'The conception of science in Galileo's work',

in *New Perspectives on Galileo*, ed. R. E. Butts and J. C. Pitt, pp. 209–57, for a similar point about Galileo.

23 The final phrase, 'que ceux qui sont ici expliqués' occurs only in the French text as an addition to the original.

24 'Certis & quotidianis experimentis confirmatas' (VIII-1, 323); in French, 'prouvée par une infinité d'experiences' (IX-2, 318).

FIVE

Explanation

If the argument of the previous chapters is at all plausible, and if Descartes can be excused of the most characteristic theses of the paradigm rationalist, then two further questions arise with almost equal importunity. One of these concerns the Cartesian understanding of a scientific explanation: what, for Descartes, would satisfy his requirements that a purported explanation is truly scientific? And secondly, in what way would the plausibility of such explanations be evaluated? The two questions are interconnected, for if one imagines that Cartesian explanations are hypothetical this has corresponding implications for any discussion of their evaluation. And if Descartes is thought to reject experiential evidence in confirming or disconfirming explanations, then this likewise has obvious implications for his understanding of explanation. For convenience of exposition, the first question – about the Cartesian concept of explanation – is discussed here, while the second question is deferred until the next chapter.

§13 *Causal explanations*

To explain a physical phenomenon, for Descartes, was equivalent to (i) specifying its efficient causes, and (ii) describing the mechanism by which the phenomenon results in some 'necessary' way from the assumed causes. If this rather general concept of explanation is combined with various other metaphysical and methodological assumptions of Cartesian science, a more specific understanding of scientific explanation quickly emerges. For example, Descartes assumes that all physical phenomena are explicable in terms of the motions and interactions of small, imperceptible particles of matter.[1] Since nothing less than a causal explanation is satisfactory, it follows that any account which Descartes might be willing to endorse must be hypothetical. On the other hand, Descartes was obviously unwilling to settle for mere conjectures, guesswork or unproven assumptions; so that even though he used the word 'hypothesis' to imply that we have no direct, experiential access to the causes or mechanisms which our scientific theories must describe, at the same time he imagined he could eliminate the uncertainty of hypotheses by a variety of different strategies. Descartes' approach to constructing hypotheses, to choosing between alternative explanations, and to confirming or disconfirming suggested scientific explanations is examined in more detail in the following chapter. For the moment it is enough to notice that the imperceptibility of the kinds of cause which are involved and of the mechanisms by which they operate implies that a Cartesian scientific explanation must be hypothetical.[2]

Scientific explanations are also a priori.[3] This is a misleading expression for the contemporary reader whose understanding of 'a priori' is so much influenced by Kant. For while 'a priori' now means something like: 'independent of experience or empirical evidence', for Descartes it meant something more like: 'causal'. This is what Descartes apparently means when he refers to his account of optical refraction in the *Dioptrics* as 'a priori'; he wrote to Mersenne in 1638: 'You should know that I demonstrated the refractions geometrically and a priori in my *Dioptrics*, and I am amazed that you still doubt it' (II, 31). Likewise for reflection, in a letter to Mersenne in 1640: 'I believe that, in the second discourse of my *Dioptrics*, I have provided an a priori explanation of why reflection takes place with equal angles' (III, 82). In each case, an a priori explanation of the optical phenomena in question is an explanation in terms of the motions of 'light' particles and of their interactions with various kinds of media or surfaces.

There are two reasons for understanding these texts as references to causal explanations rather than to explanations which are independent of empirical evidence. One reason is that Descartes openly admits that the general claims about the nature of matter and light which are found at the beginning of the

Dioptrics are assumptions or hypotheses. Thus he wrote to Plempius, in December, 1637:

> The things which I propose in the first chapters about the nature of light, and about the shape of particles of salt and fresh water, are not my principles as you seem to object, but rather the conclusions which are demonstrated by everything which follows. (I, 476).

The following year he wrote in a similar vein to Vatier, concerning the general assumptions which initiate the *Meteorology*:

> As regards what I assumed at the beginning of my *Meteorology*, I could not demonstrate it *a priori* without giving the whole of my physics; but the *expériences* which I deduced necessarily from it – which cannot be deduced in the same way from other principles – seem to me to demonstrate it adequately *a posteriori*. (I, 563).[4]

This suggests that the introductory assumptions of the two essays, the *Dioptrics* and the *Meteorology*, are not provided with an a priori demonstration, whatever that might mean; and at the same time, that they can provide an a priori explanation of refraction or reflection.

The other reason which supports the causal interpretation of the phrase 'a priori' is Descartes' use of the term in cases where empirical evidence is used as the only source of warrant for an a priori claim. For example, Descartes wrote to Mersenne in 1632 about the possibility of constructing an a priori explanation of all the terrestrial bodies:

> For, although they [the fixed stars] seem to be very irregularly scattered here and there in the heavens, nevertheless I do not doubt that there is a natural order among them which is regular and determinate. And the knowledge of this order is the key and foundation of the highest and most perfect science . . . For by means of this science one could know a priori all the diverse forms and essences of terrestrial bodies whereas without it we have to content ourselves with guessing them a posteriori, *and through their effects*. I cannot think of anything which would help me more in coming to know this order than the observation of many comets. (I, 250–51; my italics).

Descartes continues his letter by urging that someone should compile a complete inventory of anything known about the heavens, 'in accordance with the Baconian method . . . and without introducing any explanations or hypotheses' (*ibid.*, 251). If an a priori explanation of terrestrial phenomena should ideally begin with a Baconian listing of the known facts, it must be obvious that Descartes means something else by 'a priori' than 'non-empirical'. The natural reading of the text is: empirical information is a starting point for a breakthrough to understanding the order in heavenly bodies which underlies their apparent irregularity. And once such a theory is discovered one could then explain a priori why terrestrial bodies are the way they appear to be. In other words, we would know the causes which explain the observed effects.[5]

In more general terms, a Cartesian account of any physical phenomenon involves locating an appropriate description of the explicandum within a broader framework in such a way that the description is deducible (in a rather loose, Cartesian sense) from a description of parts of matter, their motions and their interactions. The relevant description of the parts of matter may in turn be located within another more general framework, so that one views the logical structure of an explanation as something like the following:

$$\ldots Q_1 \ldots Q_2 \ldots Q_3 \ldots$$

where each Q represents a group of propositions, and the connections between them are Cartesian deductions. In this model, Q_3 can be explained a priori by reference to Q_2, while Q_2 can be confirmed, a posteriori, by Q_3. However, Q_2 may be merely postulated as an assumption because one has not yet regressed as far as Q_1 in one's series of explanations, and therefore Q_2 cannot be said to be explained or demonstrated a priori. Despite its non-demonstrated status, Q_2 can still function to provide an a priori explanation of Q_3.

Although Q_3 is thus provided with an a priori explanation there is no suggestion at all that it is known a priori in Kant's sense of the term. Descartes clarified this point in the letter to Plempius:

from the oblong and inflexible shape of the salt particles I deduced . . . as many other things as possible which are obvious to the senses. I wished to explain the latter by the former as effects by their causes, but not to prove them since they were already well known (I, 476).

Nor is there any implication that Q_2 (the *explanans*) is known a priori, either in Kant's sense or in Descartes'; as in the example quoted above about terrestrial bodies, the *explanans* may be discovered empirically and, in the case of the *Dioptrics* and *Meteorology*, it may not itself be provided with an (a priori) explanation. So that for Descartes, an a priori explanation is an account of a physical phenomenon in terms of more simple and primitive concepts, namely the concepts of the size, shape and motions of the particles of matter.[6]

The postulated Cartesian causes of physical phenomena must furthermore explain, not only that physical events are as they are observed to be, but also that they could not have been otherwise than they are. This feature was underlined in a letter to Mersenne in 1645, and it is close enough to the classical Aristotelian view in the *Posterior Analytics* to seem almost like a paraphrase:

As far as Physics is concerned, I believed that I knew nothing at all if I could only say how things may be, without being able to prove that they could not be otherwise (March 11, 1640: III, 39).

This point is linked to an objection from Morin to the effect that it is very easy to construct ad hoc hypothetical causes to explain any conceivable effect. Descartes responded to the objection as follows:

Although there are truly many effects to which it is easy to match different causes, with one cause for each effect, it is nevertheless not so easy to fit one single cause to many different effects, if it is not in fact the true cause which produces them. (Descartes to Morin, July 13, 1638: II, 199).

Again this point overlaps with the discussion in the following chapter about how one might come to know which hypothesis is the correct one; however this is done, Descartes clearly intended that an acceptable scientific explanation involves specifying the unique or correct cause of any given phenomenon, and therefore an explanation of how the effect was completely determined by the hypothetical cause. Apart from latent connotations of a strictly deductive logic of explanation, this also suggests that an adequate scientific explanation must be able to specify the actual mechanism by which the effect results from a cause, rather than merely to suggest a variety of possible ways in which this might happen.

So far in this section I have ignored questions about the relationship between physical hypotheses and metaphysics, and have avoided the troublesome grey area where an *explanans* is no longer unambiguously a physical hypothesis. If we can continue this blinkered attitude for the present, it seems that a scientific explanation of something described by Qn involves $Qn\text{-}1$, and likewise an a priori or causal explanation of $Qn\text{-}1$ involves reference to $Qn\text{-}2$. The logic of specifying $Qn\text{-}1$, or $Qn\text{-}2$, etc. is, at least in part, hypothetico-deductive.[7] And besides describing the hypothetical cause of a given phenomenon, a physical explanation must also describe the mechanism by which the observed effect inevitably follows from the proposed cause. To the extent that the cause is unobservable, the mechanism by which it operates will also be unobservable and therefore the description of this mechanism is unavoidably hypothetical.

§14 *Clocks, codes and hypotheses*

The scientific essays of 1637, the *Dioptrics* and *Meteorology*, are unambiguously hypothetical. Descartes initiates each essay with various assumptions about matter in motion which are then put to use in constructing explanations of specific phenomena such as reflection, refraction or the rainbow. The logic of this approach is clarified by Descartes in Part VI of the *Discourse*:

since experience makes the majority of these effects very certain, the causes from which I deduce them are used not so much to prove them as to explain them; but, quite the contrary, it is the latter [the causes] which are proved by the former. (VI, 76).[8]

This led to further inquiries from readers, especially from Morin and Mersenne.[9] In reply to Mersenne, Descartes penned one of the clearest and best known of his attempts to analyse scientific explanations:

You ask if I believe that what I wrote about refraction is a demonstration. And I think it is, at least in so far as it is possible to give a demonstration in this kind of study, without having first demonstrated the principles of physics by metaphysics – a project which I hope to realise some day, but I have not yet done so – and also to the extent that any other question of mechanics, or of optics, or of astronomy, or any other question which is not purely geometrical or arithmetical, has ever been demonstrated. But to demand geometrical demonstrations from me in something which presupposes physics is to wish that I do the impossible. And if one wishes to call only the proofs of geometers 'demonstrations', then one must say that Archimedes never demonstrated anything in mechanics, nor Witelo in optics, nor Ptolemy in astronomy, etc.; but this is not what is said. For in these matters one is content if the authors presuppose certain things which are not manifestly contrary to experience, and if the rest of the discussion is coherent and free from logical errors, even if their assumptions are not exactly true . . . If people say that they do not accept what I have written because I have deduced it from assumptions which are not proved, then they do not understand what they are asking, nor what they ought to ask for. (II, 141–2, 143–4).[10]

Apart from the reference to providing a metaphysical demonstration for physics, this text clearly indicates that Descartes understands his procedure as a hypothetico-deductive one in which the acceptability of the hypotheses is at least partly determined by their explanatory success vis-à-vis relevant explananda. This point was developed in a letter to Plempius, for Fromondus, in 1637. Fromondus had apparently objected to the logic of Descartes' arguments in the *Meteorology*, and in reply Descartes explained that each of his various hypothetical explanations could be rewritten in the form of a syllogism.[11]

If O_1 (observed phenomenon), then probably E (likely explanation).
But O_1.
Therefore, probably E.

Descartes gives a number of examples of this form of argument, and then adds:

Although considered separately these only convince us with a certain probability, when they are all taken together they amount to a demonstration. (I, 423).

Unfortunately Descartes does not make the logic of his arguments entirely clear, because he fails to indicate the logical relationship within the major premise of each syllogism between the antecedent and the consequent. In each example he claims that the observed effects are a sign (*indicium est*) of his proposed hypothetical cause. It is not clear, for example, how the relative viscosity of water and oil 'is a sign' that the parts of water are like eels and the parts of oil are branch-shaped. This way of expressing it makes it seem as if the experiential evidence implies the hypothesis; in fact, it is quite the reverse. His argument should read: assuming that the parts of water are like eels and that the parts of oil are branched, one would expect to find observed effects O_1, O_2, etc. – the antecedents of the major premise of each syllogism. Since all of these observational statements are true, the success of a single hypothesis in explaining a diversity of empirically known phenomena amounts to a demonstration of the hypothesis in question.

Since explanations in physical science cannot aspire to providing more than hypotheses which conform to experience, it follows that the only way in which a proposed explanation can be faulted is:

(a) by showing that the initial assumptions are false;[12]
(b) by finding a logical error in the explanation; or
(c) by proving that the implications of the explanation are incompatible with experience.[13]

An alternative model for the logic of explanations is found in the discussion of clocks and codes in the *Principles*. These analogies were introduced towards the conclusion of the *Principles*, partly to explain the way in which hypothetical causes must be postulated in scientific explanations, but also to clarify the kind of certainty which Descartes claims to have realised in his physics. Only the first of these considerations is at issue here.

Article cciv of Part IV of the *Principles* begins: 'It suffices in the case of imperceptible entities if one explains how they may be, even if they are not in fact as described.' The French edition adds: 'and that is all that Aristotle tried to do'. (VIII-1, 327; IX-2, 322). Just as a watchmaker could construct two watches which were externally similar and equally accurate in keeping time, but with very different internal mechanisms, so likewise God could have chosen a variety of causal mechanisms to produce the observable effects which we can observe in nature. The implication here is that the scientist cannot unlock the causal mechanisms at work in nature by direct inspection, and he must be content with postulating the existence of some hidden causes which adequately explain observable physical phenomena. The French text makes the implication explicitly:

It is likewise certain that God has an infinity of different ways by each of which he could have arranged that everything in this world appears as it does at present, without it being possible for the human mind to know which of these many ways he chose to follow. (IX-2, 322).

Conceding this point, Descartes continues:

And I would believe that I have done enough if the causes which I have explained are such that all the effects which they could produce are similar to those we observe in fact in the world, without inquiring further if it was by these causes or by some others that they were in fact produced. . . . For medicine, mechanics, and in general all those arts for which physical science is useful have no other objective apart from applying some perceptible bodies to others so that, by a series of natural causes, certain observable effects follow. (IX-2, 322).

This text at least acknowledges that physical science depends on postulating causes which could explain observable effects; it also contains strong suggestions of a crude instrumentalism which Descartes borrows from the saving-the-phenomena tradition. I will argue in the next chapter that this is not Descartes' own position and that he is merely using references to this tradition to excuse his apparent failure to achieve the kind of certainty he promised at the outset of his career.[14]

In the subsequent article (ccv), Descartes appeals to the analogy of decoding a message to illustrate both the method and the kind of certainty one can expect in physics. If someone systematically substitutes some of the letters of the alphabet for others in a code written in ordinary language, and if the substitution makes sense of the original, he might justifiably claim to have cracked the code; likewise,

If one considers how many different properties of magnets, of fire, and of all the other things in the world have been deduced very clearly from a very small number of causes which I proposed at the beginning of this treatise, even if one imagines that I assumed them by chance and without any reason . . . he will have as much reason to believe that they are the true causes . . . For the number of letters in the alphabet is much greater than the number of first causes which I assumed. (IX-2, 323–4).

There is a more obvious concern here with establishing the certainty of Cartesian hypotheses than with acknowledging the hypothetical procedure which introduces them in the first place; but the analogy speaks for itself with sufficient clarity to suggest that the physicist is comparable to the code-breaker in postulating whatever is necessary – hypothetical causes for the scientist – to explain a given phenomenon successfully.

Although hypotheses are unavoidable in science, conjectures or unfounded guesses are unacceptable. In the Fifth Replies to Objections the attempt to guess at God's purpose in creating the universe is called a conjecture:

And although in ethics, where it is often acceptable to use conjectures, it is sometimes a mark of piety to guess what objective God has in mind in ruling the universe, it is certainly inappropriate in physics where everything should be based on most secure reasons. (VII, 375).

It is not clear whether the conjectural status of an unconfirmed hypothesis depends on either of these two factors:

(*a*) The hypothesis has no initial plausibility, prior to further examination or testing. This initial plausibility might derive from its intrinsic reasonableness, its simplicity, its coherence with a structure of scientific explanations, or even from some empirical evidence in its favour.

(*b*) The hypothesis is such that, once adopted for examination as a possible explanation, there is no further evidence available in favour of its truth, or perhaps there could never be any such evidence which could decide for or against it.

Whereas in the discussion of God's purpose in creation the second factor above seems to be uppermost in Descartes' mind, the passage at the conclusion of the *Principles* quoted above suggests that (*a*) is sufficient to reduce an hypothesis to a mere conjecture: 'even if one allows that I assumed them by chance and without any reason'. This implies that before any evidence is proposed in favour of an hypothesis one is dealing with nothing more than an unfounded guess or mere conjecture, and this has no *permanent* place in physical science. Therefore Descartes can both exclude guesswork from physical science and at the same time endorse hypotheses if either of the following conditions is satisfied: an assumption has some initial plausibility, either because of favourable empirical evidence, its simplicity, etc.; or an assumption is corroborated by experience or by reason, after its initial adoption for further examination. In this way it is possible for a mere conjecture to become a plausible hypothesis as a result of corroborating evidence, and this is the minimal claim being made for the general assumptions which were adopted at the beginning of the *Principles*. Even if they began life as mere conjectures, the evidence introduced later in the text redeemed them as acceptable physical hypotheses.

§15 *Constraints on hypotheses*

One could hardly conceive of Descartes approaching some problem in physical science with a completely open mind as to what may be legitimately postulated to provide an acceptable explanation. Some theoretical entities are excluded a priori; more importantly, there is an implicit but significant complicity on Descartes' part with a kind of crude empiricism which avoids the theoretical in favour of scaled down pictures of the objects of our ordinary perception. So that parallel to the acknowledgment that a scientific explanation must inevitably be hypothetical, Descartes relies on a number of metaphysical and methodological assumptions to specify further the range of entities which may figure in hypotheses. It is at this point that metaphysics has a decisive influence on the content of Cartesian science.

As is well known, Descartes rejected scholastic forms as non-explanatory. *Le Monde*, chapter 5, rejects such explanatory qualities as heat, cold, etc. because 'these qualities seem to me to need explanation themselves' (XI, 25–6). The *Discourse* more generally 'expressly assumes' none of the 'forms or qualities which are disputed about in the schools' (VI, 42–3).[15] It is consistent with this rejection of scholastic explanations that Descartes is not concerned to provide any explanation of the substances of physical phenomena, in so far as substances are distinct from physical properties: 'this substantial form of the sun, in so far as it is distinct from those qualities which are found in its physical nature (*matière*), is once again a philosophical entity which is unknown to me' (Descartes to Morin, September 12, 1638: II, 367; cf. *ibid*., 364, for a similar remark about the 'form' of motion).

The suggestion that scholastic forms are themselves in need of explanation perhaps implies that Descartes understood scholastic explanations as redescriptions – in an esoteric language – of *explananda* rather than as genuine explanations.[16] Whether or not he would have accepted this interpretation of his comments, it is unquestionable that his proposed alternative was to look for the efficient and material causes of physical phenomena, and that formal and teleological causes had no place in his science. The question then arises as to how he could so easily specify, apparently a priori, what could count as a cause in the kinds of explanation which he was willing to accept. The suggestion which is most often made at this juncture is that Descartes was attempting to conflate distinctions between physical and mathematical sciences, and that he therefore hoped to explain all physical phenomena in terms of the geometrically specifiable features of bodies in motion. I think this suggestion has some validity; but paradoxically, a more influential factor is Descartes' fundamental empiricism.

Descartes' most comprehensive discussions of the relevance of mathematics as a paradigm of scientific methodology are found in the *Regulae* and the *Discourse*, and these are discussed in more detail in Chapter 7. Descartes was evidently enamoured of the certainty of mathematics and its relative progress as a science compared to philosophical confusion, and there is no doubt that he recommended some adjustments in philosophical and scientific method to exploit what he considered to be the source of the mathematicians' success. On the other hand, there is ample evidence, especially in the correspondence after 1630, that Descartes had lost interest in pure mathematics; so that one needs to be especially cautious in interpreting references to 'mathematical' method in Descartes' mature physical science. For example, he wrote to Mersenne, April 15, 1630:

As far as the [mathematical] problems are concerned, I will send you a million of them to set for others if you wish; but I am so tired of mathematics and take so little account of them now that I would hardly take the trouble to solve the problems myself. (I, 139).

The same sentiment is clearly expressed in writing to Mersenne, in October or November, 1631; to Stampioen in 1633; to Mersenne in March and September, 1638: 'Please do not expect anything else from me in Geometry; for you know that for a long time I've protested that I do not wish to work at it, and I honestly think that I can give it up completely.' (II, 361–2).[17]

Descartes is obviously reluctant to spend time with purely formal, or abstract, mathematical problems. 'To tell you the truth, I am so tired of abstract mathematics that I can no longer work at it.' (To Mersenne, II, 507). The disillusionment with abstract mathematics is reflected in the *Discourse* in terms of a distinction between pure and applied mathematics (VI, 17–18). When his correspondents expressed surprise at the change of heart (for example, M. Desargues), Descartes replies:

I have decided to abandon only abstract geometry . . . and the reason for this is because I will have so much more time to cultivate a different type of geometry, which is concerned with explaining the phenomena of Nature. For if he cares to consider what I wrote about salt, the snow, and the rainbow, he will quickly realise that all my physics is nothing else but geometry. (II, 268).

The last line here is partly an attempt to placate an importunate correspondent. It is just as much a reflection of the standard distinction between pure and applied mathematics, the latter of which included music, astronomy and optics.[18] Descartes speaks of two kinds of geometry, (rather than of mathematics), where 'geometry' is understood as 'a science which, in general, teaches one to know the measures of all bodies' (VI, 389; cf. 392). In other words, any exact science is part of applied mathematics.

The correspondence after 1630 thus shows a constant disillusionment with purely formal mathematics. This is consistent with an established and predominant interest in the physical sciences and, more confusingly, with Descartes' use of the term 'mathematics' to refer to any scientific knowledge which is subject to mathematical treatment. This wider use of the term survives in a number of places where a physical explanation is called mathematical.

And surely, if we use only those principles which seem to be most evident, if we deduce nothing from them unless by mathematical arguments, and if we find that those things we have thus deduced from them correspond accurately with all the phenomena of nature, then we would seem to insult God if we suspect that the causes which we have thereby discovered are false. (VIII-1, 99).

Evidently Descartes was impressed with the rigour and certainty of mathematics, and he wished to emulate these features of the discipline in all scientific knowledge. But rather than reduce physics to abstract mathematics, he planned to minimise uncertainty by rather stringent limitations on the conceptual resources of physical science. The assumption of a viable distinction between primary and secondary qualities partly determined this move; those qualities of physical phenomena which were assumed to be a function of the perceiver's response could be reduced, within a comprehensive account of both the perceiver and what is perceived, to qualities which were not explicable in the same way. In the language of *Le Monde* (discussed above in Chapter 4) such qualities could not be used to explain anything because they were in need of explanation themselves.

When Descartes is eventually faced with specifying what kind of qualities could count as explanatory, there is a noticeable absence of arguments for his choice. There is an obvious advantage in small parts of matter exchanging motion through contact action – for this kind of explanation is subject to mathematical control. But even here the promise of a rigorous presentation of the *explanans* is more than can be realised; for Descartes recognises that he has no way of dealing with the multiplicity of factors which determine the results of collisions between moving particles.

In default of such a mathematically exact description of the parts of matter in motion, Descartes falls back on ordinary experience as a source of explanatory concepts. This is what is meant in the passage from *Le Monde*, where matter is said 'to contain nothing which is not so perfectly known to the reader that you could not even pretend not to know it' (XI, 35). The *Discourse* summary of the procedure in *Le Monde* accurately reflects the same point:

Thus, I first described this matter and tried to represent it in such a way that there is nothing in the world, it seems to me, which is clearer or more intelligible, except what was earlier written about God and the soul; for I explicitly assumed that it had none of those forms or qualities which are disputed in the schools nor, in general, anything the knowledge of which is not so natural to our minds, that one could not even pretend not to know it. (VI, 42–3).

And the kinds of qualities which are such that one could hardly pretend not to be acquainted with them are precisely those observable characteristics of bodies such as motion, size, etc. which are known through experience. The limitations imposed by this kind of conceptual empiricism only become apparent when the explanation of specific phenomena is examined. Thus, the concept of attraction at a distance would seem to be ruled out in advance by a good Cartesian; gravity must be explicable by reference to impact action. Magnetism is explained by reference to eel-like particles; muscular action is the result of contact action; in fact, no other explanatory concept is considered at a later stage of the scientific project apart from those which are initially admitted.

This feature of Cartesian science is too often absorbed by the presumed dominance of mathematics and mechanics as an explanatory model. But when it is considered in conjunction with the Cartesian reliance on models, the very rough sense in which the conceivability of these models can be thought to confirm an hypothesis, and the emphasis in both the *Regulae* and the *Discourse* on the reduction of complex problems to the simple and familiar, it may be seen just as easily as pointing towards a kind of crude empiricism in Descartes' conceptual scheme. Physical reality is much too complex to be amenable to mathematical description; there are too many factors in every physical situation to be brought within the scope of a mathematical formula. On the other hand the theoretical concepts introduced by the scholastics were considered to be suspect from the point of view of a viable explanation. For want of anything better, Descartes decided to restrict the conceptual tolerance of theories to those concepts which are known from our ordinary experience of physical bodies, and to structure theories along the lines dictated by crude models of colliding pieces of matter which are described in non-theoretical language.

§16 *Models*

There is little doubt that Descartes relies extensively on models and analogies in articulating scientific theories; he also makes the much stronger claim that the possibility of constructing a model is a *sine qua non* condition for explanations in physics.

I claim that they [i.e. models and analogies] are the most appropriate way available to the human mind for explaining the truth about questions in physics; to such an extent that, if one assumes something about nature which cannot be explained by any analogy (*comparaison*), I think that I have conclusively shown that it is false. (To Morin, September 12, 1638: II, 368).

A similar sentiment is expressed in writing to Plempius, October 3, 1637:

There is nothing more in keeping with reason than that we judge about those things which we do not perceive, because of their small size, by comparison and contrast with those which we see (*ad exemplum et similitudinem eorum quae videmus*). (I, 421).

These reflections on method coincide with Cartesian practice. As early as the *Regulae* (X, 395) the nature of light was to be explained, if necessary, by analogy with other natural powers which were already known. And the construction of a model universe in *Le Monde* is introduced as a 'fable' (XI, 31). Nor is it plausible to argue that the switch to a model was a move on

Descartes' part to avoid the kinds of difficulties encountered by Galileo – for Descartes talks about a 'fable' long before Galileo's inquisition problems (November 25, 1630: I, 179). In the second part of *Le Monde*, the 'Treatise on Man', there is a similar move to construct a model of how the body operates and to understand the body's functioning by analogy with a machine. So that there are frequent references to the machine of the body (XI, 120, 141), and the relationship between model and reality is one of 'representation' (XI, 173).

The most widely cited examples of models are the three *'comparaisons'* which are introduced at the beginning of the *Dioptrics*. As in the more general discussion in *Le Monde*, the author refuses to speculate about the true nature of light and substitutes a hypothetical approach which is comparable to the procedure of astronomers:

But, since I have no need to talk about light in this context except in order to explain how rays of light enter the eye and how they may be turned by the various bodies which they encounter, it is not necessary that I undertake to say truly what its nature is; and I believe that it will be enough if I use two or three analogies (*comparaisons*) which help us understand it in a way which is most convenient to explain all its properties which experience acquaints us with, and to subsequently deduce all those other properties which cannot be so easily noticed; in this approach [we are] imitating astronomers who, although their assumptions are almost entirely false or uncertain, nevertheless, because they agree with various observations which they have made, do not fail to draw many very true and very certain conclusions from them. (VI, 85).

Three models[19] are then introduced, in turn, before the sine law is discussed:

(*a*) a blind person's use of a walking stick as an analogy for the propagation of light by a 'force' or 'pressure' which eventually impinges on our eyes;
(*b*) the example of wine leaking from a vat, as an analogue for the linear transmission of light, and
(*c*) a tennis ball moving towards a thin sheet of material which it punctures on impact, and then continues its motion with reduced speed.[20]

The models are recognised to have some negative analogies also;[21] for example, after introducing the comparison between our perception of light and the blind person's perception of physical objects Descartes adds: 'But, because there is a great difference between this blind man's stick and the air or other transparent bodies, through the medium of which we see, I must use another analogy at this stage.' (IV, 86). Likewise, in the case of the tennis ball analogy, the weight, size and shape of the ball are excluded as irrelevant to the model, so that the change in direction resulting from impact with a permeable surface is highlighted as of primary concern (VI, 94, 99).[22]

The model-building feature of Cartesian science is much more pervasive than these few examples suggest; it would hardly be an exaggeration to say that Descartes' whole scientific project is one of imaginatively constructing descriptions of the motions of particles which might explain natural phenomena and our experience of them. The 'real world' is abandoned with unusual haste in favour of the imaginary world in almost every attempt to explain. The ease with which this is done and the value of the resulting discussions were challenged by Morin, in a letter of August 12, 1638:

Problems in physics can rarely be resolved by analogies (*comparaisons*); there is almost always some difference [between model and reality], or ambiguity, or some element of the obscure being explained by the more obscure (*obscurum per obscurius*). (II, 291).

Descartes' reply to this was not only impenitent, but boldly steadfast in defending the analogical method in explaining the motions of particles in the transmission of light:

And I was right in using these observable spheres to explain their turning motion, rather than the parts of subtle matter which are invisible, so as to submit my explanations (*raisons*) to the test of the senses, just as I always try to do. (II, 366).

Despite this methodological claim, the proposed explanation was not in fact subjected to empirical test, and Morin rightly objected on this precise point in a later reply;[23] what was done was that the invisible *boules* of subtle matter were compared with the wooden models which could be imagined more easily, without any experience of the characteristic motions of such model *boules*, and without any attempt on Descartes' part to do appropriate experiments to test his theory.

The defence of this analogical approach is interesting. A viable explanation of any natural phenomenon can be constructed in terms of the size and motions of its parts. Therefore one can always construct a large-scale model of whatever is happening at the micro-level, because the only disanalogy involved is one of size; in fact, the concepts used to describe the properties of the small particles are themselves parasitic on our everyday language for talking about the medium-sized physical objects of ordinary experience:

in the analogies I use, I only compare some movements with others, or some shapes with others, etc.; that is to say, I compare those things which because of their small size are not accessible to our senses with those which are, and *which do not differ from the former more than a large circle differs from a small one*. (II, 367–8: my italics).

The central place of models as scaled-up versions of micro-events without any corresponding change in the concepts which are used to describe both model and *explanandum*, is consistent both with Descartes' peculiar procedure for confirming explanations which are formulated by reference to a model, and with the even more surprising thesis that any model – even if not the 'true' one – is preferable to none at all in explaining physical phenomena.

One usually thinks of scientific confirmation or corroboration as establishing the truth of propositions which have a direct bearing on the truth-value of an hypothesis. What one normally expects to find is evidence which implies the truth of an hypothesis, or evidence which is consistent with it and inconsistent with its likely alternatives. Descartes stretches the already tenuous link between hypothesis and confirming evidence by substituting the confirmation of claims about models for the confirmation of claims about the *explanandum* being modelled. This is an understandable move if one believes, as he apparently does, that there is no significant difference between the model and the reality apart from obvious disanalogies of size which are already allowed for. Thus, for example, one finds the case in which heating snow in a container confirms a theory about clouds ('cecy est aysé a experimenter en la neige': VI, 292); burning earth and other chemicals together confirms an hypothetical explanation of lightning ('ainsi qu'on peut voir, par experience': VI, 320); shaking beads on a plate tests a theory about ice ('ainsi que vous pourres voir par experience': VI, 288); or the opacity of sun-spots corroborates a theory about the origin of the earth's surface (VIII-1, 205). When asked how the subtle matter surrounding the earth can push heavy bodies towards the centre he replies: get a vessel with heavy and light particles mixed together, and spin it. The heavy ones displace the light ones towards the centre. (Descartes to Mersenne, October 16, 1639: II, 593–4).

In each of these cases, and in many others which could be quoted, Descartes corroborates a description of a model rather than introduce evidence which bears directly on the hypothesis at issue. The logic of the argument seems to be:

1. To explain phenomenon ϕ, under the description D, construct hypothesis(es) H.
2. ϕ is similar to ϕ^1.
3. To explain ϕ^1, under description D^1, construct hypothesis H^1.
4. H^1 implies evidence or effects E.
5. E is true.
6. Therefore H^1 is probable.
7. Therefore H is also probable.

The plausibility of the move from 6 to 7 is a function of the similarity or otherwise of ϕ and ϕ^1 or, in other words, of the appropriateness of the model adopted.

One is initially surprised at the logic of this type of argument – for it provides little warrant for the conclusion. The simplest explanation for the poor logic is to say that Descartes is a sloppy thinker in matters physical – and this is unquestionably true. A second reason is the one already mentioned; that prior methodological assumptions about what counts as an explanation have underestimated the significance of possible disanalogies between particles of subtle matter and the everyday models which Descartes prefers to discuss. There is one further reason, however, which helps reinforce an otherwise out of character reference on Descartes' part to constructing likely stories: where an ideal, demonstrative and fully guaranteed explanation is not available, the Cartesian is apparently willing to settle for a plausible reconstruction which may not accurately reflect how matters actually stand in the real world.

This represents a further weakening of the concession already made by Descartes that, since explanation in the physical sciences is explanation of the observable in terms of non-observable causes, the construction of viable explanations is unavoidably hypothetical; that concession still held out the hope that the resulting uncertainty could be effectively minimised by discovering a small number of hypothetical causes which would explain a wide variety of disparate effects. Whether or not this ideal can be realised in practice will be discussed in the next chapter, in connection with Descartes' views on confirmation. Even if it cannot be realised, there is a persistent suggestion that when nothing better is available, any plausible hypothesis at all will do in physics.

The distinction between 'true' hypotheses and those which are acceptable despite their presumed falsehood emerges most explicitly in the Cartesian account of the evolution of the earth. Descartes seems to have believe 1 – or at least claims to have believed – that the earth was created by God, in an instant, in a fully developed state. On the other hand, he was proposing an account of a model world which might have gradually evolved from chaos to the structured natural universe we observe today:

Nevertheless I did not wish to conclude from all these things that the world was created in the way which I proposed; for it is much more likely that God made it as it should be, from the beginning. But it is certain – and this is an opinion which is commonly accepted among theologians – that the action whereby he now conserves the universe is exactly the same as that by which he created it. So that even if he had given it, from the beginning, no other form apart from chaos, provided that he established the laws of nature and gave it his concurrence to act in the way it usually does, one could believe, without denigrating the miracle of creation, that by that act alone all purely material things could have developed with time into the condition we see them in today. And their nature is much easier to understand if one sees them develop gradually in this way rather than when one thinks of them in their complete state. (VI, 45).[24]

As in the previous discussion in Chapter 4, one could construe this passage as a phony compromise between genuinely held philosophical beliefs and apparently accepted religious dogma. It seems more likely that Descartes had a genuine problem here, and that he was in fact modifying his concept of explanation in the light of irreconcilable difficulties with theology. Since the world was created in an instant by God, and one cannot understand God's creative action, the only alternative is to imagine a way in which the instantaneously implemented creative act could have been accomplished by a more gradual and autonomous[25] structuring of the physical universe under the control of the laws of nature. So that an explanation of a physical event is not necessarily an account of how it happened historically; it is rather an account of how it could have happened which is consistent with one's prior methodological and physical principles.

This point is taken up again at greater length in the *Principles*:

There is no doubt that the world was created with all of its perfection from the very beginning . . . This is what the Christian religion teaches us, and natural reason likewise convinces us of the same. For once we take account of the omnipotence of God we must conclude that whatever he created would have had its entire perfection from the beginning. Nevertheless, to understand the nature of plants or of man, it is much better to consider how they can gradually develop from seeds, than to consider how they were created by God at the beginning of the universe. Thus, if we can think of a few very simple and easily known principles from which we can show that the stars and the earth, and everything else we can observe on earth, could have developed as if from seeds – although we know they did not in fact develop in this way – we could explain their nature much better in this way than if we simply described them as they are now, [added in French] or how we believe they were created. (VIII-1, 99–100: IX-2, 123–4).

In other words, a scientific explanation of a physical phenomenon is equivalent to an account of how it could have happened as a result of the normal influence of the laws of nature.

Once this distinction between the historically 'true' and the scientifically viable is adopted – perhaps initially because of the need to compromise for religious reasons – it is difficult to contain the latent instrumentalism which begins to colour much less obvious cases. For example, astronomical hypotheses are canvassed in the *Principles* not with a view to their truth, but with an eye on their explanatory value: 'Three different hypotheses, that is suggestions, have been discovered by astronomers, which are considered not as if they were true, but merely as suitable for explaining the phenomena' (VIII-1, 85). The alternative Cartesian theory was proposed 'merely as an hypothesis and not as the truth of the matter' (*ibid.*, 86). In fact, Descartes advises the reader to understand all the explanations which are to follow the discussion in Part II of the *Principles* as hypotheses:

I wish everything I write from this point forward to be regarded as an hypothesis. Even if they are thought to be false, I think it will have been worth while if everything I deduce from these hypotheses agrees with experience. For we can see that they are as useful for life as the knowledge of the truth itself, [added in French] for one can use them in the same way to arrange natural causes to produce whatever effects one wishes. (VIII-1, 99; IX-2, 123).

There is no suggestion at this stage that the general principles themselves are merely hypotheses in this sense; nor that the facts to be explained are in some sense uncertain because they are empirically known. The status of the general principles is already agreed; and the empirical basis of our knowledge of *explananda* in no way compromises its certainty. What is at issue is the status of the intermediate claims which relate general principles of physics to the descriptions of specific phenomena:

P-principles . . . observational judgments

The Cartesian view of the dotted line is that, at least initially, it cannot hope to be anything but a plausible story which is consistent both with the P-principles and with the description of observed explananda.

It is precisely at this juncture that the Cartesian reliance on models is most evident. For in physical explanations where one has insufficient experimental evidence, 'it suffices to imagine a cause which could produce the effect in question, even if it could have been produced by other causes and we do not know which is the true cause' (to an unknown correspondent, IV, 516). The *Principles* reflects this moderate position:

As far as particular effects are concerned, whenever we lack sufficient *expériences* to determine their true causes, we should be content to know some causes by which they could have been produced . . . (IX-2, 185).

I believe that I have done enough if the causes which I have explained are such that all the effects which they could produce are found to be similar to those we see in the world, without inquiring whether they were in fact produced by those or by some other causes. (IX-2, 322).

One could not automatically conclude from these concessions that Descartes is willing to settle for a pervasive uncertainty in science. There are hints even here that the remaining uncertainty could perhaps be diminished by further empirical evidence. Whatever one decides on that point, it remains that a plausible or hypothetical account can constitute an explanation, in physical science, as long as it is 'deduced' from Cartesian P-principles and is consistent with our experience. One of the primary functions of models is to facilitate the construction of such plausible accounts and thereby complete the otherwise unfinished story of how very general and simple principles can explain the natural occurrence of specific physical phenomena.

Notes

1   *Principles*, VIII-1, 326: 'I have tried to discover, from the observable (*sensilibus*) effects and parts of natural bodies, the character of their unobservable (*insensiles*) causes and constituent parts.'
2   For a much clearer statement of this position, see Pierre-Sylvain Régis, *Cours entier de philosophie ou systeme generale selon les Principes de M. Descartes*, vol. 1, p. 274; 'in the case of physical bodies, because their parts are unobservable one cannot perceive either the order or the arrangement of the parts, and the most one could hope for would be to guess at these from the known effects'.
3   Cf. L. J. Beck, *The Method of Descartes*, p. 249, note 1: 'Descartes admits that the existence of any particular cannot be proved *a priori*; his contention is that all scientific *explanation* is *a priori*.' It appears that Beck does not understand 'a priori' as I do here.
4   Cf. also Descartes (to P. Fournet?), October 3, 1637 (I, 455); Descartes (to Boswell?), (1646?), (IV, 689), which refers to the discussion of matter on page 42 of the *Discourse*: 'As regards the subtle matter, it is true that I did not prove it a priori; since I had no intention of dealing with the whole of my philosophy in such a book, I had to begin somewhere and therefore I wrote that I assumed it. But I contend that there are more than five hundred reasons in the *Meteorology* and the *Dioptrics* which prove it a posteriori; that is, that I explain more than five hundred difficulties which could not be explained without it.' See also Descartes to Morin, July 13, 1638 (II, 201) where a similar point is made about the assumptions 'on page 42 of the *Discourse on Method*'.
5   See Descartes to an unknown correspondent (1648?); 'I have by no means described all the movements of each planet in detail, in my *Principles*, but I assumed in general all those [movements] which observers have noticed in the planets, and I attempted to explain their causes.' (V, 259).
6   In a letter to Mersenne, November 15, 1638, Descartes explains

what he means by an a priori knowledge of the lifting power of a machine: 'There is no other way ... of knowing a priori the magnitude of this effect, namely which weight and what size weight can be lifted with such a machine, except by measuring the quantity of the action which causes the effect, i.e. of the force which must be employed for this purpose.' (II, 433). Again in this case, an a priori knowledge is a causal account of it.

7   Only in part, because there is a significant input from various empirical, methodological and metaphysical assumptions already made by Descartes to what might count as an acceptable *explanans*.

8   See Descartes to Morin, July 13, 1638 (II, 198); *Principles*, VIII-1, 81, where Descartes lists some of the phenomena he hopes to explain and then adds: 'not indeed so that we might use these phenomena as explanations to prove anything; for we wish to deduce the explanations of the effects from causes and not, on the contrary, the explanation of the causes from the effects'.

9   See Descartes to Morin, February 22, 1638 (I, 536).

10 Cf. Descartes to Plempius, October 3, 1637, where he discusses his explanation of why a ray of light passes more easily through water than air, and then adds: 'That is all I wrote, and if I understand what a demonstration is, I have demonstrated it.' (I, 419).

11 'If he would be good enough to read with sufficient attention everything I wrote in the *Meteorology* and *Dioptrics*, he would find six hundred explanations from which six hundred syllogisms could be constructed to prove what I say.' (I, 422).

12 Cf. E. Gilson, *Études sur le rôle de la pensée médiévale*, pp. 128–37.

13 The three conditions are given in a slightly different form in the third part of the *Principles*. 'And certainly, if we use no principles except those which are most evident, if we deduce nothing from them unless by mathematical reasoning, and if those things we deduce from them in this way agree with all the phenomena of Nature, we would seem to insult God if we suspect that the causes of things which we discovered in this way were false.' (VIII-1, 99). Cf. *ibid.*, 101, where Descartes claims that he may assume any hypotheses which are suitable for explaining nature 'on condition that all those things which are deducible from them agree with experience'.

14 Cf. IX-2, 185: 'As regards these particular effects, of which we have insufficient empirical evidence to determine the true causes which produce them, we should be content to know some causes by means of which they could have been produced'; a letter (to Huygens ?), October 5, 1646: 'in such matters in which one has not done many experiments, it suffices to imagine some cause which could produce the effect in question, even if it could also be produced by another cause and one does not know which is the true cause'. (IV, 516).

15 See also VI, 61–2.

16 In a letter to Huygens in March or April, 1638, Descartes gave as an example of a non-explanation: 'lux est medium proportionale inter

substantiam et accidens' (II, 51). It would be difficult to resist agreeing with him!

17   Descartes to Mersenne, October or November, 1631 (I, 229–30); to Stampoien, 1633 (I, 275); to Mersenne, March 31, 1638 (II, 95); to Mersenne, April 1, 1640 (?), (III, 50); to Dozem, March 25, 1642 (III, 534); the passage quoted is from September 12, 1638 (II, 361–2).

18   Cf. VI, 19–20, and E. Gilson, *Discours*, pp. 216–17. For Descartes' distinction of geometry and mechanics, cf. VI, 389 and 392. Pierre Boutroux discusses Descartes' attitude towards abstract mathematics in *L'Imagination et les mathématiques selon Descartes*, p. 34; see also P. Golliet, 'Le problème de la méthode chez Descartes', *Revue des sciences humaines*, **61** (1951), 56–73, at p. 62.

19   The word *'modèle'* is often used by Descartes, as in *'modèle de bois'* – Descartes to Huygens, January 25, 1638 (I, 505), and to Huygens, February 8, 1638 (I, 520) – and in *'modèle de cuivre'*, Descartes to Ferrier, November 13, 1629 (I, 55). The word is also used to mean a diagram, as in VI, 215, 217, 224.

20   For earlier uses of the same analogy, see A. I. Sabra, *Theories of Light from Descartes to Newton*, pp. 93–9.

21   For the terminology of negative analogies, see M. B. Hesse, *Models and Analogies in Science*.

22   A similar recognition of disanalogy is found in Descartes to Mersenne, July 27, 1638. Descartes had tried to explain the colour of light in terms of the rotation of small spheres; he then adds the qualification: 'the spheres which are painted in the figure on this page serve only as an example, and should be taken to be spheres of wood or some other visible material, and not parts of subtle matter' (II, 269). Cf. Descartes to Mersenne, October 28, 1640: 'it is for this reason that I assumed, in my *Dioptrics*, that the surface and the ball are perfectly hard, and that the ball has neither weight, nor size (*grosseur*), etc. in order to make my demonstration mathematical [i.e. exact]. For I am well aware that the reflection of an ordinary ball never occurs at exactly equal angles' (III, 208).

23   Morin had objected to this defence in a letter of October, 1638, to which Descartes seems not to have responded. 'There is no one on earth who could perform the experiment you mention on wooden spheres . . . why have you not explained the motions which are characteristic of the spheres of subtle matter . . . neither one nor the other of these spheres can be experienced.' (II, 418–19).

24   Cf. *Principles*, VIII-1, 99.

25   The term 'autonomous' means in this context: that God does not need to intervene directly in the evolution of the universe once he established the laws of nature and imparted an initial measure of motion to the parts of matter.

SIX

Theory confirmation

Cartesian science is defined in terms of the certainty, rather than the truth, of proposed explanations. Once the possible falsity of hypotheses is acknowledged the only issue remaining in science is to tailor one's explanations to the available evidence, and then claim a degree of certainty for the resulting hypotheses which is warranted by the relevant evidence. The first section here discusses the kinds of certainty which Descartes demands as a minimum of acceptability for genuinely scientific explanations.

In §18 I look at the function of empirical evidence both in confirming and in disconfirming physical hypotheses. The evidence here points to the conclusion that empirical evidence holds a very important place in deciding which explanations should be adopted and what degree of certainty may be claimed for them. The following section, §19, examines some cases where Descartes openly disagrees with his contemporaries about the explanation of some phenomena and it concentrates especially on the disagreement with William Harvey about the explanation of the circulation of the blood. The conclusion here is consistent with the evidence in §18, namely that Descartes relies almost exclusively on putative empirical evidence to argue his side of the issue.

The final section, §20, introduces factors other than empirical evidence which could constitute corroborative arguments in favour of physical hypotheses, and these include such factors as simplicity, agreement with metaphysical or methodological assumptions, etc.; it also summarises my understanding of the status of physical hypotheses in Cartesian science.

§17 *Certainty*

There are few clear acknowledgements in the Cartesian corpus
that empirical science produces only probable knowledge, and
that this is all one could hope to achieve in any case. Instead one
gets the definite impression of an author who believes he has
access to the truth in a relatively unproblematic way, through
'clear and distinct ideas'. I wish to argue that the Cartesian
position is rather more complicated than this simple picture
suggests and that some of the complexity derives from standard
problems in interpreting Descartes' views on truth and certainty.

Since I accept the general lines of Harry Frankfurt's
interpretation of the Cartesian circle, there is no need to repeat his
arguments here.[1] Descartes does indeed make a distinction
between what is true, absolutely speaking, and what is certain. In
the Second Replies he writes:

> What does it matter to us if perhaps someone imagines that the very
> thing of whose truth we have been firmly persuaded should appear false
> to God or to an angel and is therefore false, absolutely speaking? What do
> we care about this absolute falsity, since we by no means believe in it nor
> have the least suspicion of it? For we are assuming a conviction which is
> so firm that it can in no way be challenged; and hence a conviction which
> is evidently identical with the most perfect certitude. (VII, 145).

This implies that there is a perspective on reality which is
inaccessible to man and which provides an insight into how
things are, in fact, in some absolute sense. The concept of truth
which is implicit here is a correspondence theory which assumes
that among alternative conceptualisations of the same reality, one
is absolute or true in an unqualified way whereas others may be
false despite the fact that they are the best available.

Frankfurt argues convincingly that the Cartesian distinction
between the 'absolutely true' and the 'indubitably certain' is
closely dependent on Descartes' voluntarism.[2] There is no real
distinction, in God, between the faculty of understanding and the
will; God creates the laws of nature and the eternal truths and
knows them because he creates them. There are no constraints
extrinsic to God's will on what God can create, even in creating
eternal truths; his omnipotence is not constrained by our logic,
nor by what we regard as reasonable.

On the other hand, man's understanding is very limited, and
we cannot comprehend God's nature. Hence we cannot discover

by recourse to logic or to our limited reason which eternal truths God can create.[3] All we have to guide us in our inquiries – apart from divine revelation – is the relatively dim light of reason. So that whatever we judge to be indubitably certain as a result of using our native wit as correctly as possible is all we can hope to know. Those propositions which we judge to be indubitable come as close as we can possibly come to the truth; but whether or not they are true in an absolute sense is a question we cannot answer.

It is consistent with this general epistemological position to define scientific knowledge in terms of certainty rather than in terms of absolute truth. And Descartes is definitely a rationalist if this means that he is willing to trust 'reason' as the most reliable and most critical faculty for evaluating the trustworthiness of all kinds of evidence, including empirical evidence. Thus, in default of anything better (apart from revelation) we can only put our trust in what we are led to believe by the best evidence available after a critical scrutiny by reason. Scientific knowledge is characterised by certainty rather than by absolute truth: 'Omnis scientia est cognitio certa & evidens' (X, 362). Without a high degree of certainty, it is impossible to have scientific knowledge. Accordingly the atheistic mathematician is subject to serious doubt about the reliability of reason and he cannot hope to have scientific knowledge; 'for it can be seen that no knowledge which can be made doubtful should be called scientific' (VII, 141).

One major source of doubt for any knowledge claim derives from doubts about the reliability of our cognitive faculties rather than doubts which are based on an examination of the relevant evidence. These are 'metaphysical' or 'hyperbolic' doubts (VII, 460). Once Descartes has proven to his own satisfaction that God exists and is not a deceiver, the doubts expressed in the first two chapters of the *Meditations* are shown to be very tenuous and even *'risu dignae'* (VII, 89).[4] The consideration of these extreme metaphysical sources of doubt is a project one should undertake only once in a lifetime; after which it suffices to remember one's metaphysical conclusions so as to devote one's time to physical science.[5]

Since the argument in the *Meditations* is designed to answer metaphysical doubts, there is no reason to continue doubting empirical evidence. It is no surprise therefore to find Descartes consistently rely on empirical evidence to establish knowledge-claims with certainty. This is taken for granted in the *Discourse*:

Thus, in destroying all of my opinions which I thought were poorly established, I made various observations and availed myself of many experiences which have since served me to establish more certain [opinions]. (VI, 29).[6]

In the *Dioptrics*, Descartes discusses an experimental model of the retinal image in the human eye, and twice uses the phrase 'on ne peut douter' (VI, 124). In the *Description of the Human Body*, the proposed theory of blood circulation is so consistent with the evidence that 'on ne pourra douter' (XI, 231) that the theory is correct. Descartes encourages Regius, in a letter in December 1641, to test his opinions about the human heart experimentally and, if they agree with the results, not to be afraid to claim certainty for them: 'for it is easy to experiment, and if it succeeds, you should propose it as certain and not with words like "I think" and "it seems" ' (III, 455).

While empirical evidence does provide a basis for certainty, the kind of certainty thereby achieved is not immune from later doubts. Descartes introduces this qualification in a letter to Voetius, in reference to the latter's interpretation of the Cartesian criterion of certainty.

I have not spoken about some kind of certitude which lasts for the whole life of an individual, but only about that which is had at the particular moment at which some knowledge (*scientia*) is acquired. (VIII-2, 170).

This eminently sensible qualification on the level of certainty attainable in empirical science is matched by a corresponding qualification about the certainty which results from many Cartesian 'deductions'. For since 'deductions' often depend on memory, they 'can be defective and therefore are subject to doubt' (X, 389).

A. Gewirth has distinguished three kinds of certainty which are more or less explicitly operative in Cartesian discussions: moral, psychological and metaphysical certainty.[7] Moral certainty is that which suffices for making practical decisions in those matters which we do not usually doubt even though, strictly speaking, we may be mistaken.[8] Psychological certainty is provided by clear and distinct perceptions which are such that the mind cannot resist assenting to them. Despite our inability to refuse assent, these perceptions are still open to metaphysical doubts. Metaphysical certainty is what results from showing that the sources of metaphysical doubt are irrational. Thus, the Cartesian who accepts the proposed defence of reason and of other cognitive faculties in the *Meditations* is free from metaphysical doubts and can therefore convert psychological certainty into metaphysical certainty. The possibility of being mistaken – in the absolute sense mentioned above – remains. This leaves Descartes with two kinds of certainty, moral and metaphysical; and when there is no reason to doubt a claim because the evidence is unreliable, or when the evidence seems to be conclusive, Descartes claims metaphysical certainty, even 'in rebus naturalibus' (VIII-1, 328).

Apart from the distinction between moral and metaphysical certainty, where these represent degrees of certainty in the light of the relevant evidence, there are few other indications of what is possible for a Cartesian physicist to achieve in science. The theory of clear and distinct perceptions or ideas is no help here.[9] For a clear and distinct idea is one which has been critically evaluated on the basis of the relevant evidence and found to be above suspicion. Hence, to search for clear and distinct ideas is equivalent to a search for knowledge claims which are certain, and the method proposed for achieving such clarity and distinctness is nothing else but the implementation of the Cartesian method as a whole. There is no specific kind of certitude which is characteristic of clear and distinct ideas, as such, for the kind of certainty which is possible is a function of the nature of one's inquiry; metaphysics, physics or mathematics can each provide clear and distinct perceptions, but they differ significantly in how this is realised and in the kind of certainty which is possible as a result in each.

What is manifestly lacking in the Cartesian enterprise is an appreciation of probability. Descartes' comments on probability are alarming on first reading; for example, he wrote to Mersenne to clarify his use of terms, for Fermat, as follows:

[Fermat] thought that in saying that something is easy to believe, I meant to say that it was only probable (*probable*). However he is far from my understanding of the term in this. For I treat almost as false whatever is merely probable (*vraisemblable*) (Descartes to Mersenne, October 5, 1637: I, 450–51).

This text is not as clearcut as it seems. It presumably means that Descartes rejects 'probable' propositions, in the sense in which this was used by logicians or Dialecticians, rather than that he rejects propositions which are supported by strong evidence but fall short of indubitability. Thus he wrote in another letter, possibly in the same year:

I would not dare claim that those [principles] which I propose are the true principles of nature. All I claim is that, by assuming them as principles, I have satisfied myself in all the many things which depend on them. And I see nothing which prevents me from making some progress in the knowledge of the truth. (To an unknown correspondent, IV, 690).

For lack of a concept of probability, Descartes is forced into describing hypotheses as certain, even if they are only 'morally' certain, i.e. highly probable. If this is considered together with the strong Cartesian rejection of the standard 'plausible' theories of the day and Descartes' penchant for overstating the certainty of his own theories, we have all the makings of a muddle.

To help guide us in looking at some typical Cartesian confirmatory arguments, the following points should be underlined:

(*a*) Science is knowledge which is certain, rather than merely plausible or conjectural opinions.

(*b*) Metaphysical discussions such as one finds in the *Meditations* dispel all fears of metaphysical doubt; 'reason' shows that man's cognitive faculties are reliable and capable of providing knowledge which is certain under specifiable conditions. These same metaphysical considerations show that indubitability is compatible with our opinions being false in an absolute sense. Thus indubitability is all we can hope to achieve in science.

(*c*) Corresponding to the range of sciences, from metaphysics to mathematics, and physical science, and even morals, there is a range of levels or degrees of certainty which it is possible to achieve. In the case of each discipline, the researcher must consult all the relevant evidence he has available and then make a judgment based on his evaluation of that evidence. Where the evidence is weak he can claim only a low degree of certainty; where the evidence is overwhelming, he can claim metaphysical certainty, even in physical science.

Another way of expressing the same position about knowledge and certainty is to say that, in Descartes' usage, the term 'certain' is not an absolute term.[10] Two distinct knowledge claims may each be certain, and yet one may be more certain than the other or it may be certain in a different sense. Rather than name the less certain opinion probable – because of the connotations of mere guesswork deriving from the Dialecticians' use of the same term – Descartes prefers to call any opinion which is based on reliable evidence certain. And such well-based, certain knowledge claims may still be subject to doubt on the discovery of new evidence; and every opinion, no matter how indubitable it is thought to be, may not be true in the absolute sense in which God or some other superior intelligence knows how things are in fact.

§18 *Confirmation of hypotheses*

Even in those cases where one least expects to find it, such as in the *Principles*, Descartes' approach is unambiguously hypothetical. The phenomena to be explained are first listed; the explanatory hypotheses are introduced, and they are then confirmed, at least partly, by reference to their agreement with the empirically known facts. For example, in Part III, article xlii, the author limits the scope of *explananda* to be discussed to the Sun, the fixed stars, etc. In proposing explanations of this variety of phenomena Descartes writes: 'I wish everything I write from this point on to be taken as an hypothesis' (VIII-1, 99). By assuming that matter is composed of small imperceptible particles in constant motion and that the laws of nature provide an adequate basis for explaining all natural phenomena,[11] the only remaining task for the scientist is to invent appropriate auxiliary hypotheses to link basic assumptions with descriptions of explananda. Descartes undertakes precisely that task with his characteristic confidence in the project. The text which follows is dotted with acknowledgments of the hypothetical nature of the discussion, with phrases such as: 'I propose this hypothesis' (p. 86); 'we take the liberty to assume' (p. 86); 'it should be thought that' and 'we think', 'we do not think' (pp. 89, 93, 94); 'here I assume' (p. 103); 'I think it is equally necessary that these two assumptions be admitted' (IX-2, 139). At the beginning of Part IV Descartes writes: 'I ought to retain the same hypothesis [as in Part III] to explain what is observed on earth' (VIII-1, 203); and at the conclusion of that section he reminds the reader that his assumptions may not be the true causes of observed effects (VIII-1, 327; IX-2, 322).

Descartes' prodigality in introducing such a variety of auxiliary hypotheses as one finds in his scientific essays can only be explained by his pessimism about controlling these hypotheses experimentally. It is almost as if, for want of something better, any plausible account of how the general assumptions about matter and motion might explain observed natural phenomena is preferable to none at all. In some cases Descartes admits that experience could decide the merits of an auxiliary hypothesis. For example, he is not sure if gravity is homogeneous on the surface of the earth and he could easily imagine some possible causes of a lack of homogeneity: 'but I have not yet been able to do any experiments to test this' (IX-2, 214). Likewise he is not sure if a spherical magnet rotates when floating on its pole opposite to the nearest pole of the earth, and this would also have to be decided by experiment: 'whether this is true or not, I have not yet discovered by experiment' (VIII-1, 302).[12]

There are many similar indications in the correspondence of experimental control over auxiliary hypotheses. For example, Descartes wrote to Villebressieu in 1631 encouraging him to publish his *expériences,* 'in order to construct a physics which is clear, certain and demonstrated'; to Mersenne, in 1632, requesting a full account of whatever astronomical observations were available; to Mersenne the same year, describing his own work in anatomy 'to explain the nature of imagination and of memory'; to Huygens in 1637, referring to the multiplicity of experiments which are necessary 'to examine whatever belongs to this subject [medicine]'; to Mersenne in 1640, wishing that someone could measure exactly the speed of falling bodies and their relative impact on hitting the ground, 'for one could thereby discover the speed with which a weight begins to move when it falls'; to Mersenne in 1643, bemoaning the lack of funds to 'be able to perform all the experiments which would be necessary to discover the specific nature of each body'. The same year he wrote to Mersenne declining to offer an opinion about phenomena which he had not experimentally examined. 'As regards your question about jets of water, I am unable to determine anything about it; for it depends on some experiments which I have not yet performed.' Descartes wrote to Huygens in 1645, when he claimed that the lack of experimental work hindered further progress in chemistry. 'I have not done the experiments which would have been necessary . . .'; and finally, he wrote to the Marquis of Newcastle in 1645, when the same concern about experimental work on animals is expressed.[13]

These consistent references to experimental control over auxiliary hypotheses coincide with a general policy statement in the Preface to the French edition of the *Principles*; given the generality of the initial assumptions and the plausibility of the laws of nature, the only thing which remains to be done to complete the project is to press ahead with experimental work:

The remainder of those [truths] which remain to be discovered, depend on specific experiences which one never encounters by chance, but which should be searched out with care and expense by very intelligent men. (IX-2, 20).[14]

However, despite the acknowledged need for experimental work and control over hypotheses, and despite the fact that Descartes devotes a major portion of his abundant correspondence to discussing detailed experiments, there is still a significant gap on this issue between the ideal and the reality in Cartesian science. A typical example of a scientific explanation is found in the discussion of magnetism in the *Principles*. In Part IV, article cxlv, Descartes lists thirty-four different properties of magnets which need to be explained. What follows, in approximately thirty pages of text, are rather descriptive or imaginatively constructed model explanations of how small particles of matter with unusual shapes could cause the variety of observed properties in magnets. And the fact that this account can be given, within the framework of the general theory of matter and the laws of nature adopted in Part II, is thought to *confirm* the theory.

There is no doubt that Descartes proceeds hypothetically in physical science; and there is no doubt that, ideally, he envisages a tight experimental control over auxiliary hypotheses. But the evidence also points decisively towards a very flexible use of the term 'confirm' in respect of hypotheses. And this raises inevitable questions about the consequent certainty of hypotheses and of Descartes' evaluation of their degree of certainty.

There are unexceptional uses of the term 'confirm', and its synonyms, in Descartes' writings where what is being decided is an empirical matter of fact. For example, the claim that the pupil of the eye expands and contracts is confirmed by experience (VI, 107); or that it is possible to make lenses from ice, 'ainsi que l'experience a monstré' (VI, 82); that a small sphere inside a capillary tube accelerates when one revolves the tube in a circle around one end 'hoc experientia confirmat' (VIII-1, 111); or that the bodies we find on earth are full of pores ('l'experience peut montrer fort clairement': VI, 87). What is common in this type of example is that a relatively non-theoretical, empirical claim is directly confirmed by reference to the relevant evidence or experiment. And Descartes claims maximum warrant or certainty in the case of such non-theoretical, non-experimental examples. The indubitable empirical evidence, taken in conjunction with Descartes' trust in his validation of cognitive faculties, is sufficient to generate a metaphysical certainty that, for example, physical bodies exist and that they are the subjects of relative motion.

Who has ever doubted that bodies move, and that they have various sizes and shapes . . . for we perceive this not only with one of our senses, but through many of them, by sight, by touch, and by hearing.' (VIII-1, 323).

The other kind of certitude [i.e. when we think that it is in no way possible that something is other than we judge it to be] extends also to the knowledge which we have that there are bodies in the world. (IX-2, 324).

As soon as the empirical evidence in favour of such factual claims becomes less direct, more theoretical or more experimental, there is a corresponding lowering of the level of certainty which it is possible to achieve, for reasons already outlined in Chapter 3 above.

It is much more difficult to specify the sense in which Descartes believes that theoretical claims are confirmed. They are partly confirmed by empirical evidence, and partly confirmed by other features such as simplicity, etc. I defer consideration of these other features to §20, and concentrate here on the empirical confirmation of hypotheses.

The weakest sense in which theoretical hypotheses are

confirmed is where one's theorising agrees with experience, i.e.
there is some relevant empirical evidence available and one's
hypothesis at least does not conflict with it. The usual position
here is that Descartes is already in possession of empirically
confirmed facts or, at least, of claims which he believes are true.
Then, beginning from a few assumptions about matter in motion
and the laws of nature, he weaves a likely account of how basic
hypotheses can causally explain the facts; in constructing the
likely story there is a very prodigal use of auxiliary hypotheses,
many of which have not been independently checked. At the
conclusion of the story, the agreement with the facts is noted, and
the story is thereby 'confirmed'. This approach is so *ad hoc* in
tailoring the explanation to fit the putative facts that it is hard to
see how there can be any corroboration at all derived from such
an agreement. And yet this type of argument is very characteristic
of Cartesian science.

For example, Descartes concludes the discussion of comets in
the *Principles* with the claim: 'Nor do I think that there have been
any observations of comets up to now, except for those which are
to be regarded as fables or miracles, whose cause is not found
here.' (VIII-1, 191).[15] The explanation of sun-spots agrees with
experience; likewise the hypotheses about the polarity of iron in
mines 's'accorde avec l'expérience'; while the explanation of
viscosity is confirmed by all available experiences.[16]

The mere agreement of hypotheses with empirically known
facts provides nothing more than a negative criterion for deciding
their truth. There are indications that Descartes recognises the
need for experimental tests before claiming to have verified or
confirmed an hypothesis. For example, in discussing the
magnetic properties of metals in mines, he writes of

different kinds of metal, which I might have explained in more detail
here, if I could have had the opportunity of doing all the experiments
which are necessary to confirm (*verifier*) the reasonings which I engaged
in on this subject. (IX-2, 236).[17]

In default of independent empirical control, Descartes
occasionally concedes that he has only established his opinion
with a certain probability.[18] So that a charitable interpretation of
this loose sense of 'confirmation' would be the following:
physical explanations are hypothetical claims about the way in

which the more general assumptions of Cartesian science can causally explain observed phenomena. That is, they are attempts to fill in the dotted line

P-principles . . . *explanandum*-sentence

with auxiliary hypotheses. To the extent to which there is independent empirical evidence to control such auxiliary hypotheses, the resulting explanation is more or less certain; and to the extent to which such control is lacking, the proposed explanations at least satisfy the minimal negative criterion of agreeing with the available empirical evidence.

One of the ways in which Cartesian hypotheses are confirmed in a stronger sense of the term is by standard experimental testing of predicted, quantitative implications of theories. (An alternative type of corroborative argument is discussed in §20.) There are many notable cases in Cartesian science where quantitative predictions based on a theory are confirmed by experiment. The sine law of refraction implied a constant of proportionality between the sine of the angles of incidence and refraction; a series of experiments (*expériences*) with different angles of incidence confirmed that theory.[19] The Cartesian theory of the rainbow was also confirmed by experiments (VI, 337). Experiments are invoked to confirm an hypothesis about magnets (Descartes to Mersenne, November 14, 1630: I, 172); to measure changes in the weight of a body nearer to the centre of the earth (to Mersenne, July 13, 1638: II, 225); to test the relation between the heat of the heart and the frequency of heart-beats in eels (to Plempius, February 15 and March 23, 1638: I, 523, and II, 66); to check the flow of liquid through tubes (to Huygens, February 18, 1643: III, 617, 805).

The number of examples cited here could be considerably increased by further references to Descartes' scientific essays and correspondence; and yet, despite this, one still has a dominant impression in reading Cartesian explanations that it was more important for the author to provide plausible explanation sketches rather than to follow through on a detailed testing of particular explanations. One is tempted to conclude that Descartes was not particularly concerned whether his theories were confirmed or not, and that this perhaps betrays over-confidence on his part in the plausibility of his hypotheses.

It also raises the question as to whether he might have granted that Cartesian scientific explanations were capable of being disconfirmed; it is here more than on any other issue that Descartes can reveal his stand vis-à-vis rationalism.[20]

There is a problem in requiring that a scientific theory as general and comprehensive as Descartes' assumptions about matter and motion should be disconfirmable.[21] Moreover there is reason to believe that the criterion of falsifiability is selectively applied by historians of science to the many corpuscularian philosopher-scientists of the seventeenth century. If one thinks primarily in terms of the general framework within which the science of the time was developing, there is no distinction between empiricist and rationalist among scientists of the corpuscularian tradition with respect to their convictions about basic assumptions. Like many others of the day, Descartes probably had no real doubts about the eventual success of the kind of theory of nature which he was defending. So that when the question of disconfirming theories or hypotheses is raised, it is necessary to distinguish a number of questions which might be put to Descartes with a view to disclosing his assumptions about the certainty of his scientific theories:

(a) Did Descartes accept that his scientific theories could be fundamentally mistaken?
(b) Did he think that the basic assumptions of his science (i.e. the P-principles) could be empirically disconfirmed?
(c) Would Descartes concede that hypothetical explanations of individual phenomena might be empirically disconfirmed?
(d) Are there any intimations in Descartes that there may be objections to empirical disconfirmation because of the theory-laden character of observation statements or because of some more fundamental distrust of empirical evidence as such?

The first question has already been answered in the affirmative in Chapter 4; in that case divine revelation or the theological interpretation of revelation which was current in Descartes' time was accepted by him as a possible source of disconfirmation. The second question raises a different issue entirely. In this case one needs to identify a Cartesian assumption which is so central that if it is shown to be false one has reason to doubt Descartes' whole scientific approach; and secondly, it must be possible to disconfirm such a central assumption empirically. In correspondence with Mersenne Descartes acknowledged that the motion of the earth satisfies the first condition here;[22] however, this is still an issue about which reason and revelation apparently conflict. A more appropriate example is Descartes' claim that 'light reaches the eye in an instant from a luminous source',[23] and that this is so certain that proof to the contrary would undermine his whole enterprise: 'This seems to me to be so certain that, if someone could show it were false, I would be prepared to agree that I know nothing at all in philosophy.' (I, 307–8). In this case Descartes agreed to put his theory to the test, and rather than adopt the test proposed by his adversary he suggested an alternative which would be more favourable to those who defend a finite speed of transmission of light. The alternative *experimentum* was to try to measure the speed of light when it travels between the moon and the earth during a lunar eclipse, for Descartes suspected that the speed of light was much greater than could be measured over a shorter distance. Unfortunately the instruments available at the time were not adequate to measure even this interval of time and he concludes:

Therefore your experiment is useless and mine, which is the one accepted by all astronomers, shows very clearly that light is not seen in a perceptible interval of time. Hence I consider this argument a demonstration (I, 310).

This is a rather isolated case of testing fundamental hypotheses experimentally. It is probably more accurate to say that although Descartes might be willing to agree that his basic assumptions in physics may be false, he did not anticipate experimental disconfirmation. And the reasons for this position are partly explained by over-confidence in his theories, and partly by factors which fall under question (*d*).

In contrast to his stand on the certainty of fundamental assumptions, Descartes is quick to rely on empirical evidence to challenge hypotheses about individual phenomena. For example, he appeals to *plusieurs expériences* to cast doubt on the assumption that our ideas exactly resemble the objects they signify (XI, 4); to an experimental test to disprove the claim that a certain type of stone points to the sun at all times (Descartes to Huygens, January 14, 1643: IV, 803–4, V, 548); to a 'most certain experiment' to refute the Galenic theory of blood 'circulation' (Descartes to Plempius, February 15, 1638: I, 526). Descartes writes to Ciermans that he is willing to reconsider his explanation of the colour red if there is one experience in the whole of nature which is incompatible with it (Descartes to Ciermans, March 23, 1638: II, 75). He rejects Hobbes' explanation of refraction because 'experientiae repugnat' (Descartes to Mersenne, February 18, 1641: III, 317), and he has a similar reaction to another explanation of the same phenomenon by an unknown author, whose suggestions Mersenne had forwarded to him: 'experience clearly contradicts it' (Descartes to Mersenne, June or July, 1648: V, 205). Ptolemy's planetary theory is likewise rejected because it is 'manifestly contrary to experience' (Descartes to an unknown correspondent, 1644(?): V, 550; cf. *Principles*, VIII-1, 85).

These examples show that, at least when it suits him, Descartes is not reluctant to appeal to empirical evidence or experiments to challenge the credibility of scientific hypotheses.

The final question raised about empirical disconfirmation concerned the possibility of general philosophical objections along the lines of the Duhem–Quine thesis or the theory-ladenness of observational evidence. It would be anachronistic to claim to find these objections in Descartes in their present-day formulations; at the same time I have indicated in §5 that Descartes objected to experiments on a number of grounds, some of which overlap with recently formulated reservations in the philosophy of science. For example, Descartes distrusted experiments which were not accompanied by the correct theory; and he was uncharacteristically cautious in pointing out that one may draw an incorrect theoretical conclusion from a reliable piece of empirical evidence. The main reason for this caution is that any physical situation is much more complicated than our theories recognise and there are many features of an actual physical event or situation which are not reflected in the variables of our hypotheses. Physical reality is too complex for our theories and therefore counterfactual evidence must be carefully interpreted.

Apart from this qualification of the disconfirming role of experience, Descartes is never found to reject possibly falsifying empirical evidence, and there is no evidence to suggest that he mistrusted sense-knowledge as such as a source of reliable information about the physical world. If the counter-evidence to a theory is not otherwise explicable, as where there is no parallax of the fixed stars when the earth moves,[24] the theory must be adapted to fit the phenomena.

In summary: in the case both of confirmation and of disconfirmation, Descartes' reported practice suggests that he relies almost exclusively on empirical evidence when the issue at stake is relatively non-theoretical. Factual claims about observable phenomena are most easily decided by experience.

Once a disputed opinion is theoretical, the evidence available in Descartes' writing is not unambiguous. On the one hand, he is too quick to claim that his own auxiliary hypotheses are 'confirmed' simply because they 'agree with experience'; and I have suggested that Descartes oscillates on this question between claiming more than he has proved and admitting that he has only probable arguments in his favour. On the other hand, one also finds classic examples of quantitative predictions based on theory which are found to agree with well-constructed experimental tests. And in these cases one feels that the word 'confirmation' is appropriate. A similar ambiguity obtains in the case of disconfirming theoretical claims. Descartes is rather quick to indicate how some hypotheses fail to agree with experimental evidence; and he is just as likely to claim – especially in his own defence – that experience rarely provides unqualified evidence against a theory, either because the theory is further adaptable to fit the evidence, or because 'experimental' evidence is not to be taken at face value.

§19   *Crucial experiments*

Descartes was familiar with the problem of competing scientific explanations of the same phenomenon. The choice between such alternatives was determined by a number of factors, such as the relative simplicity of the competing hypotheses, the degree of their compatibility with already accepted assumptions, and their fruitfulness in suggesting further explanations of otherwise unexplained phenomena. Empirical evidence was also a dominant factor in resolving issues of this kind. For example, Descartes comments in the *Discourse* about crucial experiments:

As regards that problem [a choice between competing explanations] I know of no other resolution except to look afresh for some experiences which are such that their occurrence is not the same if one chooses to explain it [a particular effect] in one way rather than the other. (VI, 65).

This is not equivalent to suggesting the possibility of crucial experiments in every case of conflicting explanations; Descartes is only acknowledging that he knows of no other expedient than to look for *expériences* – whether they be observations, experiments or even phenomena – which are compatible with one explanation and incompatible with the other.

The test of Descartes' commitment to such an empirical decision procedure is an examination of what he does, or proposes should be done, in those cases where his explanation of some phenomenon clashes with that of some other scientist, whether a contemporary or otherwise. Although a detailed examination of each case would be required in order to draw any definitive conclusion, only one example will be considered here as a paradigm of Cartesian procedure in a scientific controversy; some references are given to other cases where Descartes seems to follow through on his *Discourse* strategy. The case examined here is the disagreement with William Harvey in explaining how the human heart is the cause of blood circulation.[25]

In discussing Harvey's difference with Descartes the following plan is followed. A brief summary is given of the points on which the two scientists agreed, contrary to most physicians and surgeons of the day, concerning the circulation of the blood. This is followed by indicating the points about which they disagreed. In retrospect the history of physiology has evidently vindicated Harvey's position. However at the time of the dispute there is no recorded instance of Descartes appealing to anything but experience as the deciding factor between the two theories. This is clear from examining the evidence introduced by both scientists. In fact, it is interesting to notice that precisely those features of Descartes' position which seemed most counter-experiential were also found in Harvey's tentative explanation of blood circulation.

Descartes discusses the circulation of the blood in *Le Monde* (1632), the *Discourse* (1637), *The Passions of the Soul* (1646) and in his *Description of the Human Body* (1648). His explanation of blood circulation does not change during this period. Even before he read Harvey's account in 1632 in *De Motu Cordis*, Descartes had already introduced the hypothesis that blood circulates in the human body, as part of a mechanical model of man:[26]

> the greater part of it returning to the veins through the extremities of the arteries, which are found to be joined in various places to those of the veins; and from the veins perhaps some of it is used to nourish some of the body's members. However, most of it returns to the heart, and from there goes once more to the veins; so that the movement of the blood in the body is nothing but a continuous circulation. (XI, 127).

When Descartes reflects on this passage in the *Discourse* he explains that it is not a good example of his proposed deduction of particular explanations from more general principles. Rather, 'since I had not yet sufficient knowledge to speak about it [the body] in the same way as other things, that is, by demonstrating the effects through their causes' (VI, 45) he had to be content with an hypothetical starting point and then examine what could be explained subsequently. It is as an example of this hypothetical method that he discusses, at length, the circulation of the blood. 'But, so that one can see how I dealt with this matter, I wish to propose the explanation of the movement of the heart and of the arteries' (VI, 46). It is precisely because of its hypothetical character that the theory had need of empirical corroboration.

Once he read Harvey's *De Motu Cordis* Descartes consistently attributed the discovery of blood circulation to the English physician and spoke of him with praise as the man who first 'broke the ice in this place [i.e. in his book]' (VI, 50). The principal reasons proposed by Descartes in favour of the circulation theory are the same three which were used by Harvey. These were:

(*a*) A quantitative argument – the heart pumps more blood in half an hour than could be drained from the whole body and resupplied by nutrition.[27]

(*b*) The experiment of ligating the arm: a loose ligature results in a build-up of pressure in the arm, because the arteries continue to conduct the blood into the arm whereas the veins are constricted from allowing the blood to circulate back out again.[28]

(*c*) Evidence from the structure of the valves: the valves in the veins, arteries and the heart are so constructed that blood cannot pass in both directions, but only in the direction suggested by Harvey and Descartes.[29]

Descartes then proceeds to mention six other pieces of

evidence in favour of the hypothesis, and the language used here again illustrates the kind of method employed. 'But there are many other things which show that the true cause of this movement of the blood is the one which I proposed.' (VI, 52). All six are empirical 'facts': the colour of the blood, the relative hardness of the arteries and veins, the relative size of the left and right ventricles of the heart, the pressure of the blood as an index of health, the heat of the blood and the role of the lungs in cooling the blood.

Harvey and Descartes agreed on the fact of the blood's circulation and on the path followed by the blood: from the vena cava through the right auricle and ventricle of the heart and the pulmonary artery to the lungs; back through the pulmonary vein to the left side of the heart, before emerging again through the aorta to move through the arteries and return again to the veins. Descartes and Harvey disagreed about the *cause* of circulation. More precisely, they agreed that the heart was the cause of blood circulation but disagreed on the explanation of the heart's functioning.

Descartes erroneously defended a form of the Galenic theory, according to which the blood fell, one drop at a time, into the right side of the heart, and the innate heat of the heart caused a type of effervescence which expanded the volume of the blood, and caused the systole of the heart. It was at this time, he thought, that the blood was expelled from the right ventricle through the pulmonary artery. After it had been cooled in the lungs, the same process occurred again in the left ventricle, and the blood was expelled into the arteries from which it circulated back, through the veins, to the vena cava again. In this model of the functioning of the heart, the blood is expelled through the pulmonary artery and the aorta when the heart expands, and the blood enters the heart when it contracts.

Descartes' evaluation of the justification of his own position is clearly illustrated by the kinds of arguments he invokes against Harvey.[30] They differed primarily on when the systole and diastole occurred, and also on the explanation of the capacity of the heart to force the blood into the arteries and back to the heart again through the veins. The first point of difference was primarily an observational one, whereas the second one was to a great extent theoretical. Descartes appeals to the appropriate kind of evidence in his favour in both instances.

Harvey was correct in his observation of systole and diastole. Although he was not the first to distinguish correctly the two movements of the heart,[31] he was convinced by his observations and experiments that the proper action of the heart, as a muscle, was its contraction in all directions at once, and that this movement forced the blood out through the pulmonary artery and the aorta. Thus the systole of the heart corresponded with the diastole of the arteries. On relaxing again in diastole, the heart allows blood to enter from the vena cava and pulmonary vein, at which point the whole process begins again.[32]

Harvey was also correct in suggesting that the explanation of the systolic movement was nothing more than the heart's characteristic movement as a muscle.[33] As evidence for this he gave the example of the heart continuing to beat even when there was no blood in it, or even when it had been cut into pieces after excision from the body.[34] In normal circumstances, however, the heart appears to the trained observer in the following way:

2. It contracts all over, but particularly to the sides, so that it looks narrower and longer . . .
3. Grasping the heart in the hand, it feels harder when it moves. The hardness is due to tension, as when one grasps the forearm and feels its tendons become knotty when the fingers are moved.
4. . . . when the heart moves it is paler in colour, but when it pauses it is of a deeper blood colour. From these facts it seems clear to me that the motion of the heart consists of a tightening all over, both contraction along the fibres, and constriction everywhere. The motion is just the same as that of muscles.[35]

Added to these observations was the experiment of cutting the lower tip of an animal's heart while it is beating, and inserting one's finger into the ventricle; the pressure on one's finger is felt at the same time as the systole of the heart.

It is difficult to see how Descartes can ignore such clear, empirical evidence in favour of Harvey's theory. In fact, he does not ignore it but provides a careful and accurate summary of all of Harvey's evidence (in the *Description*, XI, 241-2), before proceeding to give his own explanation of the phenomenon. He finds that Harvey's theory is 'against the common judgment of sight' (XI, 241).

Descartes introduces the discussion of which explanation of blood circulation is correct with the following phrase: 'But, in order to be able to see which of these two causes is correct, it is necessary to consider some other *expériences* which cannot agree with both of them.' (XI, 242). There is no mention of his own explanation being deductively verified from first principles, confirmed a priori by Cartesian insight, or preferred despite the evidence because of its coherence with a more comprehensive theory of nature. The deciding factor between Harvey and himself will have to be empirical evidence; he proceeds to give three *expériences* which he believes are decisive in his favour:

(*a*) If the fibres of the heart contract, then the heart should diminish in size. But if the blood expands, so should the heart. 'But one can see by experience that it does not lose any of its size, but rather that it increases it.' (XI, 242).

(*b*) 'Another *expérience* which shows that its cavities do not become narrower' (XI, 243) is to cut the point of the heart of a young rabbit, and see the ventricles increase in size while the heart pumps out blood and stiffens at the same time. In fact, Harvey's similar experiment with the heart of a dog gave him the results he recorded because the fibres of such larger animals' hearts could exert pressure on an inserted finger even though the ventricle of the heart itself expands!

(*c*) 'I will add a third *expérience*' (XI, 243), which is that arterial blood has different qualities from venous blood. In Harvey's explanation, one would have to postulate some *faculté* which causes the heart to pump, and another *faculté* to explain the changed condition of the blood between the vena cava and the aorta. Descartes' theory accounts for both of them by means of the innate heat of the heart, itself not a postulate (he thought), but something which 'everyone knows is greater in the heart than in all other parts of the body' (XI, 244).

Harvey's reaction to this was to suggest, erroneously in part, that Descartes was incorrect in his observations.[36] He therefore attempted an alternative explanation, in terms of the relative thickness of arteries and veins, of why the blood in each was of a different colour. Not only was Harvey ignorant – as were all of his contemporaries – of the real cause of this phenomenon, but he later conceded most of the points that inspired Descartes' explanation even though many of them were incompatible with his own theory. For example, he granted both that the heart was a source of heat to the body, and also that the blood itself had a certain innate heat which it shared with the heart, and which triggered the ebullition of blood in the heart when it reaches the right ventricle.[37] He suggested erroneously that the blood returned to the heart cooler than when it left, and that it was so warmed by the heart that the lungs cooled it.[38] Harvey even goes so far as to explain both the triggering and continued movement of the heart by the heat of the incoming venous blood even though he had himself shown that an excised bloodless heart continues to beat.[39] In fact, this had been his most telling objection to Descartes' explanation. The final paradox of Harvey's position was that he was so adamant in denying the existence of both the anastomoses (in the Galenic sense) between the veins and the arteries, and the invisible pores in the septum of the heart, because neither one was observable; yet at the same time he had to postulate the existence of capillary connections between the veins and the arteries which were also, in his time, unobservable.[40]

It seems that at least this much is evident from the tentative investigations of Harvey and Descartes' reactions to them: there is no clear line of demarcation between theory and observational fact, and there is equal disagreement on each between the two scientists. Harvey was by far the better in physiological studies, and his observations were correct in most cases. But the significance of this disagreement between Harvey and Descartes for the present inquiry is the attempt on Descartes' part to resolve it solely in terms of the accuracy of the observations and the greater explanatory power of his own theory in accounting for what he believed to be empirical facts.[41] Descartes does not appeal to any a priori reasons in favour of his own explanation. Rather, he admits the significance of empirical evidence to decide between Harvey and himself, and believes that the *expériences* he appeals to are decisive in his favour.

One clear example from the abundance of Cartesian controversy is obviously insufficient to establish a consistent pattern of reliance on experience as a major factor in choosing between competing theories. However, there are not many other examples available in Descartes' work. The reason for this is not that one finds Descartes attempting to decide theoretical disagreements in science without reference to empirical evidence; rather, he is seldom in fact faced with the situation of having to choose between alternative explanations. When the occasion does arise, however, of arbitrating between competing theories, he is true to his stated preference for empirical evidence as a decisive factor.

For example, the dispute about the speed of the transmission of light, already mentioned above, was agreed by both sides to be empirically decidable. When Cavendish objected to his calculations of the periodicity of triangular-shaped pendula as being counter-experiential, he answered that Cavendish had failed to take air resistance into account.[42] Roberval suggested an alternative explanation of the same phenomenon, and Descartes agreed to 'decide the truth of the explanations by *expériences*'.[43] Another critic, Fabri, suggested an alternative explanation of falling bodies in terms of each body having a certain gravity, and quoted some experiments of weighing objects in dark caves as a possible objection to Descartes' explanation. Descartes accepted the experimental findings, but shows that they are perfectly compatible with his own hypothesis also.[44] Finally, in the discussion of gravity versus subtle matter and the possibility of a vacuum in barometers, Descartes claims to have suggested the Puy-de-Dôme experiment to Pascal, who had apparently expected the opposite to the results he obtained. Again, the experiment was 'entirely consistent with my [Descartes'] principles'.[45] The experiment had been proposed as a means of resolving the fundamental differences between himself and Pascal; as might be expected, experimental evidence was inadequate to the task. Nevertheless, its choice by Descartes is significant for the interpretation of his scientific methodology.

§20 *The certainty of physical explanations*

I have argued in §§13–19 that Descartes' theory of scientific explanation involved a recognition both of the need for certainty in science and of the inevitability of hypothetical reasoning. The greatest disparity between these two dominant features of explanation develops when divine revelation apparently endorses a scientific theory which conflicts with 'rational' hypotheses. In such cases, Descartes seems genuinely satisfied to accept Church teaching as if it were true, and to substitute a 'false'

but plausible account as a likely explanation of how nature would
have acted had God not intervened as he did.

As an hypothetical enterprise, physical explanation in the
Cartesian project is located in the logical space between
M-principles and empirically known physical phenomena,
where P-principles occupy a place of honour close to the
M-principles.

[M-principles . . . P-principles] . . . auxiliary hypotheses . . .
descriptions of explananda.

When the time comes to assess the certainty of Cartesian
explanations, Descartes returns to a schema something like the
one above in order to distinguish the metaphysical certainty of
basic assumptions in physics from the moral certainty of specific
explanations.

Apart from empirical evidence which has already been
discussed, and the complex relation between M-principles and
P-principles – both of which confirm the P-principles – Descartes
introduces further considerations which he thinks confirm the
truth of the P-principles. These features include: the simplicity of
the P-principles, the fact that there are relatively few principles to
explain a wide diversity of physical phenomena, and the fact that
the principles succeed in explaining phenomena which were not
considered in the initial formulation of basic assumptions.

Morin elicited some clarification of these criteria when he
objected that it is always possible to imagine a cause which could
explain any given effect. In response Descartes wrote, July 13,
1638:

Finally you say that there is nothing easier than to fit some cause to any
given effect. But although there are indeed many effects to which it is
easy to fit different causes, one to one, it is not so easy to fit a single cause
to many different effects, unless it is the true cause which produces
them. There are often effects where, in order to prove which is their true
cause, it is enough to suggest a cause from which they can all be clearly
deduced. And I claim that all the causes which I have discussed are of
this type . . . If one compares the assumptions of others with my own,
that is, all their *real qualities*, their *substantial forms*, their *elements* and
similar things which are almost infinite in number, with this one
assumption that all bodies are composed of parts: something which can
be observed with the naked eye in some cases and can be proved by an
unlimited number of reasons in others . . . and finally, if one compares
what I have deduced about vision, salt, winds, clouds, snow, thunder,

the rainbow, and so on from my assumptions, with what they have deduced from theirs . . . I hope that that would suffice to convince those with an open mind that the effects which I explain have no other causes apart from those from which I deduce them. (II, 199–200).[46]

The claim that relatively few principles or causes explain a variety of phenomena had already been made in *Le Monde* as a corroborating argument, together with the simplicity and the 'familiarity' of the assumptions:

Finally, as regards the other things I assumed which cannot be perceived by any sense, they are all so simple, and so familiar, and even so few in number, that if you compare them with the diversity and marvellous artifice which is apparent in the structure of visible organs, you will far more have reason to suspect that, rather than include some which are not genuine, I have omitted some which are in fact operative in us. And knowing that nature always operates in the most simple and easy way possible, you will perhaps decide that it is impossible to find more plausible explanations of how it operates than those which are proposed here. (XI, 201).[47]

This same point is reflected in the *Meteorology*, where the author claims: 'it seems to me that my explanations (*raisons*) should be all the more accepted, in proportion as I make them depend on fewer things' (VI, 239). The assumptions underlying Cartesian astronomy are likewise characterised as simple, plausible, and intuitively reasonable: 'And I do not think that one could think of other principles of nature which are more simple, or intellectually familiar, or even more probable.' (VIII-1, 102).[48]

The unforeseen explanatory success of a few principles constitutes an extra confirmatory argument. Thus early in Part III of the *Principles* Descartes proposes to include just a few hypothetical causes,

in order to see if we can deduce all the other more specific ones from these, even though we have not taken the latter into account in proposing the more general causes. For if we find that this procedure works, this will constitute a very strong argument that we are on the right track. (IX-2, 122).

The same point is reiterated at the conclusion of the *Principles*:

Whoever notices how many features of magnets, of fire, and of the whole fabric of the world have been deduced here from a few principles . . . will acknowledge that it could scarcely happen that so many things would cohere together if they were false.[49] (VIII-1, 328).

The use of supplementary corroborating arguments based on simplicity, explanatory power, etc. implicitly acknowledges that mere 'agreement with experience' is no guarantee that the hypothetical causes proposed in a theory are the true causes of some phenomenon. It is also clear, however, that the supplementary arguments only apply to the more general and basic assumptions which are adopted at the early stages of the Cartesian enterprise. This is exactly the position defended by Descartes at the conclusion of the *Principles*:

> [metaphysical certitude] extends to everything about physical bodies which can be demonstrated, either by the principles of mathematics or by other principles which are equally evident and certain; it seems to me that one should include, among the latter, those principles which I wrote in this treatise, at least the more important and general among them. (IX-2, 324).

In trying to get more explicit about which hypotheses are included among the 'principal and more general ones', the author refers to the theory of matter adopted in Part III, article xlvi. This is almost equivalent to an admission that the only assumption which is metaphysically certain is the hypothesis that matter is divisible into small parts, and that the motions and interactions of these parts are sufficient to explain all physical phenomena:

> I think that one should also recognise that I proved all the things I wrote by means of a mathematical demonstration, at least the more general points about the fabric of the heavens and the earth, in the way in which I described them; for I took care to propose whatever I thought was doubtful, as such. (IX-2, 325).

These remarks at the conclusion of the *Principles* illustrate the kind of dilemma which was implicit in the Cartesian demand for certainty, when coupled with the obvious hypothetical character of physical explanations. The proposed compromise is unsatisfactory; what was obviously lacking was a more nuanced concept of probability or certainty. Descartes' suggestion seems to amount to the following: M-principles have maximum certainty. The P-principles are also certain, because some of them can be directly confirmed by experience; they are consistent with the M-principles; they are so familiar, so simple, so intuitively plausible; and despite the fact that they are few in number, they provide a successful base for explaining a wide variety of diverse phenomena, including many which were not even considered at the time of initially formulating the general principles.

In contrast to the P-principles, the more specific explanations of particular physical phenomena are morally certain. The level of uncertainty involved here is remediable up to a certain point; but Descartes does not seem to be optimistic that it can be completely avoided. The reason for this has already been discussed; the explanation of particular phenomena depends on the specification of all the variables which can affect them and this seems to be a theoretically insuperable task. Secondly, even if all these factors could be specified and incorporated into a theory, Descartes is notoriously sceptical about the possibility of conducting appropriate experiments which would adequately control the variations in these factors. In default of such perfect science, Descartes proposes a likely story, or model, which is consistent with both the general principles and our empirically warranted observations.

Those who demand more than this in physical explanations 'do not know what they are asking for, nor what they should look for'. (II, 144).

Notes

1   See H. Frankfurt, 'Memory and the Cartesian circle', *Philosophical Review*, **71** (1962), 504–11; 'Descartes' validation of reason', in W. Doney, ed., *Descartes*, pp. 209–26; *Demons, Dreamers, and Madmen* (Indianapolis, 1970); 'Descartes on the creation of the eternal truths', *Philosophical Review*, **86** (1977), 36–57. See also Alan Gewirth, 'The Cartesian circle', *Philosophical Review*, **50** (1941), 368–95; 'The Cartesian circle reconsidered', *Journal of Philosophy*, **67** (1970), 668–85; 'Descartes: two disputed questions', *Journal of Philosophy*, **68** (1971), 228–96.
2   'Descartes on the creation of the eternal truths'.
3   Cf. Descartes to Arnauld, July 29, 1648: 'since every account of goodness and truth is subject to his [God's] omnipotence, I would not dare say that God could not create a mountain without a valley, nor that he could not make the sum of one and two not be three; I would only claim that he has given me such a mind that I cannot

conceive of a mountain without a valley, or of the addition of one and two not being three, etc. and that such things involve a contradiction in my understanding.' (V, 224).

4   Cf. VII, 36, 89, 460. In *Recherche de la vérité* Eudoxus encourages Polyander with this advice: 'I warn you that those doubts which frightened you at the beginning are like those phantoms and vain images which appear at night due to a weak and uncertain light.' (X, 513). Cf. also Annotations to the *Principles*, XI, 654, for a rejection of unreasonable and unfounded doubts.

5   Descartes to Elizabeth, June 28, 1643 (III, 695).

6   E. Gilson, in *Discours*, p. 269 assumes that this refers to Descartes' experimental work, especially on the sine law of refraction, which provided more certain knowledge than the opinions of philosophers.

7   See A. Gewirth, 'The Cartesian circle reconsidered', pp. 670ff.

8   E. Gilson, in *Discours*, pp. 358–9, argues that moral certainty and metaphysical certainty are not two degrees of the same kind of theoretical certainty, but rather two different kinds of certainty. However Descartes describes the results of physical explanations in terms of moral certainty (see *Principles*, VIII-1, 327–8) and this is evidently a degree of certainty in a theoretical question. Cf. III, 359; VI, 37; VII, 475, 477.

9   Cf. *Principles*, VIII-1, 21–2; A. Gewirth, 'Clearness and distinctness in Descartes', *Philosophy*, **18** (1943), 17–36; H. G. Frankfurt, *Demons, Dreamers, and Madmen*, pp. 123–45.

10   For an analysis of the concept 'certain' which would be compatible with Cartesian usage, see R. Firth, 'The anatomy of certainty', *Philosophical Review*, **76** (1967), 3–27. The contrary position is defended by Peter Unger, *Ignorance*, pp. 47ff.

11   Descartes surprisingly imagines that it is a positive feature of his assumptions that any possible condition of the universe could, perhaps with more ingenuity than usual, be explained by them. Cf. VIII-1, 103; IX-2, 126; *Discourse*, VI, 64–5.

12   VIII-1, 311: 'nor can I examine that power of attraction unless I first deduce many of its other properties from various experiments, and in this way (*ita*) investigate their innermost nature'. The '*ita*' suggests that the nature of the phenomenon is understood from the relevant experiments.

13   The references in order are to: Summer of 1631 (?), (I, 216); May 10, 1632 (I, 250–51); November or December, 1632 (I, 263); December 4, 1637 (I, 507); March 11, 1640 (III, 40); January 4, 1643 (III, 610); October 20, 1642 (III, 590); August 4, 1645 (IV, 260); October 1645 (?), (IV, 326).

14   For similar comments, see the second letter to Picot, XI, 326; *Description of the Human Body*, XI, 252–3; *Recherche de la vérité*, X, 503; Descartes to Elizabeth, January 31, 1648 (V, 112); to an unknown correspondent (1648 or 1649), (V, 261); Descartes to Henry More, April 15, 1649 (V, 344); *Principles*, IX-2, 309–10.

15   Cf. *Le Monde*, XI, 63: 'so that this model comet lacks none of the par-
      ticular properties of those which have been observed in the real
      world'. In this case, it is more obvious that the explanation was tail-
      ored to fit the facts.

16   IX-2, 158 (in the French version only). Cf. VIII-1, 99; IX-2, 241; IX-2,
      302; XI, 14. Other examples are his experiments in anatomy, *Genera-
      tion*, XI, 514, 524, 534, where the observations of various facts are
      said to confirm his opinions (in each case, the word '*confirmo*' is
      used); his theory of the location of the magnetic north pole, VIII-1,
      301; a test of a claim by Mersenne about the declination of magnets
      to see if it agreed with his theory, 'afin de voir si elle s'accordera avec
      mes raisons, ou plutost mes coniectures' (Descartes to Mersenne,
      May 30, 1643: III, 673); the examination of a calf's heart provided
      many pieces of evidence 'which agreed so accurately with my
      explanations that [I could not imagine] any better' (*Varia Anatomica*,
      XI, 552). See also *ibid.*, p. 555, and his examination of hailstones for
      their internal and external whiteness, VIII-1, 149; *Anatomica*, XI,
      617. Other examples of 'confirmation' in which the agreement of
      theory and phenomena is completely dependent on rather ad hoc
      auxiliary hypotheses are: that blowing one's breath through closed
      fingers confirms the theory that heat is the movement of small par-
      ticles (VI, 245); that the distance of the fixed stars is confirmed by the
      movement of comets (IX-2, 121); or that we can find no liquid which
      is composed of small particles, is pure, and is not transparent
      (VIII-1, Part IV, art. xvi).

17   Cf. IX-2, 17, where he talks about the need for experiences to 'sup-
      port and justify my reasoning'.

18   See *Le Monde*, XI, 20–21: 'The experiences of which I spoke are not
      enough to prove it [i.e. that there is no vacuum in nature] although
      they are sufficient to convince us that the spaces where we perceive
      nothing are filled with the same matter'; *ibid.*, p. 10, where it is said
      that several experiences 'favorisent cette opinion'. And in the *Medi-
      tations* (VII, 73), the experience of imagining probably shows that the
      body exists: 'probabiliter inde conjicio corpus existere'.

19   Cf. VI, 102, and Descartes to Golius, February 2, 1632 (I, 236).

20   For example, Gerd Buchdahl writes: 'Certainly he [Descartes] is
      never in doubt that his basic truths must be compatible with experi-
      ence. The crucial question is whether he would have admitted – a
      doubtful possibility – that these truths might be falsifiable in a novel
      context.' ('Descartes' anticipation of a "logic of scientific discov-
      ery" ', p. 417.) For a similar interpretation see M. Hesse, *Forces and
      Fields*, p. 109; Jean Rostand, *L'Atomisme en biologie*, p. 156; J. F. Scott,
      The Scientific Work of René Descartes, p. 164; E. W. Strong, *Procedures
      and Metaphysics*, p. 215.

21   For a clear statement of the Duhem–Quine thesis, see Adolf Grün-
      baum, 'Can we ascertain the falsity of a scientific hypothesis?' in
      Observation and Theory in Science, pp. 69–129.

22   Cf. Descartes to Mersenne, November 1633 (I, 271): 'I admit that if it

is false [that the earth revolves], then so are all the foundations of my philosophy because it can be clearly demonstrated from them. And it is so closely connected with all the other parts of my treatise, that I could not detach it from them without making the rest of it defective also.'

23   Descartes to Beeckman, August 22, 1634 (I, 307). This is not equivalent to saying that light travels in an instant from its source. Presumably, the distinction lies in Descartes' contention that the light does not actually travel, for it would make little sense to him that something could actually travel that quickly. Descartes corrects his correspondent on that score in the same letter.

24   VIII-1, 97.

25   A number of commentators have focused on the disagreement with Harvey as a model of Cartesian rationalism at work. See especially P. Gallois, 'La méthode de Descartes et la médecine', *Hippocrate*, **6** (1938), 77; L. Chauvois, *Descartes: sa méthode et ses erreurs en physiologie*, p. 18; A. C. Crombie, 'Descartes on method and physiology', *Cambridge Journal*, **5** (1951–2), p. 179. For a different interpretation of Cartesian physiology, see Jean Rostand, *L'Atomisme en biologie*, pp. 152–61; T. S. Hall, *Ideas of Life and Matter*, vol. I, 250–63, and 'Descartes' physiological method: position, principles, examples', *Journal of the History of Biology*, **3** (1970), 53–79.

26   'I saw the book *De Motu Cordis* about which you had previously spoken to me, and I find that I differ somewhat from it, though I had not seen it until after I had written about the same topic.' Descartes to Mersenne, November or December, 1632 (I, 263).

27   See William Harvey, *Exercitatio Anatomica de Motu Cordis et Sanguinis in Animalibus*, trans. Chauncey D. Leake, 3rd ed., Chapter 9; and *Discourse*, VI, 51–2: 'par l'experience qui monstre que tout celuy qui est dans le cors en peut sortir en fort peu de tems par une seule artere, lorsqu'elle est coupée, encore mesme qu'elle fust estroitement liée fort proche du coeur, & coupée entre luy & le lien, en sorte qu'on n'eust aucun suiet d'imaginer que le sang qui en sortiroit vint d'ailleurs.'

28   'Ce qu'il prouve fort bien, par l'experience ordinaire des chirurgiens' (VI, 51); Harvey, *De Motu Cordis*, p. 89.

29   'Il prouve aussy fort bien ce qu'il dit du cours du sang, par certaines petites peaux, qui sont tellement disposées en divers lieux ... qu'elles ne luy permetent point d'y passer du milieu de cors vers les extremitez ...' (VI, 51); Harvey, *op. cit.*, pp. 97ff.

30   Prior to discussing the nine reasons he thinks confirm his hypothesis, Descartes suggests that the motion of the heart follows from the disposition of its parts and the nature of the blood, just as simply as the movement of a clock follows from the disposition of its parts. This has been taken, on occasion, as a clear statement of Descartes' a priori explanation of blood circulation. The contrary is the case however. The 'nature of the blood' is known from experience: 'la nature du sang qu'on peut connoistre par experience' (VI,

50). Likewise the structure of the heart and the disposition of the valves is known from anatomical investigation. What Descartes is saying is: if the heart, the blood, veins, etc. are actually as described, nothing further is required to get the blood circulating. The same type of argument is proposed in the *Description of the Human Body*, XI, 231.

31 Harvey's debt to Realdus Columbus, who had been a professor of anatomy at Padua until 1547, and whose *De Re Anatomica* was published posthumously in 1559, is documented by Gweneth Whitteridge, *William Harvey and the Circulation of the Blood*, pp. 41–77.

32 The development of Harvey's theory is traced through the Lectures of 1616 to the *De Motu Cordis* by Whitteridge, *Harvey*, pp. 91–7. For summaries of observations made by Harvey and of his analysis of the heart beat, see *De Motu Cordis*, pp. 31 and 47.

33 'The motion [of the heart] is just the same as that of muscles when contracting along their tendons and fibres. The muscles in action become tense and tough, and lose their softness in becoming hard, while they thicken and stand out. The heart acts similarly.' Harvey, *De Motu Cordis*, p. 30.

34 See *ibid.*, p. 42.

35 *Ibid.*, 29, 30.

36 'That very acute and ingenious man, René Descartes, . . . and others . . . According to my light, however, their observation is incorrect.' Harvey, Second Letter to Riolan, 1649, in *The Circulation of the Blood*, trans. by Kenneth J. Franklin (Oxford, 1958), p. 65.

37 That the heart is a source of heat, see Harvey, *De Motu Cordis*, p. 71. Nevertheless, he writes to Riolan in his second letter: 'Nor is the heart, as some think, like a sort of burning coal . . . the source of heat . . . but rather the blood . . . gives to the heart (as to all the other parts) the heat which it has received.' *Circulation*, p. 63. Harvey also claims that the blood boils up by its own heat in the right auricle in a form of fermentation. 'The blood . . . slowly growing warm from its internal heat and becoming more rarefied, swells up and rises in the way that fermenting things do.' *Ibid.*, p. 57. This latter part of his theory is proposed, according to Harvey, 'without a demonstration' (*ibid.*, p. 62).

38 See the Letter to Riolan, *Circulation*, pp. 19–20. In fact, the blood is warmer on leaving the various parts of the body through which it passes. See L. Chauvois, *William Harvey*, p. 248. For the function of the lungs, see *De Motu Cordis*, pp. 59, 71 and *Circulation*, p. 20.

39 Both Sir Kenelm Digby and Plempius of Louvain pointed this out as objections to Descartes' explanation of the beating of the heart.

40 They were first observed by Malpighi, ten years after Descartes' death. See Dreyfus-Le Foyer, 'Les conceptions médicales de Descartes', p. 240.

41 This was also the interpretation of E. Gilson, in *Etudes*, pp. 93–4: 'The attitude adopted by Descartes when faced with the description by Harvey is extremely interesting. He never denied that it was coh-

erent and capable of accounting for the phenomena; on the contrary he saw in this one of those cases where two different explanations account for the same phenomenon in an equally satisfactory manner.' See also A. Gewirtz, 'Experience and the non-mathematical in the Cartesian method', p. 199, note 61. J. A. Passmore, in 'William Harvey and the philosophy of science', *Australasian Journal of Philosophy*, **36** (1958), 85–94, sees the disagreement of Harvey and Descartes as an instance of two conflicting philosophies of science, one reductionist and explanatory, the other empirical and non-systematic. While there is an element of this here, it is primarily a clash between two alternative explanations of the same phenomenon, not observed or described identically by the two contestants.

42 See Descartes to Cavendish, March 30, 1646 (IV, 380–88).

43 Descartes to Mersenne, October 5, 1646 (IV, 512). He later writes a letter to Mersenne for Roberval, and comments on the implications of his own calculations: 'Et pour ce que cela se trouve par experience, il est evident que l'experience s'accorde tres-constamment avec mes conclusions.' (IV, 547–8). He reiterates his willingness to abide by experimental tests in a letter to Mersenne, January 25, 1647 (IV, 595–7).

44 See Descartes to Mersenne, April 26, 1647 (IV, 636).

45 See Descartes to Carcavi, August 17, 1649 (V, 391). Cf. Descartes to Mersenne, December 13, 1647 (V, 98–100), where Descartes comments on Pascal's experiments, and suggests that he and Mersenne could test the influence of atmospheric changes on the readings of the barometer.

46 The objection that ad hoc explanations can always be constructed to explain any phenomenon was made by Descartes against Galileo: 'without having considered the first causes of nature, he [Galileo] has merely sought the explanations of a few particular effects, and he has thereby built without foundations' (Descartes to Mersenne, October 11, 1638: II, 380).

47 Cf. XI, 7–8.

48 Cf. *Le Monde*, XI, 80–3.

49 A similar appeal to the explanatory power of a few hypotheses is made in the discussion of magnetism (VIII-1, 284), and in explaining the dispersion of colours in the light spectrum (VI, 334).

SEVEN

Methodological Essays

I have suggested above that Descartes' two principal essays on methodology, the *Regulae* and the *Discourse*, are unreliable guides to understanding Cartesian science as long as they are considered either in isolation from the scientific practice which they purport to describe, or as the definitive expressions of views about physical science which most likely evolved between 1628 and 1650. One may not gratuitously assume that Descartes' views about scientific method are either clear or consistent; so that there is no a priori guarantee that what one finds in these essays coincides with the method apparently endorsed by his scientific work. At the same time, it does seem as if Descartes, in the mature period of his science (i.e. from about 1635 forward), was forced to come to grips with a variety of methodological issues which easily escape readers of the *Regulae* or the *Discourse*. The fact that these issues – such as problems about hypotheses, certainty, models – are often discussed in incidental passages or, at greater length, in correspondence only confirms the suspicion that their author was seriously concerned with the implications of his scientific experience for his views about method. The close liaison, in the mature period, between scientific practice and methodological discussion provides a reasonably sure foothold for plausible interpretation. And the interpretation which seems most plausible in this context is not the classic picture of a narrow rationalist devoted single-mindedly to a priori explanations and chains of logical deductions.

The question which was mentioned at the outset, and deferred, must now be faced however; and that concerns the extent to which the methodological essays represent a different view of scientific method from the one so far ascribed to Descartes in these pages. If Descartes is not a stubborn rationalist in the face of experiential evidence, perhaps the *Regulae* exhibits early rationalist tendencies which were abandoned in the mature period; or perhaps the *Discourse* even more acutely illustrates some kind of evolution from rationalism to moderate empiricism in the apparent discrepancies between Parts II, V and VI.

§21 *The* Regulae

Rather than even appear to propose a commentary on the *Regulae*, which deserves a much more comprehensive treatment than could possibly be attempted here, I wish to isolate a number of points which support the thesis that this early methodological essay is consistent with the view of Descartes already outlined.

The first point to be noted is that the *Regulae* was originally planned as a general discussion of method in three parts or three books,[1] each of which would contain twelve rules. The first twelve rules are concerned with the use of our cognitive faculties in general and are not meant to give detailed or specific indications of how the rules proposed here could apply in different disciplines. So that one might anticipate, as a result, that the discussion is so general as to give very few indications of how one might solve a mathematical problem or how one might discover or test an explanation in physical science. Thus, at the conclusion of rule 7 one finds this comment:

Finally, it is important not to separate these last three propositions, because in most cases one must consider them all together and they all contribute equally to the perfection of the method. And it would make little difference which one is taught first; we have only discussed them briefly here because this is the main topic in the rest of the treatise, where we will present in detail what we have proposed here in general (X, 392).

What one finds in rules 1 to 12 is indeed so general that it is difficult to get any clear ideas about the proposed method. Partly as a result of this vagueness and partly because of Descartes' tendency to extol the merits of mathematics, one is tempted to assume that Cartesian method involves an extrapolation to a variety of disciplines of a method which is peculiar to mathematics. And in a sense this is true – but only in the unusual sense that analysis and synthesis was originally conceived of as a geometrical method. But with the exception of the claimed ancestry in Greek mathematics, there is one characteristic of Cartesian method which emerges very clearly in the *Regulae*, and that is that it is *not* an extrapolation of mathematical techniques to other disciplines.[2]

The certainty of mathematical reasoning had been conceded in rule 2; however the conclusion to be drawn was not that this is the only discipline worth studying:

> And one should conclude from all this, certainly not that one should study nothing but Arithmetic and Geometry, but only that those who seek the straight path to the truth should not study anything of which they cannot have a degree of certitude which is equal to the demonstrations of Arithmetic and Geometry. (X, 366).

Those who pay close attention to the text are told, in rule 4, that Descartes is not proposing a theory about 'common mathematics', but 'some different discipline' (X, 374), of which the figures and numbers of mathematics are only the 'outer garments'. The new discipline is the *mathesis universalis* of rule 4:

> these thoughts turned me from a particular study of Arithmetic and Geometry to look for a certain general *mathesis* . . . because the word '*mathesis*' means the same as discipline, the other disciplines may be called 'mathematics' with as much right as Geometry. And yet there is hardly anyone . . . who does not easily distinguish, among whatever is presented to him, between what falls under '*mathesis*' and what belongs to other disciplines. . . . only those things in which order and measure are involved belong to *mathesis*, and it makes no difference if one looks for such a measure in numbers, or in figures, or in the stars, or in sounds, or in whatever object one wishes. Hence there must be a certain general science which explains everything one can learn about order and measure and which is not tied to any particular subject matter; it is called *mathesis universalis* . . . because it contains everything on account of which all the other sciences are likewise called mathematical. (X, 377–8).

Asking questions about relative measures in the correct order is the whole of 'pure mathematics' (X, 385). This is a much wider or more basic enterprise than merely studying what is commonly called mathematics (i.e. questions of order and measure when applied to numbers and figures alone). Hence, if someone merely studies mathematics in the restricted sense just mentioned, he will not be able to resolve the problem of finding the anaclastic, for that depends not only on such mathematics but on 'physics' (X, 394).

The distinction between Cartesian *mathesis universalis* and the common mathematics of the seventeenth century is even more obvious in rule 14 when Descartes expressed the preference that his readers not have studied mathematics at all. The method of the *Regulae* was not devised for solving mathematical problems; quite the contrary, the mathematical puzzles are only proposed to provide the reader with practice in the new method.

[these rules] . . . are so useful for achieving a very deep wisdom that I do not hesitate to say that this part of my method was not discovered for the solution of mathematical problems, but rather that one should almost not bother learning mathematics except to practice this method (V, 442).

The constrast being suggested here is a contrast between the more or less unmethodical mathematics which Descartes is criticising and, on the other hand, a method or procedure which is claimed to be more basic than mathematics in so far as it applies generally to every scientific discipline. *Mathesis universalis* is what makes mathematics as certain or scientific as it is; it is incidental that common mathematics is concerned with numbers and figures, for if one properly understands the method being proposed by Descartes (he thinks) then one can hope to have discovered the key to a scientific understanding of anything, including numbers and figures, but also sounds, and stars, and . . . . The first twelve rules of the *Regulae* then are supposed to explain the central idea of this generalised method. The subsequent group of twelve rules was meant to indicate how this method applies to numbers and figures; and the third part, again containing twelve rules, was intended to show how the *mathesis universalis* could just as easily be accommodated to the problems of physical science.

The distinction between problems which are appropriate to Part II and those which belong in Part III is drawn in terms of the distinction between perfect and imperfect problems.

Among these questions, some are perfectly understood even if we do not know their solution, and we treat of these alone in the twelve rules which immediately follow; finally, there are other questions which are not perfectly understood, and we reserve them for the final twelve rules. (X, 429).

The concept of a perfect problem is explained as follows:

It should be noted that, among the questions which are perfectly understood, we number only those in which we distinctly perceive three features, namely: by what signs one can recognise what is sought, however it is discovered; what precisely it may be deduced from; and how one should prove that these questions so depend as much on one as the other [i.e. the starting point and the conclusion or solution] that it is completely impossible to change one without a corresponding change in the other. Thus we possess all premisses and nothing remains to be shown except how to reach the conclusion . . . Questions of this type which are mostly abstract, and which are rarely found except in Arithmetic and Geometry, will appear to those who are not well versed in them to be of little use. But I would advise those people that they should apply themselves for a long time to learning this art and to practising it, if they wish to grasp perfectly the subsequent part of this method in which we discuss all other kinds of problems [i.e. those which are not perfect]. (X, 429–30).³

This distinction is repeated in rule 17, where the functional dependence of a solution to a problem on what is already given defines the questions which are relevant to Part II:

we have assumed from the beginning of this part [of the book] that there is such a dependence between those things which remain unknown in a question and those which are known that the former are completely determined by the latter. (X, 460–61).

The distinction between perfect and imperfect problems is best explicated in terms of Descartes' understanding of analysis and synthesis, which is discussed below. For the present it suffices to underline the point that the method being proposed in the *Regulae*, in so far as it can be understood at all, is not simply an extrapolation of the methods of arithmetic and geometry to other disciplines. Descartes' objective was to explain in Part I what it was about any scientific knowledge which made it scientific; and then to illustrate in Parts II and III how these general methodological remarks could be applied both to mathematics and to physics.

There is a second point to be noted about Cartesian method in the *Regulae*; that is, the dominating theme of the simplicity of basic ideas and the obviousness of the starting point for scientific explanations. There are seventy-four references to the concept of simplicity alone in the text. Many of these are concerned with the so-called simple natures, where 'simple' vaguely means 'conceptually basic'. However many other references involve the suggestion that a scientific knowledge or explanation of something ought to begin with those things which are known to the common man rather than the learned. A few quotations illustrate this point.

And although the learned may perhaps convince themselves that there is very little such (simple and certain) knowledge, because they have not bothered to consider such knowledge, thinking that it is too easy and available to everyone like some kind of vice common to all men; I propose that there is much more such knowledge than they think. (X, 362).

the learned, not content to recognise things which are obvious and certain, have presumed to affirm things which are both unknown and obscure . . . there are many more [truths which are obvious] than most people recognise, because they do not deign to give their attention to such simple things. (X, 367–8).

the learned are often so subtle as to find a way of making obscure what is self-evident and never unknown to peasants; this happens every time they try to explain something which is self-evident by means of something else which is more evident. (X, 426).

Nevertheless, because the learned often use such fine distinctions . . . they dissipate the natural light [of reason] and discover obscurities even in those things which peasants are never ignorant of . . . (X, 442).

This general contrast between the spontaneous and primitive capacities of the human intellect when left to its own resources and the obfuscations introduced by phony learning is consistent with the underlying assumptions of the *Regulae*: book learning, philosophical conundrums, dialectic and syllogistic logic, all of these conspire to extinguish the natural light of reason. Descartes' project is fundamentally an attempt to rid us of intellectual accretions and bad habits, including those developed by practising mathematics, and to return instead to what he considers to be the more powerful capacities of our native intelligence. Peasants or rustics are paradigms of those whose minds have not been corrupted by unmethodical learning.

This point is even more explicit when applied to problems in the physical sciences. Here one might expect – in line with the general Cartesian criticism – that the 'learned' would try to resolve problems in physics by reading other authors or by juggling a priori arguments about what must be the case, given their obscure understanding of simple terms like 'extension', 'movement', etc. Descartes' reaction here is refreshingly outspoken and moderately empirical.

Rule 5 proposes that one analyse complicated questions into simpler parts, and then proceed from the simple to the complex. Among those who break the rule are a priori physicists:

This is the way all those astrologers operate who, without knowing the nature of the heavens and without even carefully observing their motions, hope to predict their effects. This is also the way most of those operate who study mechanics apart from physics, when they rashly try to construct new engines to produce motion. Likewise those philosophers [are included] who neglect experience (*expériences*) and think that the truth will emerge from their own heads as Minerva did from that of Jupiter. (X, 380).

Not only should one first be familiar with the relevant observations or experiential evidence, but the most appropriate empirical evidence is that which is simple, familiar and known to everyone. This point is made at length in rule 9:

It is a common vice among mortals to find those things which seem more difficult the most attractive; and most people think they know nothing when they see the obvious and simple cause of something, while at the same time they admire certain sublime explanations which the philosophers look for further afield . . . There is one point which I should emphasise here more than any other, that is, that everyone should be firmly convinced that even the most obscure sciences should be deduced, not from lofty and obscure things, but only from those things which are the most easy and simple to discover.

Therefore if, for example, I wished to discover if a natural power can travel to a distant point and pass through all the intermediate points in an instant, I would not immediately turn my attention to magnetic forces, or to the influence of the stars, or even to the speed of the action of light, . . . that would be more difficult to establish than the original question. Instead I would reflect on the local motions of bodies, for one could not find anything more accessible to experience (*sensibile*) in this category . . .

In the same way if I wished to know how two contrary effects can be produced by the same simple cause at the same time . . . I would not proceed to speculate about the moon, saying that it heats by means of its light and cools by a certain occult quality; but I would consider a balance. (X, 401–2).

Descartes' point is not only that we should establish some very simple, empirically known truths as the basis for physics; we should also rely on our ordinary experience as a source for the 'simple concepts' which constitute the explanatory framework within which explanations of physical phenomena are generated. Thus the concept of motion is more clearly understood from the experience of moving than from definitions such as 'the potency of a body in so far as it is in potency' (X, 426), and the concept of place is clearer than 'the surface of a surrounding body' (X, 433). The exorcism of scholastic philosophical entities goes hand in hand with a paradoxical Cartesian reliance on the deliverances of common sense.

Cartesian method as a general *mathesis* proposes that any problem should be tackled by starting from what is simple, where 'simple' may mean what is conceptually simple, or what is obvious or self-evident, even if the latter may appear to be embarrassingly trivial. Once the correct starting point is found, then one should proceed in an orderly fashion towards the discovery of what is unknown. The twin procedures of discovering the simple and obvious and arguing towards a solution are compared by Descartes to the ancient mathematical method of analysis and synthesis.[4]

When Descartes talks about analysis and synthesis he is much closer to the original mathematical understanding of this method than has usually been assumed. For what is being analysed or synthesised are not propositions but, more generally, *things*. Just as the ancient method was primarily concerned with the analysis of geometrical objects or figures, so likewise Descartes' discussion of analysis and synthesis in rules 5, 6 and 7 concerns the analysis of things, '*rerum*'. The things in question are found to be mathematical objects in Part II, and physical phenomena in Part III. In either case a major part of one's work is the discovery of the steps by which one can argue from what is already known to a solution of any given problem. This discovery process is the analysis, and the synthesis is the resulting 'proof'. In mathematical work the analysis may take the form of constructing geometrical diagrams and arguing, in the course of the construction, from one step to another in preparation for the eventual solution. In physical problems, one hopes to discover not only the basic causes which explain any given phenomenon but also the auxiliary hypotheses by means of which one may explain the mechanism through which the causes operate. The discovery of such appropriate auxiliary hypotheses and the supporting evidence which justifies them is part of what Descartes means by 'analysis'.

As already mentioned above, precisely those rules which were planned to explain the application of this general method to physics were never written. Despite that, Descartes gives at least two good examples of analysis and synthesis at work in physical explanations: one in optics, and the other in magnetism. The optical example is especially relevant because it involves a scientific discovery which Descartes was probably working on about the time he wrote the *Regulae*. The vague references to analysis and synthesis might therefore be elucidated by a brief examination of the method Descartes claims to have used in discovering the sine law of refraction.

The logic of the search for the anaclastic is described as follows in rule 8 of the *Regulae*:

he will find that the proportion between the angles of incidence and refraction depends on variations in these angles according to the variety of media [involved]; and furthermore, that this change depends on the way in which the incident ray penetrates through the whole transparent body. The knowledge of this penetration presupposes that the nature of the action of light[5] is also known. Finally, to understand properly the action of light it is necessary to know what, in general, is a natural power – and this is the final term which is the most absolute of the whole series. Therefore when he has clearly understood this by a mental *intuitus*, he will retrace the same steps according to the fifth rule; and if he cannot understand the nature of the action of light in the second step, he will enumerate (according to the seventh rule) all the other natural powers so that he can at least understand it by comparison with the knowledge of something else, as will be seen below. Once that is done he will try to understand how the ray penetrates through the whole transparent body. And thus he will follow through all the other things in order, until he arrives at the anaclastic itself. (X, 394–5).

What this proposed method amounts to in practice can be illustrated by Descartes' discussion of the discovery of the sine law of refraction in the second discourse of the *Dioptrics*.

In the *Dioptrics*, Descartes explicitly refuses to speculate about the true 'nature of light' and concentrates instead on an examination of how light acts;[6] the action of light in turn is understood by analogy with other well known phenomena which are familiar from ordinary experience. This is consistent with the advice quoted above from rule 9 for understanding a natural force. The discussion divides naturally into an analytic and a synthetic phase.

The analytic part of the method is first applied to the case of a tennis ball striking a permeable surface. Assume the ball strikes the surface at B in Fig. 1, and loses a fraction of its speed, for example a half. Secondly, assume that we can distinguish between the movement of the ball and 'its determination to move in one direction rather than another'. (VI, 97). From this it follows that the quantity of these determinations must be independently considered. The determination of the ball to move from left to right is not opposed by the impact with the cloth at B, whereas its determination to move from above to below, in the direction HB, is. Since the ball loses half its speed on impact, it must take twice

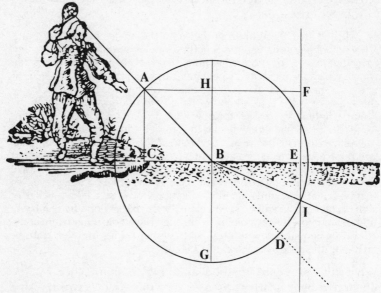

Fig. 1

as much time to reach any point on the circumference of the circle – for example at D – as it does to travel from A to B. In twice the time it will have travelled twice the distance from left to right, since this determination of its motion has not been impeded. Therefore it must move towards I, rather than towards D, where BE = 2 CB.

Examples of striking different surfaces are then considered where the ball is reflected or where its speed changes at the point of refraction.

Finally, in so far as the action of light follows in this respect the same laws as the movement of the ball, one must say that when its rays pass obliquely from one transparent body to another one which receives them more or less easily than the first body, they are deflected in such a way that they are always less inclined on the surfaces of these bodies on the side of the body which receives them more easily than they are on the other side; and that this occurs precisely in proportion as one receives it more easily than the other. (VI, 100).

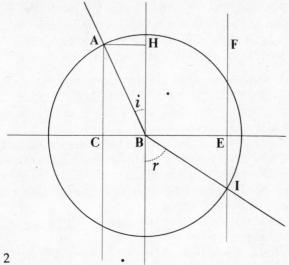

Fig. 2

The analogy between the tennis ball and the ray of light gives the following analysis of optical refraction (see Fig. 2): If V_i and V_r represent the speed of the incident and refracted rays respectively, then

$$V_r = KV_i$$

where the constant, K, equals one-half in this example. Also, since the horizontal speed is not affected by the impact,

$$V_i \sin i = V_r \sin r.$$

Thus, $\sin i / \sin r = K$.

To determine the value of K for a given combination of media one must have recourse to experience:

And although in order to determine their quantity [i.e. of refractions], in so far as it depends on the particular nature of the bodies where they occur, it is necessary to have recourse to experience, one can still do so rather easily and certainly, because they are all reduced to a common measure. Because it suffices to examine them [refractions] in only one ray. (VI, 102).

The results of one experiment can be extrapolated to all others with the same media, and this inductive step can itself be checked by experience.

There is an even better example of analysis and synthesis in Descartes' explanation of the rainbow, and this is discussed below as a paradigm of the method of the *Discourse*. The example from the sine law only resolves the first step in the problem posed in the *Regulae*, and yet it provides a good example of Cartesian method at work. Analysis and synthesis, in this case, involve:

(*a*) abstraction from the nature of light to concentrate on its action;
(*b*) the use of models to focus on this action and, in turn, abstraction from the disanalogies in the models such as the weight, size, etc. of the tennis ball (VI, 94);
(*c*) conceptual analysis of the 'force' of the motion of the ball, and the distinction between motion and the determination of motion;
(*d*) a deduction from the assumptions made up to this point that the relative speed of light in different media is a constant which is a function of unknown factors;
(*e*) the geometrical analysis of the path of a light ray and the resulting sine law;
(*f*) the confirmation of this law by experiment (VI, 102).[7]

This explanatory, constructive and experimental approach is presumably what Descartes means by 'analysis'. It involves deductions, but deductions from assumptions and models among other things. A synthesis would merely consist in re-ordering the various pieces of the puzzle which have been unearthed here to provide a continuous argument from basic assumptions to the description of the *explanandum*, i.e. refraction.

This account of analysis and synthesis is consistent with Descartes' attitude to mathematics; one ought not to apply the methods of common mathematics to physics. Rather, one needs to discover a more fundamental method which, with appropriate qualifications, is applicable to both mathematics and physics. Analysis and synthesis is such a method.

One final point should be made here before looking at the method proposed in the *Discourse*. The *Regulae*, as already noted, relies heavily on the role of *intuitus* in all scientific knowledge.

When *intuitus* is defined in rule 3 it is contrasted with the 'fluctuating faith of the senses or the false judgment of the imagination when composing badly' (X, 368).[8] The question arises as to whether this definition precludes any significant role for the senses and the imagination in science, or whether it merely rejects a particular use of sense and imagination. Rule 12 makes it clear that the latter is the case, and the extant portion of Part II is explicit about the function of the imagination in mathematics.[9]

Apart from the knowledge of simple natures by *intuitus*, all other knowledge is knowledge of composites; and these are known either: (i) through experience or (ii) because we have composed them ourselves.[10] Both of these can lead to error. Experience is a source of error whenever one hastily argues from one's sensation to a knowledge claim about the objects of sensation without some other independent evidence.[11]

But these same things will not deceive the understanding of the wise man because he will judge that everything he learns from the imagination is indeed depicted there in that way; but he never assumes that it has passed intact, without any change or alteration, from external objects to the senses and from the senses to the imagination, unless he had previously known this by some other means (*ratione*). (X, 423).

This account of the fallibility of sense agrees entirely with that outlined above in §5.

The other kind of knowledge of composites results when we compose something in our minds without any experiential basis for it (X, 423). And, with one exception, this inevitably leads to error. Composition may be realised in three ways: under impulse, by conjecture, or by deduction (X, 424). The fallible composition of the first type – as a result of impulse – occurs when someone believes something 'without having been persuaded by reason' (X, 424), either because he was urged towards belief by some disposition of his imagination or because he freely chose to believe. The second kind of composition does not deceive as long as it is recognised as hypothetical; however, as hypothetical knowledge, it is uncertain and therefore it fails to provide a method for knowing composite entities with certainty. Deduction, in the Cartesian sense, is the only remaining alternative which is a reliable source of knowledge.

Descartes concludes, on the basis of the distinction between composition based on experience and experience-free composition, that error arises only when we compose things ourselves. In other words, the erroneous use of experiential evidence and composition without experiential evidence (except by deduction) are both instances of 'composing things ourselves'. It follows that the only possible way of reliably knowing composite objects is through experience which is carefully monitored or interpreted (deduction).

It is clear from this summary that the definition of *intuitus* in rule 3 represents a contrast between the fallibility of other cognitive faculties, such as sense and imagination, and the reliability of intellectual understanding. Experience does not necessarily deceive, nor is imagination dispensable; but both are liable to deceive the unwary whenever we naively assume that what is presented in sense or imagination corresponds exactly to an objective state of affairs.

Rule 12 thus confirms the interpretation of *intuitus* proposed above in §7, where I argued that *intuitus* is not independent of sense. It is now clear that *intuitus* is not independent of imagination either. The point is simply that *intuitus* is a kind of understanding which successfully avoids the deceptive tendencies both of sense and of imagination when they are misused in the cognitive enterprise.

I have isolated four points from the *Regulae* as anticipations of positions which Descartes adopted after 1628. These four points are as follows:

(a) The method proposed in the *Regulae* is not an application of current mathematical procedures to other scientific disciplines; rather, it is a new attempt to understand what it is about any scientific enterprise, including mathematics, which makes it so certain.

(b) An important feature of this method is to initiate inquiries with the most simple and obvious truths available. This point was perhaps originally fostered by Descartes' anxiety about certainty. However, it quickly developed into a much wider thesis to the effect that even the basic explanatory concepts of physical explanations, the models which could facilitate discoveries, and the truths which could best serve as starting points can all be known by ordinary experience rather than from book-learning or experiments.

(c) The method of analysis and synthesis exploited by ancient geometers provided a paradigm for Cartesian method. This ancient method was a method for discovering proofs; it involved the analysis of geometrical figures and the construction of whatever auxiliary figures seemed appropriate for developing a proof. Likewise for Descartes, analysis and synthesis is a method of discovery; its primary function is the identification of the intermediate steps between what we already know and what is to be discovered. In physical science this is equivalent to the discovery of appropriate auxiliary hypotheses.

(d) The method of analysis and synthesis is also applied by Descartes to the elucidation of epistemological problems in the *Regulae* itself, in Part I, especially to the question of analysing the role of different faculties or cognitive procedures in acquiring scientific knowledge. In this analysis, *intuitus* is defined by contrast with deduction, and with the fallible use of sense and imagination. I have argued that none of the terms for cognitive procedures in this discussion means what it apparently suggests; just as 'deduction' includes what we call induction, so likewise *intuitus* does not exclude the controlled use both of sense and of imagination. Here I have argued that it is only the imaginative composition of complex natures, i.e. the assumption that composite objects are as we imagine them to be, without the critical control of reason, which is liable to error.

Descartes abandoned writing the *Regulae* in favour of doing scientific experiments. It is reasonable to assume that he would have expanded considerably in the projected Part III on the characteristics of physical science which distinguished it from perfect problems. He comes close to this in the *Discourse*, which represents a significant evolution or clarification of what might have been written in Part III of the *Regulae*.

One can only speculate as to why the *Regulae* was left unfinished. The correspondence suggests that the burden of experimental work precluded any other writing, including work on metaphysics. Descartes, however, returned to the metaphysics in 1634 and completed his discussion of metaphysical questions in 1641. He had an ideal opportunity of doing

the same for the *Regulae* in 1635-7; yet he passed up this
opportunity, nor did he return to the distinction between perfect
and imperfect problems. It is at least tempting to assume that
Descartes' views on scientific method were modified by the
experience of involvement with scientific work. The adoption of a
hypothetical approach in the 1637 essays and the defence of this
approach in the *Discourse* are likewise consistent with this
assumption. It is almost as if what was written in the extant
portion of the *Regulae* was not so much incorrect but too vague or
general to be of use in explaining the method to be used in
physical science. What was needed was not to rework the idea of
a *mathesis universalis* but to acknowledge unambiguously that
physical explanations are unavoidably hypothetical. And this is
exactly what one finds in the *Discourse on Method* in 1637.

§22   *The* Discourse on Method

The text of the *Discourse* which was published as an introduction
to the scientific essays of 1637 was not written as a coherent or
integrated account of scientific method in the way in which the
Regulae was at least planned. In fact, it is an edited version of
various texts and/or drafts from as early as 1628, and it includes a
discussion of rather disparate topics. From the variety of
problems broached by the text I wish to select two only, and to
discuss them in some detail. The first is the method proposed in
four rules in Part II of the *Discourse*; the other question concerns
Descartes' reference to 'seeds of truth which are naturally in our
souls' (VI, 64) as a foundation for scientific explanations. Before
looking at these two issues it is necessary to indicate how the
present text apparently evolved between 1635 and 1637.

At various times between 1628 and 1636 Descartes was
engaged in writing a short intellectual autobiography, a treatise
on metaphysics, the *Regulae, Le Monde,* a treatise on meteorology
and another one on optics, together with ongoing work on
various problems in geometry. Although the text of *Le Monde* was
the first one prepared for publication, that project was
abandoned by Descartes in 1633 after hearing of Galileo's fate.[12]
The first serious plans for publication that emerge after that
episode are mentioned in 1635, when Descartes proposed to
publish the *Dioptrics.*[13] By November of the same year he had

decided to publish his *Meteorology* also, and to write a short introduction to both essays. This introduction survives in the final section, section *C* (p. 187 below), of Part VI of the *Discourse.*

Some time between November 1, 1635 and March of the following year Descartes changed his mind again and decided to include some of his work in geometry in the projected publication.[14] Evidently the preface already written for the two scientific essays was inappropriate to the method used in geometry and this prompted a rewriting of the preface to accommodate the enlarged contents. Rather than write something completely new Descartes consulted the unpublished *Regulae*; since the first part of that manuscript included four rules which were applicable to any discipline, these were excerpted and rearranged as Part II of the *Discourse.* The general applicability of the proposed method provided the cue for including some other parts of earlier unpublished manuscripts as illustrations of its resourcefulness in physics and metaphysics.

The final text which emerges from this curious procedure is not entirely coherent. It includes a section from the *Histoire de mon esprit* in Part I, and a summary of the four principal rules of Cartesian method from Book I of the *Regulae*. Part III is a relatively new piece on morals, while Part IV reproduces some of his earlier work on metaphysics and was only included in the final text while the publisher was pressing Descartes for completion of the manuscript.[15] Part V is a summary of some of the work on physics and meteorology which is found in *Le Monde*.[16] Despite the fact that Descartes explains in Part V why he abandoned plans for publishing *Le Monde*, he repeats this explanation at the beginning of Part VI and then adds the originally written preface for the two essays on *Dioptrics* and *Meteorology*.[17]

If one assumes that the *Discourse* was compiled in some such way, then it is possible to explain the inconsistencies and repetitions in the text, and to give a plausible account of the disparity between the method outlined in Part II and the more hypothetical method proposed in Part VI. Some of Descartes' early readers had noticed this disparity and brought it to his attention. One of them, Vatier, got this reply to his queries:

I was not able to illustrate the use of this method [i.e. the method of Part II of the *Discourse*] in the three essays which I published, because it prescribes an order for discovering things, which is rather different from what I believed should be used to explain them. However I did provide a sample of this method in discussing the rainbow. (I, 559).

This is consistent with the fact that there are no references to the method of the *Discourse* in the essays, with only one exception, namely in the *Meteorology*, where Descartes introduces his discussion of the rainbow:

The rainbow is such a notable marvel of nature and its cause has been so diligently sought after and yet so little known by the best minds from the very beginning, that I could not choose a more appropriate example to show how, by means of the method which I use, one can attain knowledge which was not available to those whose writings we possess. (VI, 325).

Thus, when Descartes talks about his method, without qualification, he means the method of discovery which is briefly summarised from the *Regulae* in Part II of the *Discourse*; by contrast, the *Dioptrics* and *Meteorology* are hypothetical essays which, with the exception just mentioned, do not purport to illustrate a method for the discovery of scientific explanations.

I shall assume then that Descartes consciously adopted the principal rules of the *Regulae* for inclusion in Part II of the *Discourse*.[18] Accordingly the introduction refers to Part II in terms of *rules*: 'one finds in the second part the principal rules (*règles*) of the method which the author has searched for' (VI, 1). Likewise, Part II introduces the method as a substitute for the 'precepts' of logic (VI, 18). What follows are summary versions of rules 3, 5, 6 and 7 which the *Regulae* had earlier characterised as the essence of the Cartesian method (X, 392).

However the four methodological rules which are proposed in the *Discourse* provide almost no information at all, even to the sympathetic reader, about Descartes' famous method. The brief examples of the method at work in physics, medicine and metaphysics which are provided in Parts IV and V are meant to fill out the bare essentials of the earlier description. From the point of view of physical science the references to *Le Monde* are helpful and these will be further considered below. But the primary example on Descartes' own admission of the method of discovery is the discussion of the rainbow in the *Meteorology*. This is worth considering both as an example of the method of the *Discourse*, and as a further clarification of what Descartes means by analysis and synthesis in the *Regulae*.

The Cartesian examination of the phenomenon of the rainbow takes place within a tradition which had already provided a partial explanation of its occurrence: it includes the hypothesis of Theodoric of Freiburg (1304) that the two bows are formed by two refractions and one or two reflections of light within individual raindrops.[19] On the other hand, Descartes failed to explain either the dispersion of colours in refraction, or the reverse order of colours in the primary and secondary bows.[20] His specific contribution was to provide an explanation, in terms of the sine law of refraction, of the angles at which the two bows appear in the sky, in such a way that the hypothesis is capable of quantitative confirmation. The order of his discovery, according to the *Meteorology*, was the following:

(1) *Expérience* (observation) shows that the rainbow appears in fountains as well as in showers ('l'expérience fait voir': VI, 325). This suggests the initial hypothesis, that the rainbow is formed from the combined effects of light and drops of water.

(2) A model of a raindrop is constructed, and an experiment is performed to measure the angles at which colours appear. They are found at 42° and slightly less, or at 54° and slightly more, with red appearing in each of these positions and the other colours in a series at angles greater than 54° or less than 42°.

(3) A further experiment is performed on the model raindrop by covering the model completely with an opaque material except at those places where the two kinds of incident ray and refracted rays are thought to enter and emerge. This confirms the hypothesis that the primary and secondary bows are explained by two refractions and either one or two internal reflections of the incident rays of light.

(4) Another experiment is performed with a glass prism, and this also produces the colours of the rainbow. This shows:

(a) that the surface of the rainbow-causing medium need not be curved;

(b) that reflection of the light rays is not necessary to cause colour dispersion;

(c) that the angle of incidence does not have to be any particular size, since many different angles of incidence produce the same effect;

(d) that more than one refraction of the light is not necessary for colour dispersion; and

(e) that at least one refraction is necessary, because experiment shows ('l'expérience montre': VI, 330) that if the sides of a medium are parallel, the refraction caused at the incident face is neutralised on exiting from the second face, and there is no colour dispersion as a result.

(5) Taking a cue from the prism experiment, Descartes calculates from the refractive index of rainwater what would be seen by an observer when light strikes the raindrops at different angles of incidence and is refracted and reflected as suggested. Calculation shows that the optimum differences between incident and refracted rays for visibility are precisely those which had been found earlier, through experience, from the primary and secondary bows of the rainbow ('ainsi qu'il se voit par expérience'; VI, 337).

It is clear that some kind of experience is significant at every stage of this process, whether it is simple observation, accurate measurement or constructed experiment. If one numbers these experiences 1 to 5, the logic of the discovery could be diagrammed as follows:

Experience 1 → Hypothesis

→ {
Experience 2 (measurements)
Experience 3 → theory of refraction and internal reflection
Experience 4 → conclusions (a) to (e)
}

→ Experience 5: measuring the angles at which the bows appear. These coincide with what one would anticipate if the Cartesian hypothesis is correct.

It would seem impossible to make sense of Descartes' discussion of his discovery without some recognition of the close liaison between developing theory and the auxiliary experiments and observations which supported the logic of his evolving explanation.

As already noted, Descartes explicitly appeals to this example as a sample of what he meant by the method proposed in Part II of the *Discourse* (VI, 325). When considered in conjunction with the discussions of magnetism and the anaclastic in the *Regulae* it must be obvious that analysis and synthesis, in physical science, rely significantly on experiment and observation. This would approximate to Hintikka's account of how Newton understood analysis and synthesis:

Instead of such a simple schema:
    observations of particular data → inductive leap to a general law
Newton's double (or triple) method requires a more sophisticated
schema:
    'analysis' of a complex phenomenon into ingredients
→ experimental or observational discovery of dependencies between
    different ingredients
→ inductive generalization of these dependencies to all similar cases
→ deductive application of the generalization to other cases.[21]

There are obvious problems involved in assuming that the
description found in Discourse 8 of the *Meteorology* represents
an accurate account of experimental work actually done by
Descartes. However that issue might be resolved by more
detailed historical scholarship, it is abundantly clear that the
reconstruction of the discovery by Descartes is an accurate
example of what he means by the method of discovery which is as
much concealed as revealed in Part II of the *Discourse*. That means
that we can confidently abandon the idea that Cartesian method
in physical science is non-experiential or unacceptably a
priori. Just as in geometrical proofs one first introduces new
constructions and draws conclusions from them, and these in
turn suggest further constructions and deductions, until
eventually one discovers a means of arguing from what is given
to what is required through the mediation of extra constructions,
so likewise in physical science; one draws conclusions from
what is observed, and these suggest further experiments or
observations, which in turn generate other conclusions. The
systematic introduction of auxiliary assumptions and models and
the appropriate use of experimental testing at each step of this
procedure is what Descartes means by 'analysis'. Synthesis is the
rather simple task of rewriting one's discovery, by analogy with
proofs in geometry, in a way which makes explicit both what is
initially assumed as one's most fundamental concept or
hypothesis, and the 'rational' connection between the steps of the
resulting argument.

If Part II of the *Discourse* can be faulted as a commentary on
method in physical science, then it suffers from the same defects
as the first book of the *Regulae* which inspired it: it is too vague to
be either plausible or implausible! When interpreted in the light
of the rainbow discussion, however, it is clear enough to be
manifestly not unappreciative of the role of experience, models,

and hypotheses in scientific discoveries.

The other issue raised above about the *Discourse* concerned the role of 'seeds of truth' in the formulation of basic laws of physics. The language of seeds of truth has obvious Platonist and Augustinian connotations and, without a further examination of the context, lends support to the thesis that Cartesian science is fundamentally a priori. I wish to argue that 'seeds of truth' refers, rather, to reflection on ordinary experience and that it is consistent with the theme, already outlined in the *Regulae*, that the scientific explanation of obscure or complex phenomena should begin with an understanding of familiar physical phenomena.

The reference to seeds of truth occurs at the beginning of Part VI of the *Discourse*. It is important to establish first the context of these remarks before attempting to explain them; the evidence suggests that they occur in a commentary on the scientific procedure adopted in *Le Monde*, and they parallel a similar discussion in Part V which may be exploited in clarifying the enigmatic 'seeds of truth' of Part VI.

According to the Preface to the *Discourse*, Part V is a review of 'the order of questions which he [the author] researched in physics' (VI, 1). On reading the text one finds a reasonably short but accurate review of the contents of *Le Monde*. Part VI is structurally more complicated, in so far as it refers both to earlier work and to the essays which follow. The text of Part VI divides naturally into three sections, which reflect the author's indecision about publishing *Le Monde* and the eventual decision to publish the 1637 essays. The three sections are as follows:

Section A: VI, 60 to VI, 65 (line 25). This is essentially a summary of Descartes' work in preparing the manuscript of *Le Monde* for publication. It begins with the sentence: 'It is now three years since I reached the end of the treatise which contains all those things [mentioned in Part V], and since I began to review it in order to submit it for publication . . .' (VI, 60). Since this section is a narrative of his state of mind and of his discoveries prior to 1633, all the verbs are in the past tense until Descartes comes to a transitional paragraph concerning his current evaluation of the importance of more experiments.

Section B: VI, 65 (line 26) to VI, 74 (line 2). This section is a long

discussion of why Descartes changed his mind about publication
and why he decided not to publish anything during his lifetime. It
begins: 'But since that time I had other reasons which made me
change my mind . . .' (VI, 65). The most prominent of these
reasons was fear of a fate similar to Galileo's.
Section C: VI, 74 (line 3) to VI, 78. In the final section Descartes
explains why he changed his mind for the second time, between
1633 and 1635, and decided after all to publish the *Dioptrics* and
the *Meteorology* despite the fact that the basic principles on which
the theories discussed in those essays depended were not yet
published. This third section naturally contains the most explicit
references to the scientific essays (VI, 74, 76 and 77) and
Descartes' account of the hypothetical method adopted in them.

The reference to seeds of truth occurs in the first of these
sections, section (*A*). Most likely the other two sections, *B* and *C*,
represent the final edited version of the preface originally written
for the *Dioptrics* and *Meteorology* in 1635. Thus, the appropriate
context for explaining the seeds of truth is *Le Monde*. And since
there is a remarkable similarity between this passage and a text in
Part V which also describes the method of *Le Monde*, it is helpful to
examine both passages together, beginning with the introductory
paragraphs of Part V.

According to Part V, Descartes initiated his scientific studies in
Le Monde by noticing certain laws which God had established
in nature: 'j'ai remarqué . . . ' (VI, 41). He adds the comment
immediately that the ideas of these laws were 'imprinted in our
souls', and this suggests that the laws were known a priori
and independently of any experiential input. Despite first
impressions, there are reasons for adopting an alternative
interpretation of the phrase 'imprimé en nos ames' which would
be more consistent with Descartes' actual method in *Le Monde*:

(*a*) In Part IV of the *Discourse* Descartes claims that God is the
cause of everything and, since our ideas are entities of some kind,
that God is also the cause of our ideas. 'From which it follows that
our ideas or notions, since they are real things . . . come from
God' (VI, 38). The operation of God's causality in no way precludes the agency of more proximate causes, such as physical
objects, in the origin of our ideas. Thus Descartes wrote to Vatier
after publishing the *Discourse*:

I assumed that . . . since our ideas could receive neither their forms nor their being except from some external objects or from ourselves, they would not be able to represent any reality or perfection which was not present in these objects or else in us. (I, 560–61).

This text leaves open the possibility that, whatever God's part in the causality of ideas, they must also be caused either by external objects or by our own minds, and this corresponds to the distinction between innate and acquired ideas already discussed in §6 above. There is no competition between God and the objects of our perception in the causality of our ideas, and hence any mention of God's agency cannot reasonably be construed as exclusive of the influence of physical objects in explaining the origin of corresponding ideas.

(b) In the text of the *Discourse* Descartes said that he noticed (*remarquer*) these laws, presumably in some experience of physical objects in motion. The use of ordinary experience as a source of warrant for the basic laws of nature would be consistent with Descartes' procedure in that section of *Le Monde* which he is summarising, and his later elaboration of the same point in Part II of the *Principles*. For example, he claims that 'quotidiana experientia . . . regulam nostram omnino confirmat' (VIII-1, 63) in reference to the law of inertia, and that the law of rectilinear motion 'experientia confirmatur' (*ibid*, 64).

Thus it is possible to interpret Descartes' claim that the laws of nature are imprinted in our souls in a way which is consistent with his theory of knowledge outlined above. God is the source of our knowledge to the extent that all clear and distinct ideas may be converted into reliable knowledge-claims, because knowledge of God's existence is incompatible with metaphysical doubts. In the second place, God's causality is involved in the existence of our ideas just as God's agency is involved in the existence of anything else. But the agency of God in causing ideas and his function as divine guarantor do not imply that our ideas are not proximately derived from our experience of physical nature.

As already mentioned, the first section of Part VI of the *Discourse* gives a second summary of the scientific method which the author had followed in writing *Le Monde*. He introduces the discussion with the following paragraph on the role of experience in science:

Indeed I noticed that, as regards experiences, they are more important in proportion as one is advanced in knowledge. Because it is better, at the beginning, only to use those [experiences] which present themselves to our senses of their own accord, and which are such that we could not be unaware of them provided that we perform even the slighest reflection on them, than to look for other more infrequent or studied experiences. (VI, 63).

This paragraph again suggests that the initial stages of any scientific enterprise should be based on those observations which are 'common to all men' (VII, 580), whereas the more advanced stages of scientific explanation rely on experiments to choose between alternative possible explanations.

The reference to reflection in this passage should not be misunderstood as an intuition of first principles through some kind of purely intellectual reflection. This can be supported by comparing this text with the corresponding discussion in Part V, where the author was describing the initial chaos from which the world was said to have developed:

Thus I first described this matter and tried to represent it in such a way that there is nothing in the world, it seems to me, which is clearer or more intelligible, except what was already said about God and the soul; for I even expressly assumed that it contained none of those forms or qualities which are disputed in the schools nor, in general, anything the knowledge of which is not so natural to our souls that one could not even pretend not to know it. (VI, 42–3).

The primitive matter of the universe was supposed to have no properties 'dont la connoissance ne fust si naturelle a nos ames, qu'on ne pust pas mesme feindre de l'ignorer' (VI, 43). In discussing the foundations of science in Part VI Descartes similarly restricts his inquiries to those experiences 'qui se presentent d'elles mesmes a nos sens, & que nous ne sçaurions ignorer, pourvû que nous y façions tant soit peu de reflexion' (VI, 63). The similarity between the two passages, the reference to sensory knowledge in the second one, and the methodological rule in both the *Regulae* and the *Discourse* that any scientific investigation should begin with what is most simple and easy to understand, make it plausible to suggest that what is at issue here is the role of ordinary experience, critically evaluated by reflection, in determining both the basic explanatory concepts and the fundamental principles of any scientific explanation. If the text is understood in this way, it also corresponds to the use of the same phrase in *Le Monde*, where Descartes describes the primitive matter of the universe in terms of concepts which are known to all, for 'it contains nothing which is not so perfectly known to the reader that you could not even pretend not to know it' (XI, 35).

Descartes continues the narrative in Part VI by suggesting that he moved on from simple truths to more complex problems, and that this approach was in accordance with the third rule of the *Discourse*. Then, almost as if he is anticipating himself in an orderly review of his work in *Le Monde*, he adds: 'However, the order which I followed in this material was the following. . .' (VI, 63). What follows is a description of his procedure in two stages, the first of which was the discovery of basic principles or first causes. These were drawn from certain 'seeds of truth which are naturally in our souls'.

The historical connotations of the phrase 'seeds of truth' and the canonical interpretation of the *Discourse* as a whole suggest that this is a further reference to an a priori justification of the basic laws of physics. However it may just as naturally be understood to mean that these first principles were derived from reflection on ordinary experience. Consider the following indications from the text:

(*a*) Descartes rejects any theory that the human mind is endowed with innate, actual ideas. As long as the seeds of truth are only potential ideas, they need to be actualised by an appropriate efficient cause. The observation of physical objects and events would be an appropriate cause to explain our understanding of the basic laws of physics, according to Descartes' theory of the origin of acquired ideas.

(*b*) Descartes is here again describing his procedure in *Le Monde*, and he invokes our ordinary experience of objects in motion to confirm his choice of first principles in that treatise.

(*c*) In the passage quoted above about the role of experience in science, Descartes distinguished those experiences which were appropriate 'pour le commencement' from those which were necessary when one is 'plus avancé en connoissance'. In the passage under discussion here there are also two stages in science. The first is the discovery of first principles, and the second one is involved 'lorsque i'ay voulu descendre a celles [choses] qui estoient plus particulieres'. Since this second stage requires 'plusieurs experiences particulieres', it is probable that the first stages of each description of his method also correspond and that ordinary experience plays the same important role in each in the discovery of first principles. If this is the case then Descartes can quite reasonably refer to these ideas as being 'naturally in our souls'; this is consistent with his suspicions about complicated experiments and his preference for the judgment of men of common sense, both of which are mentioned in the *Discourse*.

(*d*) This interpretation is also consistent with Descartes' thesis that any scientific explanation of complex phenomena should begin with the simple and obvious. The third rule of the *Discourse* method was to begin any investigation with 'those objects which are the most simple and most easily known' (VI, 18). This is reinforced with the suggestion that these simple and knowable things are accessible to ordinary observers of nature rather than to the book-learned.

It seemed to me that I could discover more truth in the reasonings which everyone undertakes about matters which are important for themselves, and which are such that one's conclusions can soon be to one's detriment if one judges poorly, than in those which a man of letters undertakes in his study about speculative matters which have no palpable effects. (VI, 9–10).

And thus I considered that the sciences of books, at least those in which the explanations are only probable . . . are not as close to the truth as the simple reasonings which a man of common sense can naturally make about those things which he experiences (*qui se presentent*). (VI, 12–13).[22]

The repetitions about the order of discussions in *Le Monde* are readily understood if the text was compiled from earlier manuscripts and the new preface for the *Meteorology* and *Dioptrics*, as suggested above. This accounts for the fact that we find two accounts of the same procedure: one in Part V which is a summary of *Le Monde*, and another one at the beginning of Part VI which is meant to contrast the author's approach in the earlier treatise with what is about to be introduced, in section *C*, as an outline of a more hypothetical approach in the accompanying essays. In both reviews of the method of *Le Monde* there is mention of:

(1) a distinction between the discovery and justification of basic principles and the method which is appropriate for more detailed scientific explanations; and

(2) vague references to 'seeds of truth' and the laws of nature being 'imprinted in our souls' in describing the discovery or confirmation of the laws of nature.

However there is one passage – VI, 63 – which is quite explicit on the role of ordinary experience at the first level of Cartesian science. Besides, since all these summaries are reviews of the method adopted by Descartes in *Le Monde*, it is plausible to assume that what Descartes means by 'seeds of truth' is to be understood by reference to the discussion of the laws of nature in *Le Monde*. And here one finds an exact match between the language of the earlier treatise and the language of the *Discourse*. Some concepts (rather than propositions or principles) are so well known to us from ordinary experience that one could not even pretend not to understand them. And these are 'seeds of truth' for physics. And secondly, the basic laws of physics are so intuitively intelligible and so consistent with ordinary experience that they are beyond doubt. The method of discovering and defending the basic principles of physics is no different in the *Discourse* from that proposed in *Le Monde* and the *Principles* and discussed in detail above in Chapter 4. What is naturally in our souls is what we know by reflection on unambiguous, ordinary experience.

The identification of basic concepts and the discovery of basic laws, whether by reflection on ordinary experience or by some more sophisticated application of Cartesian analysis, still leaves open the task of applying these concepts and laws to the explanation of particular phenomena. Descartes is overoptimistic about the feasibility of this project; only the shortness of his life or a dearth of experimental work could hinder the inevitable discovery of truth:

> . . . having discovered a path which seems to me to be such that, by following it, one could infallibly discover it [scientific knowledge], unless one were hindered either by the shortness of life or by a lack of experiences. (VI, 63).

Descartes tries to cope with both impediments at once by sharing his work with others in a common venture; and for this reason he must publish what he considers to be unfinished work.[23]

The ideal scientific explanation would consist in a coherent and systematic account of how each particular phenomenon is an effect of some known cause. If the a priori chain of causes and effects from the simplest and best known to the most complex is interrupted, then the only other option available, as a short-term measure, is to introduce hypotheses which can at least be fashioned to explain any given *explanandum* (VI, 45–6). This is what emerges most clearly in the third section of Part VI of the *Discourse*. A scientific explanation of particular phenomena depends on 'suppositions' (VI, 76), although even these hypotheses are 'so simple and so conformable to common sense' (VI, 77) that they will appear less incredible to the reader than the assumptions of other authors.

The optimistic side of this discussion is in Descartes' assumption that hypotheses are only a short-term concession, and that crucial experiments could be designed to chart systematically the course between 'simple natures' and complex natural phenomena. This problem had already surfaced in the *Regulae* where we are promised a method, using adequate enumerations, for converting imperfect problems into perfect ones. The publication of the essays in 1637 amounts to a recognition that this is not as easy as it may theoretically appear to be; for they come with a preface, the *Discourse*, which acknowledges their hypothetical character. The covering clause to the effect that this hypothetical element can be minimised by experimental work only serves to underline some progress in Cartesian thought. Even a hypothetical explanation is better than none at all. And the degree of confirmation realised by explaining phenomena which would otherwise have been inexplicable, while it falls short of a full-scale 'deduction' from simple natures, is sufficient to warrant publication and public discussion.

This interpretation provides an easy way of accounting for the methodological discrepancies between Parts II, V and VI of the *Discourse*. Part II is a summary of Descartes' logic of discovery, or the method of analysis and synthesis, already outlined in the *Regulae*. Part V and the introductory section of Part VI are both reflections of the approach adopted in *Le Monde* and, later, in the *Principles*. This includes the suggestion that the basic principles of Cartesian physics can be established by reference both to ordinary experience and to metaphysical first principles. Descartes seems not to have seriously doubted the possibility that these principles could, within a short space of time, be systematically applied to the explanation of every conceivable physical phenomenon.

However, in the interim period, and for reasons already mentioned, Descartes decided to publish sections of the incomplete scientific project. Since these explanations were not appropriately related to the first principles (by 'demonstration'), they could only be published by making initial assumptions about the action of light, etc. In fact, even in the discussion of blood circulation in Part V the author acknowledges that the proposed explanation relies on assumptions which had not been adequately integrated into a coherent world-view. This interim hypothetical approach is even more obvious in the *Dioptrics* and *Meteorology*, and it is correspondingly more openly acknowledged in section C of Part VI of the *Discourse*, i.e. in the originally written introduction to these essays.

The discrepancies in the method proposed in the *Discourse*, therefore, result from: (i) a distinction between a logic of discovery and a logic of explanation, and (ii) Descartes' ideal of a comprehensive, 'deductive' science of nature on the one hand and, on the other, the recognition that at least in the short term physical explanations must begin from hypotheses or assumptions which have not been adequately 'deduced' from basic assumptions about matter and the laws of nature. The ideal of a complete science is compromised, in practice, by the necessity to settle for something less in the short term. The history of methodology was to extend this 'short term' into the indefinite future and the limitations imposed by practice were to be given a new theoretical basis. What Descartes hoped to accomplish in his lifetime would now be possible only in the abstraction of a Peircian limit to human science.

Notes

1 X, 399 and X, 432 refer to a proposed second and third book, whereas X, 459 refers to a projected third part.

2 This point is discussed at length by J.-L. Marion, in *Sur l'ontologie grise de Descartes*.

3 Cf. X, 441, where mathematical problems are distinguished from 'all other considerations' until the twenty-fifth rule.

4 For a comprehensive discussion of this topic see J. Hintikka and U. Remes, *The Method of Analysis*, and J. Hintikka, 'A discourse on Descartes's method', in M. Hooker, ed., *Descartes*, pp. 74–88.

5 Descartes is explicitly prescinding here from a discussion of the nature of light; he concentrates, instead, on understanding how light acts, hence the cumbersome phrase, 'the nature of the action of light'.

6 The nature of light is not at issue: 'there is no need that I undertake to say what its [light's] true nature is' (VI, 83); 'the question here is not one of looking so closely at this issue, and none of these things is relevant to the action of light with which we are concerned here.' (VI, 94).

7 Cf. Descartes to Golius, February 2, 1632 (I, 236–40).

8 'Per *intuitum* intelligo, non fluctuantem sensuum fidem, vel male componentis imaginationis judicium fallax.'

9 Cf. X, 441, 443–8.

10 X, 422–3.

11 Experience does not deceive if four conditions are satisfied:

(*a*) if the intellect only intuits what is actually presented to it. Error can arise when the intellect predicates a quality of something which is not actually given in experience, 'quoties in illis aliquid inesse credimus, quod nullo experimento a mente nostra immediate perceptum est' (X, 423);
(*b*) if the intellect does not judge that the imagination faithfully reflects the objects of sensation;
(*c*) if it does not judge that the senses are endowed with the true shape of physical objects of sensations; and
(*d*) if one does not judge that physical objects are always as they appear to us.

12 See Descartes to Mersenne, July 1633 (I, 268), and Descartes to Mersenne, November 1633 (I, 270–71).

13 See Descartes to Mersenne (?), Spring 1635 (I, 322).

14 Gadoffre, in 'Sur la chronologie', p. 49, suggests that the *Geometry* was written between December 1636 and January 1637. See Descartes to Deriennes, February 22, 1638: 'That is a treatise which I

more or less put together while my *Meteorology* was being printed, and I even devised a part of it during that time.' (I, 458). Cf. Denissoff, *Descartes*, pp. 18–19.

15   Descartes to Vatier, February 22, 1638 (I, 560).

16   See Descartes to Mersenne, April, 1637: 'I included something about metaphysics, physics and medicine in the first Discourse to show that it [i.e. the method] applies to all kinds of subject matter.' (I, 349). See also Descartes to an unknown correspondent, May 1637 (I, 370).

17   This is consistent with the fact that there is no mention of the *Geometry* in this part of the *Discourse*, although the other two essays are mentioned a number of times.

18   In a letter to Mersenne, March 1636 (I, 339), Descartes writes about the contents of the *Discourse*, which were in process of being written at that time: 'In this project I reveal a part of my method, I try to demonstrate the existence of God.' The reference to an already existing method suggests an earlier methodological essay, presumably the *Regulae*.

19   Theodoric's contribution, and the history of the explanation of the rainbow, are examined by Carl B. Boyer, *The Rainbow: From Myth to Mathematics* and A. C. Crombie, *Robert Grosseteste and the Origins of Experimental Science, 1100–1700*. Kepler's theory of double refraction and single reflection was not published until 1718. It should be noted also that Descartes was not anticipated by Antonius de Dominis, as Newton suggests in the *Opticks* (English trans., p. 169, 172). Cf. R. E. Ockenden, 'Marco Antonio de Dominis and his explanation of the rainbow', *Isis*, **26** (1936), 40–9, where it is shown that de Dominis was mistaken in his explanation of both the primary and the secondary bows.

20   Cf. Boyer, *Rainbow*, pp. 217–18, and 344, note 26, where he disputes Crombie's claim (*Grosseteste*, p. 275) that Descartes either measured or recognised the significance of the dispersion of colours in refraction.

21   J. Hintikka, 'A discourse on Descartes's method,' in M. Hooker, ed. *Descartes*, p. 82.

22   See also VI, 20, 63, and 64.

23   Cf. VI, 63.

EIGHT

Descartes: an innovative Aristotelian

Prior to the scientific revolution of the seventeenth century, the ideal of an Aristotelian, demonstrative science dominated and thereby inhibited the development of scientific methodology. It was necessary for science to emancipate itself from the methodological restrictions of its Greek origins and achieve some notable successes as a radically hypothetical discipline before it found an adequate reflection in the philosopher's evaluation of its epistemological status. This level of independence in scientific inquiry was beginning to be realised when Descartes pledged himself to devote his life to the development of science.

This is not meant to imply that no one prior to 1600 recognised the significance of hypotheses and experimental procedures in the study of nature. Robert Grosseteste, for example, is a notable exception. However, the most prevalent interpretation of scientific knowledge was rooted in the Greek bequest of an unbridgeable gulf between demonstrated, certain propositions and mere saving-the-phenomena hypotheses. Thus, Neal Ward Gilbert was able to summarise the methodological contributions of the Renaissance period in this way: 'With regard to experimentation as a confirming stage in the application of scientific method, we have found no evidence of an explicit formulation of such a doctrine in our period.'[1]

Galileo represents an interesting shift in scientific methodology in the gradual evolution of a new concept of science. There is still clear evidence here that nothing short of a 'demonstrated' science, in the Aristotelian sense, is adequate to change one's views, for example, about the status of Copernican theory. And at the same time Galileo endorses the view that successful hypotheses are the most one could ever hope to achieve in physical science.[2] This is a very good example, from the history of science, of methodology lagging behind scientific practice. It was not just a time-lag in new ideas being accepted; what was needed was a significant conceptual change both in the concepts involved in scientific theories and also in the philosophical or methodological concepts in terms of which the method used in the new science was described. Galileo's ambivalence on this latter point is not explicable merely as a dishonest attempt to win support from both sides in the dispute about Copernicanism, from the church authorities and the scientific community. Galileo was not sufficiently clear himself about the issues involved to be so self-consciously calculating in his pleading. For the idea of a new hypothetical science was only emerging very slowly, in part within Galileo's work, and this implied many more concealed inconsistencies than one might retrospectively anticipate.

Thus Ernan McMullin correctly characterised Galileo (and Descartes) as rather reluctant champions of a new concept of science:

> We can hail Galileo and Descartes as the pioneers in the development of a new conception of science that would ultimately replace the older demonstrative one. But if we do, we ought to recognize how reluctant Galileo would have been to accept this honor.[3]

Descartes would have been less reluctant than Galileo to claim originality for his scientific method; but whether or not such a claim is warranted, either by his scientific practice or by his methodological discussions, very much depends on which features of his science he might emphasise to demonstrate a clear apostasy from the influence of Aristotle. For even if he would not agree with the description, Descartes the campaigning anti-Aristotelian is still significantly influenced, in his understanding of scientific knowledge, by the Aristotelian ideal of demonstration and certainty.

The dominant feature of Cartesian science was the demand for certainty. The requirement that a scientific claim be certain, rather than true, was maintained by Descartes despite concessions that physical explanations are unavoidably hypothetical. To accommodate this overriding ambition for science Descartes

An innovative Aristotelian 199

needed to clarify what kind of certainty was at stake here, and how it might be realised in the context of physical science. Not surprisingly, he approached the methodological issue through Aristotelian categories.

The Aristotelian tradition with which Descartes was familiar explained the certainty of scientific knowledge by reference to the certainty of its first principles, which were known through intuition, and the certainty of the demonstrative reasonings which are based on these principles. Descartes adopts a similar strategy in explaining the methodology of his own science. The distinction between basic principles and deduced conclusions is maintained by Descartes, as is the language of 'intuition' and 'demonstration'. However, the underlying metaphysical theory of essences and forms is eliminated in favour of observable properties which are explained by matter in motion. And with this change in ontology comes a corresponding change in the meanings of 'intuition' and 'demonstration'.

As regards the 'intuition' of first principles, Descartes is a qualified Aristotelian. Greek science, especially with Aristotle, relied heavily on accurate observations of common natural phenomena. As Crombie remarked, 'the main defect of the method was that it contained no procedures for dealing with problems involving many variables. As a result, the Greeks formed the habit of basing theories about complicated phenomena on casual and commonsense observation.'[4] With the development of scientific method, one would expect a heightened awareness of the role of empirical evidence and of experimental procedures, and a corresponding distrust of metaphysical speculation in empirical inquiries. Paradoxically, perhaps, experiment and metaphysics both assumed a new significance for science at the same time. Mary Hesse has drawn attention to this development in the new science.

Comparing the arguments by which Aristotle reaches his primary qualities with those by which the atomists reached theirs, it is remarkable that Aristotle relies on common experience of actual properties of bodies, however superficially he may interpret this, while the atomists on the other hand were influenced by the most sophisticated metaphysical speculations. This example and others like it make it somewhat ironical that in the seventeenth century it is atomism which is regarded as progressive and empirical, while the Aristotelian tradition carries the stigma of non-empirical speculation.[5]

Descartes is interestingly ambivalent about this development in favour of metaphysics and experiment. On the first point, he leans more towards Aristotelian practice – i.e. the accurate observation of common natural phenomena – rather than towards a metaphysics of matter. And this is a feature of Cartesian science which is commonly underestimated, although it is evident in his writing from as early as 1629.

Mersenne wrote to Descartes, in that year, about the possibility of a universal language for mankind. In reply he received many reservations about the proposed language, but he also got some suggestions about another way in which the project might possibly be accomplished, namely by inventing basic terms for common or simple natures.

> And if someone adequately explained those simple ideas which are in the imagination of men and from which they compose everything they think about, I would then hope for a universal language ... Now I believe that this language is possible and that one could discover the science on which it depends, by means of which [science] peasants could better decide the truths of things than the wise (*philosophes*) do at present. (Descartes to Mersenne, November 20, 1629; I, 81–2).

This is an early indication of a theme which permeates the whole of Cartesian science. From its dominant position in the *Regulae* under the guise of 'simple natures' and '*intuitus*' through *Le Monde* and the scientific essays of 1637 to the *Principles*, Descartes consistently proposed the theory that the observation of common natural phenomena, accompanied by critical reflection, could provide both the basic concepts and the fundamental laws which would explain all natural phenomena, no matter how esoteric or complex. I have argued in §7 that reflection on ordinary experience is what Descartes means by '*intuitus*' in the context of constructing a foundation for physical science, and that he puts this understanding of *intuitus* to work in both *Le Monde* and the *Principles* when he eventually introduces and defends his basic laws of nature.

The reliance on ordinary experience derives from a sense of security in the deliverances of common sense – or the natural light of reason – by contrast with the obfuscations of the learned. This contrast is repeatedly invoked in favour of peasants and the common man. It also underlies Descartes' reservations about experiments, in so far as they are not easy to interpret, they depend on a variety of factors which can interfere with results, and they demand a level of theoretical and technical expertise which renders any conclusions one might hope to draw at least uncertain. The dominance of ordinary experience also affects Descartes' concept of explanation; to the extent to which a concept is alien to common experience, or to the extent to which a theoretical mechanism cannot be modelled in a simple mechanical device, they have no place in Cartesian science. In this respect, Descartes is a naive empiricist.

The devotion to ordinary experience in pursuit of certainty and intelligibility is only one side of the Cartesian ambivalence about metaphysics and experiments. It has been highlighted here because it is the least recognised dimension of his ambivalence. However, as a man of his time, Descartes was equally involved in clarifying the role of metaphysics in a scientific world view, and in identifying the significance of experiments for the development of science.

By analogy with Aristotelian *epagoge*, Descartes established the first principles of physical science by reflection on ordinary experience. To proceed beyond first principles he relied, as Aristotle had, on demonstration. However, Cartesian demonstration shared little more than the name with its Aristotelian counterpart. The rejection of syllogistic logic and of middle terms, and of natures and forms in physics, was sufficient on its own to accomplish this change. As in the case of *intuitus*, so likewise Cartesian demonstrations were surprisingly flexible and tolerant towards what we would now classify as analogical, inductive or hypothetico-deductive reasoning. 'Demonstration', Cartesian-style, had one thing in common with Aristotelian demonstrations, or at least Descartes believed it had: it preserved the certainty of the first principles in their application to explaining particular phenomena.

How this certainty was preserved through the complexities of what Descartes calls 'enumerations' remains unexplained. The transition from any one point to another in the course of a given argument could, theoretically, be seen to be self-evident by the natural light of reason and this is another way in which *intuitus* functions in science. However when more than such simple transitions are considered, all arguments are compromised by their reliance on memory. Besides, in many examples of scientific reasoning, one argues from similar cases by analogy, from a limited sample by induction to the general case, from models and hypotheses, etc. Surely such arguments, as illustrated as early as the *Regulae* discussion of magnetism and the anaclastic, are not guaranteed to preserve the certainty of one's first principles!

There is no significant conceptual change, between 1628 and 1650, in the Cartesian understanding of certainty which can harmonise with the obvious uncertainty of physical explanations. Scientific knowledge was still understood, at the conclusion of the French edition of the *Principles* in 1647, as knowledge which was certain. There was an interesting evolution however in this period in how this certainty might be realised in physical science. Because many explanations of physical phenomena involved reference to mechanical interactions between unobservable particles of matter, they are inevitably hypothetical. That means that the descriptions of the properties and interactions of such particles are assumptions, even if they are assumptions which are consistent with the general laws of physics. And Descartes is not especially reluctant to concede this point.

The role of hypothetical explanations is to fill the gap in a comprehensive account of nature between basic principles which are otherwise established as certain, and the description of particular physical phenomena which are unproblematically known by experience. Ideally, the uncertainty resulting from this hypothetical procedure would be eliminated by a variety of strategies. Crucial experiments bear part of the burden here. However, Descartes also appeals to the simplicity, intelligibility, fewness and explanatory resourcefulness of his own principles – by contrast with those of others – to confirm his explanations. And while it was clear enough that even these supplementary arguments do not deliver the kind of certainty which one anticipates from the *Regulae* discussion, especially when one takes account of the frequent comparisons with mathematics, Descartes was still unable to change his view of science as knowledge which is certain. Instead we are offered a distinction, within certainty, between moral and metaphysical certainty which was also borrowed from the scholastic tradition. So that eventually the explanations of particular phenomena which are introduced as assumptions or hypotheses are redeemed, in the context of a comprehensive account of nature, as morally certain.

The recognition of a more fundamental and ineliminable uncertainty or hypothetical character in physical science was not an easy achievement in the history of science; and it continued to elude seventeenth century science, even in Newton.

The function of a metaphysical foundation for science is likewise treated by Descartes as if there is no problem either in his understanding of the issue or in his explanation of what he takes to be the correct solution. For here again Descartes is tantalisingly vague about what kind of foundation is necessary, and in what sense whatever is proposed as such provides a foundation for science. As one might anticipate, the language of 'deducing' or 'demonstrating' physics from metaphysics predominates.

On closer examination, at least some features of the metaphysical foundation of science become clear. For example, metaphysical or epistemological argument establishes against the sceptics that scientific knowledge is possible. Secondly, metaphysical or methodological arguments exclude some kinds of entities as explanatory at all, such as scholastic forms, intentional objects, etc., and also indicate that teleological accounts must be converted into explanations in terms of material and efficient causes. Thirdly, metaphysical considerations – for example, the principle of sufficient reason, or the Cartesian concept of God as a first cause – clearly influence both the discovery and the justification of the three laws of nature in *Le Monde* and the *Principles*. However, the extent to which these laws are also confirmed by reflection on ordinary experience makes it implausible to suggest that they were adequately or exclusively warranted by metaphysics. Descartes himself was unclear about such distinctions; he thought that the laws of nature were intuitively self-evident, and empirically warranted, and metaphysically demonstrated.

The actual practice of science and the kind of detailed discussions of experimental procedures which are widely reported in correspondence had obvious effects on Descartes' understanding of explanation. One of the most striking consequences of his research was the recognition of the baffling complexity of apparently simple phenomena. As in the tension between certainty and hypotheses, there was room for evolution here in Descartes' ideas from the concept of a general science or *mathesis universalis* to a more nuanced or sophisticated view of

204 An innovative Aristotelian

scientific explanation. Unfortunately the tension tended to be resolved in favour of the earlier view rather than the later, so that a number of interrelated features re-occur throughout his career in the Cartesian account of explanation.

One of these predominant features is the adequacy of ordinary experience to provide the conceptual framework within which explanations can be articulated. A relatively few, simple and almost crudely empiricist concepts are all one needs to explain anything. Secondly, explanation normally requires a mechanical model; at least, if one cannot imagine such a model one has failed adequately to understand a given phenomenon. Thirdly, experiments are less trustworthy than the observations of common natural phenomena which are available to any normal observer in standard conditions.[6]

On the other hand, it is manifestly clear even to a prejudiced Cartesian that physical reality is much more complicated than such a simple view of reality tolerates. And one might wonder about the fate of a mathematically inspired physics and of the inevitable complexity which such an ideal suggests. I have argued above that Descartes was only enamoured of the certainty of mathematics and not significantly impressed by the possibility of applying mathematics to the solution of physical problems. There is an unexpected lack of theorising about why mathematics is inappropriate for the resolution of physical problems. It seems almost as if two factors alone influenced the development of the Cartesian concept of explanation on this point. One was the complexity of physical reality vis-à-vis the three laws of nature. The second one was the resulting uncertainty of experiments. In default of a more quantifiable or mathematical account of nature, Descartes seems to have been willing to settle for a likely account, expressed in mechanical models, of how the laws of nature might have given rise to whatever particular phenomenon one encounters in nature, even if such an account is not in fact true. Plausible explanation sketches, consistent with the laws of nature, replace quantitative and disconfirmable explanations.

If one were to isolate one axiom or basic assumption which influenced the Cartesian concept of scientific explanation at almost every turn it would be this: something close to a naive and proselytising trust in the efficacy of common sense and ordinary experience as an adequate basis for scientific knowledge. This belief colours the Cartesian sense of *intuitus*, of simple natures, of metaphysical axioms, of *expérience* as a source of warrant for the laws of nature, etc. In a paradoxical way, Descartes is more crudely empiricist than Newton or Huygens or many of his scientific contemporaries such as Harvey.

On the central question of rationalism in science, Descartes is unquestionably innocent at least of traditional charges that he ignores or distrusts experiential evidence as a basis for knowledge claims about physical nature. As early as 1629 he visited the local butcher almost daily to provide the prerequisites for anatomical experiments, a period in his career which he recalls for Mersenne ten years later:

I passed one winter in Amsterdam in which I went almost daily to the butcher's house to see him kill the beasts, and I used to carry home with me those parts which I wished to anatomise at my leisure. This is something which I did a number of times in all the places where I lived. (Descartes to Mersenne, November 13, 1639: II, 621).[7]

Where the context is sufficiently unambiguous, it is difficult to match Descartes for blunt statements of the necessity of experience:

That is a question of fact, where reasoning is useless without experience.

I have nothing to say about the declination of the magnetic needle: that is a question of fact.

These things, on the contrary, can only be determined by experience, and the only thing I learn from my little reasoning is that I wish the inventor would make a small model, as I have already suggested to him . . .

And although reason seems to persuade us that the least force is able to move them [particles of subtle matter], one finds on the contrary, by experience, that this force must be proportional to their size and to the speed with which it moves them.

As regards the nature of quicksilver, I have not yet performed all the experiments which I would need to understand it exactly.[8]

The Cartesian distrust of *expériences* is, in part, a suspicion about the complexity and uncertainty of experiments; paradoxically, the Cartesian preference for reason rather than experience is, at least in physical science, a preference for one kind of experience rather than another. Ordinary experience, critically evaluated by reflection, is the paramount source both of explanatory concepts and of empirical warrant in scientific explanations.

Notes

1 Neal Ward Gilbert, *Renaissance Concepts of Method*, p. 223.
2 For the mix of Aristotelian ideals and hypothetical methodology in Galileo, see Ernan McMullin, ed., *Galileo: Man of Science*, pp. 3–51.
3 E. McMullin, 'The conception of science in Galileo's work', in R. E. Butts and J. C. Pitt, eds., *New Perspectives on Galileo*, p. 252.
4 A. C. Crombie, *Robert Grosseteste*, p. 7.
5 Mary Hesse, *Forces and Fields*, pp. 62–3.
6 Cf. Descartes to Mersenne, December 18, 1629 (I, 84–5), and again to Mersenne, December 23, 1630 (I, 195–6): 'you wish to know how to do useful experiments. I have nothing to say about that after what Bacon wrote about it, except that, without being too curious to look for all the little details of a given subject matter, it would be better to make general synopses of all the more common things, which are very certain, and which can be known without expense. Such as that all shells are turned in the same direction, . . . that the body of all animals is divided into three parts, the head, the chest and the stomach, and other similar things. For it is such things which may be used infallibly in the search for truth.'
7 Some of the results of the visits to the butcher emerge in the fifth discourse of the *Dioptrics*, where Descartes uses the eye of an ox to study the optics of vision. See VI, 115.
8 Descartes to Mersenne, March 11, 1640 (III, 35); to Mersenne, June 11, 1640 (III, 85); to Huygens, November 15, 1643 (IV, 762); to Cavendish, November 2, 1646 (IV, 560); to the Marquis of Newcastle, November 23, 1646 (IV, 571–2).

A note on deduction

Although Descartes could hardly be said to have relied extensively on 'ordinary language' considerations to support philosophical arguments, he was not beyond exploiting the ambiguity of non-technical language to express what he considered to be philosophical insights. His sensitivity to ordinary usage is evident both when he hesitates to conflict with it (as in VII, 32 or VIII-1 56, 57), and when he invokes it in favour of his own position on some question (as in VII, 175, or Descartes to Morin, July 13, 1638: II, 198). In fact, an appropriately ambivalent attitude towards the demands of ordinary language is precisely what Descartes needed in order to escape the limitations of the philosophical Latin which he inherited from scholastic philosophy.

One way of dealing with the inherited restrictions of scholastic language was to explicitly reject both the normal meaning of a term and the philosophical theory which was implicit in it; this was Descartes' choice in the case of the troublesome term 'intuitus'. A different approach was adopted in the case of various Latin terms which denote logical inferences, especially in the *Regulae*. In these cases Descartes used the terms available from the scholastic tradition in such a flexible way that, even though there was no acknowledgement of the change in meaning, the context in which the terms occur implies that they are no longer being used in an exclusively scholastic sense. I have argued above in §8 that Descartes used '*deducere*' in such a flexible way in the *Regulae*; and one possible source of the revised use of '*deducere*' was the rather more ambiguous term, '*déduire*' in French.

The word *'déduire'* was used in the seventeenth century primarily in the sense of 'to deduct', as in deducting expenses from a financial account. *'Déduire'* was also used in a slightly different sense of 'drawing out something', as in drawing out one's discussion at length and boring one's listeners or readers. It was this second sense which eventually took on more precise logical connotations. Thus Jean Nicot's French–Latin dictionary, published in 1605, gives 'deduct' as the first meaning of *'déduire'* and then adds a second meaning: 'déduire un affaire tout au long & le déclarer amplement'. The latter is then translated into Latin as: 'pertractare rem'.[1] Randle Cotgrave's French–English dictionary, published in London in 1632, gives the following meanings for *'déduire'*: 'to deduct, to draw out, to discourse of' and *'déduisant'* is translated as 'discoursing of something'.[2] Finally, the first edition of the French Academy dictionary (1694) lists deduct or subtract as the first meaning of *'déduire'* and then adds: 'il signifie aussi, narrer, raconter au long & par le menu', as in 'déduire son fait, ses raisons'. A *déduction* is explained as a 'narration, enumeration en detail' as in 'faire une longue déduction de ses raisons'.[3]

Thus apart from the primary meaning, 'deduction' means something like a long detailed narration of the kind which tends to be given when one is giving one's reasons for something or explaining it. This rather loose sense of *'déduire'* is what one might expect to find in Descartes' writings on condition that we do not transfer uncritically our contemporary usage back on to the seventeenth century. In fact, there are a few texts which are sufficiently clear to indicate that the non-rigorous use of *'déduire'* is sometimes the only one which makes sense of a given text. For example, Descartes wrote to Ferrier on November 13, 1629, thanking him for explaining his objections at length and in detail: 'Vous m'avez fait plaisir de me déduire tout au long vos difficultéz sur ce que je vous avois mandé, & je tascheray d'y répondre suivant le mesme ordre que vous les proposez' (I, 53). Likewise, in the *Dioptrics*, Descartes asks the reader to consider what he had explained earlier so that he would not have to delay himself 'à vous déduire la preuve plus au long' (VI, 210). There is a similar example in a letter to Mersenne, in 1637, in which Descartes claims that the question of God's existence had been sufficiently dealt with in an earlier treatise: 'Eight years ago, however, I wrote in Latin the beginnings of a treatise on metaphysics in which *cela est déduit assez au long'* (I, 350). In each of these texts *'déduire'* means to explain, with connotations of explaining something by going through the various steps which would lead the reader gradually to understand whatever is at issue. It is significant also that in each case the use of *'déduire'* is accompanied by phrases such as 'assez au long', 'tout au long' or 'plus au long'.

It is impossible to avoid the conclusion that Descartes uses the term *'déduire'* to mean a detailed enumeration of steps in an argument in such a way that the term no longer characterises the logic of the argument but rather the step-by-step narration which is involved in its articulation. Once this is granted there is no difficulty in conceding that a deduction may be either a proof (as in corroborating an hypothesis) or an explanation (as in proposing an hypothesis or series of related hypotheses). And in this respect the Cartesian term *'déduire'* corresponds to *'démontrer'*.

This interchangeability of terms is reflected in many Cartesian texts. For example, in discussing the explanation of certain phenomena by reference to hypothetical causes the French version of the *Principles* uses the word *'démontrer'* whereas the original Latin had *'deduci'* (IX-2, 126, VIII-1, 102). And in contrasting explanation and proof where one might expect to find the ambiguous 'demonstrate' at work, one finds instead that Descartes uses 'deduce': 'for we are trying to deduce (*deducere*) the explanation of the effects from their causes and not, on the contrary, the justification of the causes from the effects' (VIII-1, 81).

Thus both terms, 'to deduce' and 'to demonstrate', may mean either: to prove or to explain. The only difference between deduction and demonstration, for Descartes, seems to be that the term 'deduction' has connotations of a lengthy discourse. And for that reason one can sympathise with what might otherwise look like total confusion on Descartes' part in his use of 'induction' or 'enumeration' in place of 'deduction'. These terms emphasise the long narrative overtones of 'deduction'; and they are therefore appropriate synonyms for either 'explanation' or 'proof', especially in the *Regulae*. Only the context can tell us, in most cases, whether a deduction or induction or enumeration is a proof or an explanation. And even then we still have to investigate the logical character or structure of such deductions/inductions.

Descartes' need for a more flexible inferential logic was at least facilitated by transferring some of the ambiguity of the French term *'déduire'* on to the relatively inflexible Latin term *'deducere'*; the almost reluctant, subtle changes in the *Regulae* eventually yield such flexibility in using either *'déduire'*, *'deducere'*, and their respective synonyms that the logic of Cartesian arguments can only be explained by the almost limitless ingenuity of their author's *intuitus*.

Notes

1   Jean Nicot, *Le grand dictionaire françois–latin* (Paris, 1605).
2   Randle Cotgrave, *A Dictionarie of the French and English Tongues* (London, 1632).
3   *Le dictionnaire de l'Académie françoise, dedié au roy*, 1st edn (Paris, 1694).

The impact rules of Cartesian dynamics

In Part II of the *Principles* Descartes develops seven rules for predicting what happens when one body collides with another and changes its speed or direction as a result of the impact. Since Descartes implies that these rules are derived from the three 'laws of nature' of the *Principles*, and because the rules themselves appear to be evidently counter-experiential, two problems arise in attempting to understand the significance of these rules for Descartes' science:

(*a*) How does Descartes 'deduce' the rules from the laws of nature?
(*b*) To what extent do these rules provide strong evidence that Descartes' scientific method is non-empirical?

To facilitate discussion of the first question, a translation of relevant sections of the laws of nature is provided. They are referred to as P3–P5.

P3: 'Everything, in so far as it is simple and undivided, always remains in the same condition as long as it can, and it is never changed except by external causes'. (VIII-1, 62).
P4: 'No piece of matter, considered on its own, tends to continue its movement in a curved line, but only in a straight line; although many pieces of matter are often forced to deflect because of contact with others so that . . . in every movement there is a kind of circle created from all the pieces of matter simultaneously moved' (*ibid.*, 63).
P5: 'When a moving body encounters another, if it has less force

to continue in a straight line than the other body has to resist it, then it is deflected somewhere else, and while it retains its motion, it loses only the determination of its motion; if, however, it has a greater force, then it moves the other body with itself, and it loses as much of its own motion as it transfers to the other body' (*ibid.*, 65).

Rather than translate the full text of Descartes' rules, the following summary is provided and the abbreviated rules are named R_1–R_7. The original text is considered in more detail in the discussion which follows whenever it is relevant to deciphering Descartes' argument.

Consider two bodies, B and C, which are moving with initial speeds of V_B and V_C before impact. After colliding with one another, their speeds will be V_B' and V_C'. The symbol Q, with appropriate subscripts for B and C, is used to refer to what Descartes calls the size or quantity of matter of a body. Using these symbols, the impact rules are as follows:

R_1: If $Q_B = Q_C$, $V_B = V_C$, and if B and C are moving in opposite directions, they are reflected on impact with no change in speed.
R_2: If $Q_B > Q_C$, and if the other conditions are identical with the previous case, then both bodies travel after impact in B's initial direction with no change in speed.
R_3: If $Q_B = Q_C$, $V_B > V_C$, and if B and C are moving in opposite directions, then both bodies travel in B's original direction after colliding, and $V_B' = V_C'$.
R_4: If $Q_B < Q_C$, and if $V_C = O$, then B will always be reflected on impact with C no matter what its initial speed, and $V_B = V_B'$.
R_5: If $Q_B > Q_C$, and if the other conditions are the same as in R_4, then both B and C move in B's initial direction after impact, and $V_B' = V_C'$.
R_6: If $Q_B = Q_C$, and the same conditions prevail as in R_4, then B is reflected on impact with C, and C begins to move in B's initial direction; $V_C' = \frac{1}{4} V_B$ and $V_B' = \frac{3}{4} V_B$.
R_7: If B and C move in the same direction, and if B follows C in such a way that $V_B > V_C$, then three possibilities arise:

(i) if $Q_C < Q_B$, or if $Q_C > Q_B$ and $Q_C/Q_B < V_B/V_C$,[1] then B and C continue to move in the same initial direction after impact, and $V_B' = V_C'$;

(ii) if $Q_C > Q_B$, and $Q_C/Q_B > V_B/V_C$, then B is reflected from C on impact, and retains all of its original motion;

(iii) if $Q_C > Q_B$, and $Q_C/Q_B = V_B/V_C$, then B transfers part of its motion to C on impact, and is reflected from C with the remainder of its initial motion.[2]

A number of commentators have suggested that the rules cannot be derived from the laws without introducing some auxiliary hypotheses or principles.[3] Descartes himself however contends that 'all the particular causes of the changes that occur in bodies are contained in the third law' (VIII-1, 65). Hence, to determine 'from these laws how individual bodies increase or decrease their motion or change direction as a result of colliding with other bodies, it is only necessary to calculate the amount of force in each one to move or to resist motion, and to assume that the more powerful one will always produce its effect' (VIII-1, 67). This implies that, if Descartes' concept of force is clarified, and if a method is provided for measuring the force both of the resisting motion and of the causing motion, it is relatively easy to determine the results of collisions under different conditions.

This is not as easy a task as Descartes apparently assumes it to be, and it is even difficult to imagine that he could have thought otherwise himself. A large part of the problem here is that Cartesian science is constructed on the basis of everyday sensory experience, and this explains why many of the fundamental explanatory concepts of Descartes' dynamics are derived in a rather uncritical manner from our ordinary experience of physical bodies in motion. In the absence of well-defined theoretical concepts it is inevitable that the apparent clarity of Cartesian science masks deep conceptual confusions which come to light only on close inspection. This is especially true in contexts where the concepts are subject to mathematical control, as is the case in the impact rules.

The concept of force, for Descartes, is conceptually related to the possibility of calculating the quantity of matter in any given body whether it is in motion or at rest. Descartes does not distinguish between matter and mass, nor between the mass and the weight of a body. Besides, he notoriously defines matter in terms of extension, and this apparently precludes any distinction between more or less dense bodies. Despite this, one finds frequent references in his work to the relative density of different bodies or, more often, to their relative solidities.[4] There is little direct evidence in Descartes that he noticed any conceptual confusion in this situation and consequently there is scarcely any effort on his part to explain the consistency of his concepts of matter and density. And the concept of matter does need clarification as a precondition for explaining the Cartesian concept of force.

One way in which the Cartesian concepts of matter, density and force may be consistently understood is the following. Matter is defined by extension; i.e. being extended is a necessary and sufficient condition of materiality, so that there is only a distinction of reason between the two concepts.[5] Since a piece of matter has some size, it cannot be indivisible in principle; since an extended entity has some matter in it, there cannot be a pure vacuum. This kind of conceptual analysis, however, is inappropriate for discovering how many kinds of fundamental particles one must postulate in order to explain the variety of properties which matter exhibits. Therefore, one is justified in postulating whatever particles are necessary to explain our experience of nature, and in this project 'we cannot decide by reason alone' (VIII-1, 100–101). The concept of matter does not provide any a priori insight into the kinds of particles one needs for the success of a scientific theory; nor does the concept of matter determine in advance what it means for a particle to occupy a given space (or have a determinate extension).

Descartes postulates the existence of at least three kinds of matter to account for the variety of phenomena one observes in nature. These particles are primarily distinguished by their size and relative motion. Thus as early as *Le Monde* he imagines he can explain the fluidity of some bodies compared to the 'hardness' of others by reference to his theory of small particles of matter moving relative to one another with more or less ease (XI, 11–13). But how can this theory explain relative density if there are no gaps between the particles, or if the particles themselves are not more or less dense? It seems as if Descartes is doomed by the logic of his own concepts to 'a world of a single continuous matter of uniform density'.[6]

Descartes defines 'solidity' in the *Principles* in terms of the proportion between the quantity of matter of the third kind, in any given body, and the size of its surface area.[7] This is developed further in Part III, article cxxii:

Thus we see . . . that pieces of lead and other metals, once they are moved, retain a greater motion or a greater force to continue in motion than stones or pieces of wood of the same size and shape, and for that reason they are thought to be more solid; in other words, they contain more matter of the third element and fewer pores which are filled with matter of the first and second elements. (VIII-1, 172).

The rest of the article clearly implies that this is not a modern concept of density. The operative image is that of a sponge which has a very large surface area compared with its quantity of matter. Thus a compact piece of gold may be very solid; whereas the same quantity of gold can be drawn out into very fine sheets and refashioned into a structure with a significantly larger surface area, while still retaining exactly the same quantity of matter as the original solid piece of gold. In the second state, the same gold is 'less solid' than in its first state although it obviously has the same density in both states.

This model might be useful if Descartes could explain the lower density of the particles which fill the interstices in the sponge-like bodies. If not, we have a regress in his explanation which only postpones the problem at hand. It is a fact of our experience, he thinks, that some bodies are more difficult to move than others despite the fact that they are equal in size. Descartes accounts for this by saying that apparently solid bodies are more or less sponge-like; those which are more sponge-like are less solid, and vice versa. But this obviously explains nothing unless he can account for the difference in relative density between the various kinds of matter which fill the interstices in less solid pieces of matter.

Descartes seems to assume that the different particles of matter are, in fact, more or less 'solid' and that they can pack together more or less closely to constitute the macroscopic bodies which we observe.[8] But how can particles be more or less solid if matter is defined by extension? Perhaps a very small particle of matter can occupy more or less space, or have a greater or smaller extension, by moving more or less fast within a determinate place. If it is objected that there must be a vacuum in such a place to permit movement, Descartes could respond that since the place in question is occupied by the particle of matter there is no sense in describing the particle's immediate environment as a vacuum. Therefore one could conceive of bodies having different solidities in proportion to the relative number of small interstices in their structures which are occupied by small imperceptible particles. This would mean that different bodies could have different degrees of compactness, but it would not necessarily imply that there is a small vacuum in each gap occupied by small particles. And since different bodies could have varying degrees of compactness in this sense, one body may contain a greater quantity of matter than another either because it is larger in size or because it is more solid than the other. Thus Descartes wrote to Mersenne, February 23, 1643: 'if two bodies travel equal distances in the same time, one says that they have the same speed; but whichever of the two contains more matter, either because it is more solid, or because it is larger, requires more force (*impression*) and motion to travel as fast as the other one' (III, 636).

Thus the amount of matter in a given body is proportional to its volume and solidity. The weight of a body is the force it exerts in its motion towards the centre of the earth, and is a function of its quantity of matter, its size and the resistance of the surrounding medium.[9] Thus, the force of gravity of a body is relative to its solidity, and one could not determine the quantity of matter it contains from its weight alone. 'Hence, from the weight alone one cannot easily estimate the amount of terrestrial matter in each body' (VIII-2, 215). A less dense body might contain more matter than another more dense body and still exert less force of gravity because of the greater resistance of the medium to its larger surface area.

Descartes' analysis of the force of a body in motion applies equally to gravitational and impressed motion because the former is, for him, a special case of the latter. Consequently the solidity of a particular body, its size, its speed and the resistance of other bodies it encounters determine the kind of force it can exert on impact with other bodies.

Size and speed are evidently significant factors in determining the force of a body in motion. Descartes writes, in *Le Monde*, of 'the more forceful [bodies], that is to say the larger ones among those which were equally moved and the more moved ones among those which were equally large' (XI, 50).[10] Relative solidity is also a factor, because Descartes supposes that every body on earth moves in an environment which more or less impedes its motion. This is borne out by the experience of moving more or less solid objects in a liquid.

When two bodies move equally fast, it is true to say that, if one contains twice as much matter as the other, it also has twice as much motion; that is not the same as saying that it has twice as much force to continue to move in a straight line. But it would have exactly twice as much force if its surface were also exactly twice as large, because it would always encounter twice as many other bodies which resist it. (XI, 66–7).[11]

In other words, the product of quantity of matter and speed determines the measure of the motion of a body, but the relation between the motion and force of a body depends on its surface area (among other things). 'Consider that this force does not depend only on the quantity of matter of each body, but also on the extension of its surface' (XI, 66).

Descartes is evidently trying to come to terms with our experience of moving very dense objects and the exertion this requires compared with our experience of moving objects with more or less facility in fluids of differing viscosities. The details of his theory are never sufficiently developed, so that one finds the same rather vague references to size, surface area, resisting media and speed in that section of the *Principles* between the laws and the rules in which he explains the theory underlying the derivation of the impact rules:

This force [of a body to continue in motion] should be determined both from the size of the body in which it inheres and the surface by means of which it is separated from other bodies, and also from the speed of its motion, and the nature and degree of contrariety of the way in which different bodies oppose and are opposed by it. (VIII-1, 67).

Since Descartes' physics was much too undeveloped to consider all these factors in his theory of colliding bodies, he proposes the construction of an ideal situation in which two perfectly hard bodies collide, without interference from other bodies or the medium in which they move. The impact rules are applicable 'if only two bodies collide, if they are perfectly hard and if they are so separated from everything else that their motion is neither hindered nor assisted by anything in their environment'. (VIII-1, 67). In this situation, the only relevant factors which remain for calculating the relative forces of two colliding bodies are their speed and quantity of matter. If Q is the quantity of matter of a body and V its speed, then QV is the measure of its quantity of motion. The relative forces of two colliding bodies in the ideal conditions proposed by Descartes are therefore proportional to their quantities of motion, QV.

To determine what happens when bodies of differing speed and quantity of matter collide, one need only consult P5. However, to apply this law of nature one needs to measure the force with which stationary bodies resist motion. Once a method is developed for making this kind of measurement, it is relatively simple to determine which of two colliding bodies has the greater force, whether the force in question is one which tends to cause motion or resist motion.

Descartes' concept of inertia is a corollary of his understanding of the force of a moving body. Assuming that one wishes to move two bodies, M and N, with a given speed S, by colliding some other bodies with them, then more force is required to move a body with a greater quantity of matter or a larger surface area. The reason for this is obvious, given the Cartesian concept of matter. If M and N both move after impact with speed S, and M has a greater quantity of matter than N, then M has a greater motive force than N (all other things being equal). Since M can only have acquired this force when it began to move and according to P3 it tends to conserve its force intact, then a greater force must have been initially necessary to move M relative to N.

On the other hand, if M has a larger surface area than N, then it will encounter more resistance from the medium in which they move, and to compensate for this M needs a greater impressed force to maintain the same speed as N. Since the first kind of resistance to motion is a characteristic of a body apart from the medium in which it moves, Descartes reluctantly calls it the natural inertia of a body. The second type of resistance to impressed motion depends more directly on the medium in which a body moves, but it still represents a part of the inertia which must be overcome in changing the condition of a body at rest or in motion.

In either case, there is no such thing as an active resistance to motion in a body. Rather, the force required to impart a certain motion to a body by impact is equal to the force of the motion of the same body after impact. Because it requires a given measure of force to achieve a certain degree of motion, a moved body is considered to resist motion with that same degree of force.

If two unequal bodies receive the same amount of motion, since this equal quantity of motion does not give as much speed to the larger as to the smaller body, one could say, in this sense, that the more matter a body contains, the more natural inertia it has. To this one might add that a large body can more easily transfer its motion to other bodies than a small one can, and that it can be less easily moved by others. So that there is one kind of inertia which depends on the quantity of matter, and another which depends on the extension of their surfaces.[12]

In the idealised conditions in which Descartes' impact rules should apply, only the so-called natural inertia of bodies is relevant in determining the results of different collisions.

Hence to calculate the results of an impact between two perfectly hard bodies in a non-resisting medium, the only forces one needs to take account of are both functions of the speed and quantity of matter of the bodies in question. The force of a moving body to continue in motion in a straight line is a function of its speed and quantity of matter; and the 'inertial' force of a body to resist motion is a function of its quantity of matter and the speed it would acquire if it were successfully moved by some other body as a result of impact. This way of calculating forces, however, ignores the direction in which the forces act, and Descartes takes this factor into account in his use of the concept of *'determination'*.[13]

In Part II, article xliii of the *Principles*, Descartes explains that there are two modalities in the way in which moving bodies can be said to be contrary; one is with respect to their relative speed, and the other concerns the determination of their motions. The subsequent article explains this in more detail:

It should be noted that one motion is not contrary to another motion of the same speed, but we can properly discover only two kinds of contrariety in this context. One is between motion and rest or between the speed and slowness of motion in so far as slowness participates in rest. The other contrariety is between the determination of a motion towards a certain place and meeting a second body either at rest in that place or moving in a different direction; and depending on the direction from which the colliding body is moving, this contrariety can be greater or less. (VIII-1, 67).

The determination in question in this text is the determination of the direction in which a body moves, or the direction in which the force of motion of a moving body acts. Thus two bodies which come into contact will be contrary, in some sense, if they travel either with speeds or in directions which are incompatible. The purpose of the impact rules is to supply a procedure for calculating the resolution of such incompatible motions; in the first three rules the determinations of the bodies are contrary, while in the final four rules their speeds are contrary.

If we assume that Descartes has adequately clarified the concepts of 'force of motion' and 'natural inertia', and that he has explained the two ways in which the motions of colliding bodies can be incompatible, it may seem as if all he needs to do is to apply P5 to the different impact situations envisaged by the rules. This is what he attempts to do in the subsequent articles of Book II of the *Principles*; however, Descartes' discussion at this point seems to run in two parallel lines, and the available evidence of the texts is insufficient to determine which line of thought is primary. The first side of his discussion is a qualitative and almost philosophical account of how the two modes of contrariety can be made compatible in the various situations envisaged by the impact rules. This line of thought becomes especially significant in the case of R4, where a principle of economy is introduced to explain why one possible resolution of a contrariety in speed is adopted rather than another. The attempt to represent mathematically the forces involved in each collision situation gives rise to a second, almost independent, approach to the rules. This alternative approach is demanded by P5, which requires an estimation of the initial forces of each body and a redistribution of these forces, after impact, according to a conservation principle. For the successful application of P5 presupposes a calculation of which of two colliding bodies has the most force, and a precise description of the final states of the two colliding bodies after impact presupposes a correspondingly precise calculation of their initial and final forces.

For ease of application to the different impact situations, P5 can be re-written as two theorems, the first of which is

> Th I: When two bodies collide, the body with the greater
> force of motion or natural inertia predominates.

The word 'predominates' here is used to refer to the outcome of a collision where one body imposes either its direction or its speed on another. Thus if two bodies B and C collide, B is said to predominate over C if: (i) B causes C to change the direction of its motion while the direction of B's motion remains unchanged or (ii) B causes C to increase the speed of its motion or to begin to move if it is initially at rest. The actual manner in which the more forceful body predominates over the other depends on the conditions of impact, and especially on the direction in which the bodies are moving relative to each other before impact. If the more forceful body must transfer some of its motion to the other body in order for its motion to predominate, then the total quantity of motion of the system remains unchanged. If V and V' are the speed of a body before and after impact respectively, and the subscripts 'B' and 'C' denote the two bodies in question, then the conservation of motion in the system of two colliding bodies is expressed by the theorem,

$$\text{Th II: } Q_B V_B + Q_C V_C = Q_B V_B' + Q_C V_C'.$$

Using these two theorems, we can derive the rules from Descartes' description of the seven different sets of conditions he considers.

In the situation envisaged by R_1, neither B nor C has more force, since they are exactly equal in size and speed. Hence, neither one can predominate according to Th I. Also, by Th II, they must retain their original speeds if the total system is not to lose any motion in the collision. Since they are moving in opposite directions before impact, there is no other possibility available except that two bodies be reflected on impact and move in opposite directions with the same speed.

R_2: The conditions are similar to those in R_1, except that B has a greater quantity of matter and, as a result, has a larger measure of motion than C. Consequently, when they collide, B continues to move in the same direction as prior to impact, and C is forced to move in the same direction as B. Once C is reflected, it moves in its new direction with its original speed, V_C. Because B and C are then moving in the same direction with equal speeds, C does not obstruct the passage of B. Therefore, no transfer of motion from B to C is required, and the final conditions are as described in R_2.

R_3: In this case, V_B is larger than V_C and both bodies have the same quantity of matter. Hence, B has more force than C and causes C to be reflected. If this were the only effect of impact, C would then be moving immediately in front of, and with a lower speed than, B. By applying Th I, we find that B must transfer part of its motion to C in order to predominate in the collision; otherwise C would effectively be impeding the motion of B. The minimum amount of motion transferred from B to C enables both bodies to move in B's initial direction with the same post-impact speed. [14]

R₄ and R₆: Descartes gave two different resolutions of the impact conditions to which these rules apply and one can only speculate about the source of the inconsistency in the two versions. One account is found in the *Principles*, in the same place as the other impact rules; the other version is found in his correspondence. Since the latter is apparently more consistent with our experience of collisions between a moving and a stationary body, it is best to examine it first and then investigate why Descartes changed his mind in formulating R₄ in the *Principles*.

R₄ applies when C is at rest and B moves towards C with an initial speed of V_B. Q_B is less than Q_C. If V_B is sufficiently high and if the difference in quantity of matter between B and C is not very large, experience seems to indicate that the two bodies would move after impact in the same direction as B moved initially. Following the line cf argument involved in R₃, the two bodies would have the same terminal speed, $Q_B V_B/(Q_B + Q_C)$.

In the situation to which R₆ applies, the conditions are the same as in R₄ except that $Q_B = Q_C$. In this case, B would transfer half of its initial quantity of motion to C, and both B and C would move in B's initial direction, after impact, with a speed of $\frac{1}{2}V_B$.

Descartes summarises this solution to such impact conditions in a letter to Mersenne, December 25, 1639:

As regards inertia, I think that I have already written that in a completely frictionless space, if a body of a given size and speed collides with another which is equal in size and without motion, it will transfer to it [the second body] half the initial speed of the first body. However, if it collides with another which is twice as large as itself, it will transfer two-thirds of its motion and both will move afterwards with only one-third of the initial speed of the first body. And in general, the greater the body, the slower it will move when pushed by the same force. (II, 627).[15]

This represents one possible interpretation of P5 when applied to these impact conditions. For Th I suggests that in deciding the consequences of this type of collision, one need only consider the force of the moving body and the inertial force of the body at rest. Thus, no matter how large the body at rest is and no matter how small or how slow the moving body is, the latter can always transfer a sufficiently large portion of its initial motion to the former so that both move, after impact, with the same velocity.

However, it is also possible that at a certain critical point the inertia of C relative to the moving force of B is such that B is reflected on impact with C. It was apparently a consideration of this latter alternative which gave rise to the version of R4 and R6 which is found in the *Principles*. The following conjectured reasoning on Descartes' part explains the derivation of these two controversial rules.

R4: Assume that B does transfer some of its motion to C and that both bodies move, after impact, in B's initial direction. As in previously considered similar situations, B must transfer enough of its motion to C to make their final speeds equal; otherwise, C would be impeding B and this contradicts Th I. We can assume that

(i) $Q_B V_B = Q_B V_B' + Q_C V_C'$ (from Th II),
(ii) $V_B' = V_C'$,
(iii) $Q_B V_B = Q_B V_C' + Q_C V_C'$ (from (i) and (ii)),
and since
(iv) $Q_C > Q_B$,
it follows that
(v) $Q_B V_C' < Q_C V_C'$ (from (ii) and (iv))
(vi) $Q_B V_B' < \frac{1}{2} Q_B V_B$ (from (ii), (iii) and (v)).

In other words, if B transfers the minimum amount of its motion necessary to move C the residual quantity of motion of B is less than half its initial value.

If this were to happen, Descartes considers that such a collision would contravene Th I above. For if B must lose more than half of its initial motion in order to predominate in a collision, then C has a greater natural inertia to resist motion than B has force to cause

C's movement. This situation obtains no matter what initial speed *B* has as long as *C* has a greater quantity of matter than *B*, because the natural inertia of *C* increases in proportion to the increase in the speed of *B*. If one simply measures the moving force of *B* and the inertial force of *C*, then the former is greater than the latter. However, *B* has two alternatives available – either to force *C* to move, or to be completely reflected. As soon as the first of these alternatives involves overcoming an inertial force which is more than half of its own moving force, then *B* is reflected on impact with *C* and retains its motion intact. At this critical point, although the force of *B* is still greater than the inertial force of *C*, it is not large enough, relative to the force of *C*, to cause the first rather than the second of the two possible results. This is the version of R4 which is found in the *Principles*.

Descartes suggests this kind of reasoning in defence of R4 in a letter to Clerselier, February 17, 1645:

The reason which prompts me to say that a body which is at rest could never be moved by another body which is smaller than it, no matter how fast this smaller one moved, is that it is a law of nature that a body which moves another one must have more force to move it than the body at rest has force to resist motion. This excess of force can depend only on its size; for the body which is at rest has as many degrees of resistance as the other one, which moves it, has degrees of speed. The reason for this is that if it is moved by another which has twice as much speed as a third body, then it must receive twice as much motion from it; and it resists twice as much this double increment of motion.

For example, *B* cannot push the body *C*, unless it moves it as fast as it would move itself after the impact; that is, if *B* is to *C* as 5 is to 4, of the nine degrees of motion in *B* it would be necessary to transfer 4 to *C* to move it as fast as itself. This is easy for *B* because it has enough force to transfer up to 4½ degrees of motion (i.e. up to half of its total motion) rather than be reflected in the opposite direction. But if *B* is to *C* as 4 is to 5, *B* could not move *C* unless it transferred five of its nine degrees of motion to *C*, which is more than half its motion. Consequently, *C* resists this [imposed motion] with more force than *B* has to act; that is why *B* must be reflected in the opposite direction rather than move *C*. (IV, 183–5).

This explanation of R4 is consistent with the French version of the *Principles* which, according to the *Conversation with Burman*, was specifically amplified to elaborate on those rules which posed special problems for readers.[16]

The fourth [rule] is that if the body *C* were even slightly greater than *B* and at rest, . . . no matter with what speed it approaches it, it would never have the force to move it; instead it would be forced to rebound towards the same place from which it had come. For in so far as *B* could not push *C* without making it move as fast as it would move itself after impact, it is certain that *C* must resist more in proportion as *B* comes towards it more quickly; and that its resistance must prevail over the action of *B* because it is larger than *B*. Thus, for example, if *C* is double the size of *B* and if *B* has three degrees of motion, it could not move *C* which is at rest unless it transferred two of these degrees to it – that is to say, one [degree] for each of its halves – and it retains only the third [degree] for itself, because it is no greater than each of the halves of *C* and it could not move any faster than them after impact . . . so that to the extent that *B* has more speed, it will find correspondingly more resistance in *C*. (IX-2, 90–91).

However, neither the text quoted from the letter to Clerselier nor the revised French text of the fourth rule explains satisfactorily why *B* cannot lose more than half its force to *C*. Experience seems to show that if *C* is large enough relative to *B* then *B* is reflected in certain cases; but why must it be reflected in every case in which it can only move *C* by losing more (by even the slightest fraction) than half its own force?

A relatively novel consideration enters the discussion at this stage – Descartes' principle of least action. In the subsequent paragraph to the one already quoted from the February 17th letter to Clerselier, Descartes wrote that the reason why people found difficulty understanding the rules was because they failed to notice that the rules

depend on one single principle, which is that when two bodies with incompatible modes collide, some change in these modes must truly occur to make them compatible, but that this change is always the least possible; that is to say, if these modes could become compatible by having a certain quantity of these modes changed, then a greater quantity of the same modes would not be changed.

Descartes goes on to say that this resolves the difficulties encountered by readers in rules 4, 5 and 6. In rule 4 for example, since a change in the speed of either body is equally difficult to a change in the directional determination of motion, the moving body *B* has two options available: either to transfer more than half its motion to *C*, or to reverse its direction and be completely reflected on impact. Apparently the loss of more than half its force is 'more difficult' than a change in direction.

The fact that Descartes gives different solutions to the collision described in R4 and that he gives somewhat different reasons for the solution proposed in the *Principles* suggests that he was genuinely groping his way towards a satisfactory dynamical account of familiar natural phenomena. However he has not quite succeeded here, or elsewhere, in matching his philosophical approach to physical problems with the mathematical analysis which he so often recommends. The two levels of discourse, intuitive/philosophical and mathematical, inevitably intersect at precisely that point in the *Principles* where, for the first time, he attempts to apply his general principles to provide a mathematical or quantitative theory of what happens in simple collision situations.[17] The principle of least change is part of a philosophical discussion which describes collisions between physical bodies in terms of the mutual accommodation of two kinds of contrariety, in speed and determination of motion. This principle is susceptible to mathematical application when the inertia of a body at rest is measured because, for Descartes, this inertia can be quantified only as a function of the loss of force by whatever body moves another at rest. Descartes needs to compare the relative force of a body in motion with the inertial resistance of a body at rest in order to apply P5 and predict the outcome of a collision. But since a moving body, no matter how small, can always lose enough of its force to communicate some motion to a body at rest, this would seem to imply that the inertial force of a body at rest is never sufficient to resist imposed motion.

The principle of least action is Descartes' 'philosophical' justification for setting the threshold of a moving body's tendency to lose force somewhat arbitrarily at one-half. If there is no upper limit to the fraction of force capable of being lost by a moving body to another body at rest, inertial force would always be less; if, however, a moving body must lose more than half of its force to a body at rest in order to move it by impact, then we might consider the inertia of the body at rest to be greater than the force of the moving body and, according to P5, to prevail in a collision.

An obvious objection to establishing the threshold at one-half the force of the moving body is: why not some other fraction? The answer to this question depends on how one understands Descartes' rules – as a priori specifications of what must be the case, or as tentative hypotheses which represent the application of the laws to various ideal conditions. Before looking at this it is appropriate to conclude the application of the laws to the conditions described in rules 5, 6 and 7.

In rule 5, $V_C = 0$ and Q_B is greater than Q_C. Therefore B moves C by transferring enough of its motion to C to cause both bodies to move after impact with the same final speed. Since Q_C is less than Q_B, the terminal quantity of motion of C is less than half the initial quantity of motion of B. Hence C has a lower inertial force to resist motion than B has force to cause C's motion. The final speed of B and C is determined by applying Th II.

R6: This is a limiting case of the conditions which obtain in applying R4 and R5. If B is even slightly less than C in its quantity of matter, it is reflected with its speed unchanged; if B is slightly larger than C, it moves C so that the two bodies have a final speed of $Q_B V_B/(Q_B + Q_C)$. As Q_C tends to equal Q_B, then $Q_B V_B/(Q_B + Q_C)$ tends to $\frac{1}{2}V_B$. Descartes appears to resolve the question as follows: if B is slightly smaller than C, it transfers none of its motion to C. If B is slightly larger than C, it transfers almost half of its motion to C. If B and C have the same quantity of matter the result of impact is the mean of the two previous cases. Thus, B transfers only one quarter of its motion to C and is reflected with three-quarters of its initial speed. This is consistent with Th II, and agrees with the *Principles* version of R6.

R7: Parts (i) and (ii) of this rule are derived from Th I and Th II as in previous cases. If Q_C/Q_B is less than V_B/V_C, then $Q_B V_B$ is greater than $Q_C V_C$, and consequently B transfers enough motion to C to enable both bodies to move in B's initial direction, with equal final speeds. If B has a smaller quantity of matter than C, it cannot change C's motion, according to Th I. The only other possibility available is for B to be reflected with its speed unchanged.

Part (iii) of R7 is unsatisfactory because it gives no measure for the amount of motion transferred from B to C. Since both B and C have equal force there should be no transfer of motion according to Th I, and B should be reflected on impact with C. The justification of this part of R7 is apparently derived from two sources. On the one hand, it conforms to our experience of such collisions. On the other hand, it represents a limiting case between $R_7(i)$ and $R_7(ii)$, where B has a greater or lesser quantity of motion than C. When their quantities of motion are equal, Descartes suggests that part of the effects of $R_7(i)$ and $R_7(ii)$ occur.

The discussion to this point has been confined to the first question posed at the outset, namely in what sense does Descartes think that the impact rules of the *Principles* are deducible from the laws of nature? I have argued that the rules do indeed follow from the laws, but only in the rather tolerant Cartesian sense of deduction discussed above in Chapter 3. For at least in the case of R_4 and R_5 a supplementary hypothesis is introduced to help specify when the inertia of a body at rest is greater than the force of a moving body which collides with it. The second question concerns the extent to which the counter-experiential character of the rules supplies convincing evidence that there is something significantly wrong with Cartesian methodology. Descartes' readers pointed out to him that the rules seem to be contrary to experience. His response, unfortunately, seems only to confirm one's suspicion that he ignored relevant experiences and framed the rules completely a priori; and this, in turn, raises similar doubts about the validity of the laws of nature from which the rules are claimed to have been derived. For in the amended version of the rules in the French edition of the *Principles*, Descartes wrote in response to this type of objection: 'And the demonstrations of all this [i.e. of the rules] are so certain that even if experience seemed to indicate the contrary, we would be obliged to place more trust in our reason than in our senses'. (IX-2, 93).

On closer examination it becomes apparent, however, that the impact rules do not contradict experience at all and that Descartes was aware of this. For this reason he wrote: 'if experience *seemed* to indicate the contrary.' When confronted with experiments which do not correspond to the predictions of the rules, Descartes concedes that all the bodies which we experience are somewhat elastic and that the rules, therefore, do not apply to them.[18] Thus the most obviously counter-factual rule, R_4, must be balanced with Descartes' admission that the whole earth can be imperceptibly moved by the impact of something falling to the ground under the weight of gravity.[19] Besides, there are no actual collisions in a Cartesian world in which the viscosity of the medium and interaction with other bodies do not play a significant role in determining the results of collisions between bodies.

The objections to the rules on the basis of our experience of colliding bodies and Descartes' response to these objections explain why he takes the opportunity of underlining the theoretical or abstract character of the rules in the French edition of 1647. The revised version of R_4 elaborates on the description of C 'at rest'; where the Latin text said only 'si corpus C plane quiesceret', the French adds:

That is to say, not only that it has no apparent movement, but also that it is not surrounded by air nor by any other liquid bodies which, as I have explained below, dispose the hard bodies which they surround to be capable of being moved very easily. (IX-2, 90).[20]

The discussion of R_5 adds a similar qualification: 'one sometimes imagines that one observes the contrary on this earth, because of the air or other liquids which always surround hard bodies which are moving and which can greatly increase or decrease their speed . . .' (*ibid.*, 92). Article liii of Part II, which follows the discussion of the seven rules, summarises this point for the reader:

That the explanation of these rules is difficult; because every body makes contact with many others at the same time. Indeed, it often happens that experience can seem initially to be incompatible with the rules which I have just explained, but the reason for this is obvious. For they [the rules] presuppose that the two bodies B and C are perfectly hard and so separated from all other bodies that there is none other in their vicinity which could either help or hinder their movement. And we see no such situation in this world. That is why before one could decide if the rules are observed here or not, it is not enough to see how two bodies such as B and C can act on one another when they make contact; but it would also be necessary to consider, besides, how all the other bodies which are close to them increase or diminish their action. (IX-2, 93).

These qualifications imply that the rules appear to contradict experience simply because they fail to take account of all the factors which determine the result of collisions between actual physical bodies. Chief among the factors which are not considered by the rules are (i) that no physical bodies are perfectly hard, and (ii) that there are no actual cases in our experience of two bodies colliding in a context where they are completely removed from either an interfering medium or the influence of other bodies. But that is not quite the same as saying: the rules are hypothetical.

The February 17th (1645) letter to Clerselier comes closer to this kind of admission. After explaining R₄ and R₅ at length and also showing how the rules are not inconsistent with our experience, Descartes adds: 'Despite that, it is necessary here that I admit that these rules are not without difficulty; and I would try to clarify them even further if I were able to do it now. But because my mind is taken up with other problems . . .' (IV, 187). This suggests that the rules are more like a sketch or rough draft of how the laws of nature can be applied to specific problems in dynamics. The laws themselves, as I have argued above in Chapter 4, are proposed as very general hypotheses which are consistent with our experience of simple physical phenomena; the impact rules which are derived from the laws must represent an equally hypothetical or tentative effort to formulate a dynamical account of simple collision situations.[21]

If the rules are read as the expression of Descartes' tentative efforts to formulate a dynamics rather than as unwarranted a priori specifications of what must be the case, then one can more easily understand R₄ and R₅ and even accept the unsatisfactory character of many of the other rules as well. For Descartes changes his mind about how best to formulate rules 4 and 5 – he could attempt to describe how physical bodies in our experience actually react on impact, or he could formulate abstract rules which prescind from some of the factors which are assumed to determine the result of collisions between bodies. Descartes did both. R₄ can be seen as tentative and reasonable; and establishing the fraction of its moving force which *B* can lose to *C* at rest as one half can be seen to be guesswork which is designed to cope with a real experience of cases where inertial resistance to impressed motion prevails.

Does Descartes think that his efforts involve guesswork? Hardly. Besides, there is a danger at this point of excusing the impact rules by claiming that they are not counter-factual because they do not even purport to describe real collisions between physical bodies in motion. So that Descartes' methodology in science in not a priori, not so much because the rules do not conflict with our experience but because they are not even envisaged as applicable to experience. But surely this is a new kind of apriorism – constructing rules which one knows cannot even be tested in experience.

These problems cannot be easily avoided in Descartes' methodology. The examination of the impact rules shows only that he did not stubbornly insist that the rules do apply to physical phenomena despite the testimony of experience. On the other hand, he exhibits an unwarranted conviction that his rather convoluted guesswork on the subject is on the right track. This, however, is merely another instance of the general thesis proposed above, that the disparity between personal conviction and objective warrant is greater than Descartes' theory of science could cope with. The impact rules are not unique in this respect; they are neither more nor less a priori than the rest of Cartesian science.

Notes

1   This possibility is considered only in the French version of the *Principles*; see IX-2, 92.
2   R₇ (c) occurs only in the French edition, in IX-2, 93.
3   See, for example, D. Dubarle, 'Remarques sur les règles du choc chez Descartes', *Cartesio*, pp. 325–34, and Richard J. Blackwell, 'Descartes' laws of motion', *Isis*, **57** (1966), 220–34.
4   See Descartes to Mersenne, January 21, 1641 (III, 290); VIII-1, 43; XI, 17, 72–3.
5   This is discussed above in Chapter 4.
6   G. Buchdahl, *Metaphysics and the Philosophy of Science*, p. 95.
7   VIII-I, 170 and IX-2, 174.
8   See the discussion in the *Principles*, Part III, article cxxiii where the particles of the second element are described as 'omnium solidissimi qui esse possent', although the French changes this to read: 'ces petites boules sont aussi solides qu'aucun corps de mesme grandeur' (IX-2, 175).
9   See *Le Monde*, XI, 72–3: 'the weight of this earth, that is to say the force which unites all its parts and makes them tend towards its centre, each part more or less according as it is more or less large and

solid'. In the *Meteorology*, weight is said to be a function of surface area also: 'the pieces of ice ... having a very large surface in proportion to the quantity of their matter, the resistance of the air that they would have to divide could easily have more force to stop them than their weight has force to cause them to descend'.

10   See *Conversation with Burman* (Cottingham, p. 42): 'the larger a body is, the more easily it continues its motion and resists other bodies.' See also VI, 235; VIII-1, 140.

11   See also the example of ships moving with more or less force, in *Le Monde*, XI, 58.

12   Descartes to Debeaune, April 30, 1639 (II, 543–4). In a letter to Mersenne, December 1638 (II, 466–7), Descartes rejects the idea that bodies have some kind of natural inertia (*inertie ou tardiveté naturelle*) which opposes impressed motion and consequently must be overcome if the speed of a body is increased by contact action. If equal forces are applied to a large body and a small one, the former moves more slowly than the latter although it acquires exactly the same quantity of motion. Hence the concept of natural inertia is redundant to explain the different effects of similar causes. This principle is repeated in a letter to Mersenne, December 25, 1639 (II, 627) and in a letter to an unknown correspondent in 1644 (V, 551). Despite the fact that the concept of inertia is not an independent explanatory concept for Descartes, he is still willing to accept the term 'natural inertia' to refer to the force with which a body resists an increase in its speed, even if this force of resistance is nothing else than the force transferred to the body in question when its speed is increased.

13   For the concept of *'determination'* see the very useful discussion of Pierre Costabel, in his 'Essai critique sur quelques concepts de la mécanique cartésienne', *Archives internationales d'histoire des sciences*, 20 (1967), 235–52, esp. pp. 236–40.

14   Descartes describes the resolution of this collision in a letter to Mersenne, October 28, 1640: 'I understand that this ball [*B*], making contact with the other [*C*], pushed it in front of itself in such a way that they moved together after collision' (III, 210).

15   See Descartes to Mersenne, October 28, 1640 for a similar resolution of the conditions to which R4 applies. (II, 211).

16   'Since many were complaining of the obscurity of these laws, the author supplies a little clarification and further explanation in the French edition of the *Principles*.' (Cottingham, p. 35).

17   P. Costabel, in the article cited above, suggests that the philosophical approach which includes the principle of least action in resolving incompatible motions is more profound than the mathematical attempt to express this insight in rules (p. 249). He goes on to say that the principle of conservation of motion is, in some sense, the result of inductively surveying what happens in different impact situations (p. 250). In other words, Descartes first elaborated the rules and then proposed the principle of

conservation as somehow warranted by the rules. I find this interpretation of Descartes difficult to reconcile with the texts, for two reasons: (*a*) how could Descartes have formulated the rules without being in possession of a conservation principle? In other words, how could one discover from such rules that the quantity of motion of a system is conserved? (*b*) Descartes mentions a conservation principle as early as 1629 and repeats it often in correspondence and later in *Le Monde*, as I have argued in Chapter 4. I would prefer to interpret the introduction of the principle of least action as Descartes' effort to come to terms with the concept of inertia; without some idea of when inertial forces resist motion and when they cede, Descartes could never have formulated the rules at all. And he could not give any quantitative estimate of the inertia of a body at rest without first deciding how much of its force a moving body could transfer to another at rest as a result of a collision.

18   See Descartes to Mersenne, February 23, 1643 (III, 634). On April 26th of the same year Descartes wrote to Mersenne: 'I add also that these balls must be perfectly hard; for if they are made of wood, or of some other elastic material, as are all those we find on earth, then . . . ' (III, 652).

19   Descartes to Debeaune (April 30, 1639): 'When a stone falls from a high altitude to the ground, if it does not rebound but is stopped instead, I believe that this results from the fact that it shakes the earth and thereby transfers its motion to the earth.' (II, 543).

20   In the letter to Clerselier already cited, Descartes included a similar qualification of what he meant by 'at rest':

by a body without motion I understand a body which is not in action to sepa-rate its surface from the surfaces of the other bodies which surround it and, consequently, which is part of another hard body which is larger. For I said in another place that when the surfaces of two bodies separate from each other, whatever is positive in the nature of motion is found as much in the body which is commonly said not to move at all as in the one which is thought to move; and I explained later why a body which is suspended in the air can be moved by the least force. (IV, 187).

21   I agree with the hypothetical interpretation of both the rules and the laws proposed by P. Costabel on p. 246 of the article already cited:

On a dit et redit que les règles cartésiennes du choc ne sont qu'une esquisse, mais on l'a fait en sous-entendant que les principes dont elles seraient l'esquisse étaient déja fermes dans la pensée de Descartes. La réalité nous paraît différente. Ces règles ne sont qu'une esquisse parce qu'elles sont l'expression d'une pensée en état de recherche.

List of references

Adam, Charles. 'Descartes: ses trois notions fondamentales', *Revue de philosophie de la France et de l'Étrangère*, **123** (1937), 1–14.

Agassi, Joseph. 'The nature of scientific problems and their roots in metaphysics', in *The Critical Approach to Science and Philosophy*, ed. Mario Bunge, pp. 189–211. New York: Free Press; London: Collier-Macmillan, 1964.

Aiton, E. J. 'The Cartesian theory of gravity', *Annals of Science*, **15** (1959), 27–50.

—*The Vortex Theory of Planetary Motions*. London: Macdonald, 1972.

Allard, Jean-Louis. *Le Mathématisme de Descartes*. Ottawa: Editions de l'Université d'Ottawa, 1963.

Alquié, Ferdinand. *La Découverte métaphysique de l'homme chez Descartes*, 2nd ed. Paris: Presses Universitaires de France, 1966.

Anderson, Wallace E. 'Cartesian motion', in *Motion and Time*, ed. P. Machamer & R. G. Turnbull, pp. 200–223. Columbus, Ohio: Ohio State University Press, 1976.

Armogathe, J. R. & Marion, J. L. *Index des Regulae ad directionem ingenii de René Descartes*. Rome: Edizioni dell' Ateneo, 1976.

Beck, L. J. *The Method of Descartes: A Study of the Regulae*. Oxford: Clarendon Press, 1952.

Bernard, Claude. *Introduction à l'étude de la médecine expérimentale*. Paris: Ballière et fils, 1865; Rpt. Brussels: Culture et Civilisation, 1965.

—*An Introduction to the Study of Experimental Medicine*, translated by Henry Copland Greene, with an Introduction by Lawrence J. Henderson. New York: Macmillan, 1927.

Birault, Henri. 'Science et métaphysique chez Descartes et chez Pascal', *Archives de philosophie*, **27** (1904), 483–526.

Blackwell, Richard J. 'Descartes' laws of motion', *Isis*, **57** (1966), 220–34.

Blake, Ralph M. 'The role of experience in Descartes' theory of method', *Philosophical Review*, **38** (1929), 125–43, 201–18. Reprinted in *Theories of Scientific Method*, ed. Edward Madden, pp. 75–103. Seattle: University of Washington Press, 1960.

Boas, Marie. 'The establishment of the mechanical philosophy', *Osiris*, **10** (1952), 412–541.

—*The Scientific Renaissance, 1450–1630*, vol. II of *The Rise of Modern Science*. London: Collins, 1962.

Bourassa, André. 'Descartes et la connaissance intuitive', *Dialogue*, **6** (1967–8), 539–54.

Boutroux, Pierre. *L'Imagination et les mathématiques selon Descartes*. Université de Paris, Bibliothèque de la Faculté des Lettres, No. 10. Paris: Alcan, 1900.

—'L'Algèbre cartésienne', in *L'Idéal scientifique des mathématiques*, New ed. Paris: Presses Universitaires de France, 1955.

Boyer, Carl B. *History of Analytic Geometry*. New York: Yeshiva University, Scripta Mathematica Series, 1956.

—*The Rainbow: From Myth to Mathematics*. New York and London: Thomas Yoseloff, 1959.

Bracken, Harry M. 'Innate ideas – then and now', *Dialogue*, **6** (1967–8), 334–46.

—'Chomsky's variations on a theme by Descartes', *Journal of the History of Philosophy*, **8** (1970), 181–92.

Braudel, Fernand (ed.). *L'Aventure de l'esprit*, vol. II of *Mélanges Alexandre Koyré*. Paris: Hermann, 1964.

Brunschvicg, Léon. 'Mathématique et métaphysique chez Descartes', *Revue de métaphysique et de morale*, **34** (1927), 277–324.

Buchdahl, Gerd. 'The relevance of Descartes' philosophy for modern philosophy of science', *British Journal for the History of Science*, **1** (1963), 227–49.

—'Descartes's anticipation of a "logic of scientific discovery"', in *Scientific Change*, ed. A. C. Crombie, pp. 399–417. London: Heinemann, 1963.

—*Metaphysics and the Philosophy of Science*. Oxford: Blackwell, 1969.

Bunge, Mario. *Scientific Research II. The Search for Truth*, vol. 3/II of *Studies in the Foundations; Methodology and Philosophy of Science*. New York: Springer-Verlag, 1967.

Burke, John G. 'Descartes on the refraction and the velocity of light', *American Journal of Physics*, **34** (1966), 390–400.

Burtt, E. A. *The Metaphysical Foundations of Modern Physical Science*, revised ed. Anchor Books: New York: Doubleday & Co., 1954.

Butler, R. J. (ed.). *Cartesian Studies*. Oxford: Blackwell, 1972.

Cahné, Pierre-Alain. *Index du Discours de la méthode de René Descartes*. Rome: Edizioni dell' Ateneo, 1977.

Carteron, H. 'L'Idée de la force mécanique dans le système de Descartes', *Revue philosophique*, **94** (1922), 243–77, 485–511.

Cassirer, Ernst. 'Mathematical mysticism and mathematical science', in *Galileo: Man of Science*, ed. Ernan McMullin, pp. 338–51. New York: Basic Books, 1967.

Caws, Peter. *The Philosophy of Science*. Princeton, New Jersey: Van Nostrand, 1965.

Chauvois, Louis. *William Harvey: His Life and Times; His Discoveries; His Methods.* London: Hutchinson; New York: Philosophical Library, 1957.

—*Descartes. sa méthode et ses erreurs en physiologie.* Paris: Les Editions du Cèdre, 1966.

Chisholm, Roderick M. *Perceiving. A Philosophical Study.* Ithaca, New York and London: Cornell University Press, 1957.

Chomsky, Noam. *Cartesian Linguistics.* New York and London: Harper & Row, 1966.

—'Recent contributions to the theory of innate ideas', in *Boston Studies in the Philosophy of Science,* ed. Robert S. Cohen & Marx W. Wartofsky, vol. III, pp. 81–90. Dordrecht: Reidel, 1967.

Collins, James. *Descartes' Philosophy of Nature.* Oxford: Blackwell, 1971.

Coolidge, Julian Lowell. *A History of Geometrical Methods.* Oxford: Clarendon Press, 1940.

Costabel, Pierre. 'Essai critique sur quelques concepts de la mécanique cartésienne', *Archives internationales d'histoire des sciences,* **20** (1967), 235–52.

—'Physique et métaphysique chez Descartes', in *Human Implications of Scientific Advance,* ed. E. G. Forbes, pp. 268–77. Edinburgh: Edinburgh University Press, 1978.

—'La Propagation de la lumière sans transport de matière de Descartes à Huygens', in *Roemer et la vitesse de la lumière,* pp. 83–91. Paris: Vrin, 1978.

Cotgrave, Randle. *A Dictionarie of the French and English Tongues.* Two Parts. London: Islip, 1632. Reproduced by University Microfilms Library Services, Ann Arbor, Michigan.

Cottingham, John. *Descartes' Conversation with Burman.* Oxford: Clarendon Press, 1976.

Crombie, A. C. *Robert Grosseteste and the Origins of Experimental Science, 1100–1700.* Oxford: Clarendon Press, 1953.

—'Descartes on method and physiology', *Cambridge Journal,* **5** (1951), 178–86.

—*Medieval and Early Modern Science.* 2 vols., 2nd ed. Anchor Books; New York: Doubleday & Co., 1958.

—'The mechanistic hypothesis and the scientific study of vision: some optical ideas as a background to the invention of the microscope', in *Historical Aspects of Microscopy,* ed. S. Bradbury & G. L'E. Turner, pp. 3–112. Cambridge: W. Heffer & Sons, 1967.

Dambska, Izydora. 'Sur certains principes méthodologiques dans les *Principia Philosophiae* de Descartes', *Revue de métaphysique et de morale,* **62** (1957), 57–66.

Debus, Allen G. *Man and Nature in the Renaissance.* Cambridge: Cambridge University Press, 1978.

Denissoff, Élie. *Descartes, premier théoricien de la physique mathématique.* Louvain: Publications Universitaires de Louvain; Paris: Béatrice–Nauwelaerts, 1970.

De Waard, C. 'Le Manuscrit perdu de Snellius sur la refraction', *Janus,* **39** (1935), 51–73.

Dictionnaire de l'Académie françoise, dedié au roy. 1st ed. Paris, 1694.

Dictionnaire de L'Académie Française. 6th ed. Paris: Firmin Didot Frères, 1835.

Dictionnaire Universel François et Latin, New ed., vol. I. Paris: Compagnie des Libraires Associés, 1771.

Dijksterhuis, E. J. 'La Méthode et les essais de *Descartes*', in *Descartes et le cartésianisme hollandais.* Paris: Presses Universitaires de France; Amsterdam: Editions françaises d'Amsterdam, 1950.

—*The Mechanization of the World Picture,* translated by C. Dikshoorn. London: Oxford University Press, 1969.

Dobzhansky, Theodosius. 'On Cartesian and Darwinian aspects of biology', in *Philosophy, Science and Method,* ed. Sidney Morgenbesser, *et al.,* pp. 165–78. New York: St. Martin's Press, 1969.

Doney, Willis, (ed.). *Descartes: A Collection of Critical Essays.* New York: Doubleday & Co., 1967.

—'Descartes's conception of perfect knowledge', *Journal of the History of Philosophy,* **8** (1970), 387–403.

Dreyfus-Le Foyer, H. 'Les Conceptions médicales de Descartes', *Revue de métaphysique et de morale,* **44** (1937), 237–86.

Dubarle, D. 'Remarques sur les règles du choc chez Descartes', *Cartesio* (supplement to *Rivista di Filosofia Neo-scolastico*), pp. 325–34. Milan: Vita e Pensiero, 1937.

Duhem, Pierre. *The Aim and Structure of Physical Theory,* translated by Philip P. Wiener. New York: Atheneum, 1962.

Feldman, Fred, & Levison, Arnold. 'Anthony Kenny and the Cartesian circle', *Journal of the History of Philosophy,* **9** (1971), 491–6.

Feyerabend, Paul. 'Attempt at a realistic interpretation of experience', *Proceedings of the Aristotelian Society,* New Series, **58** (1958), 143–70.

—'Explanation, reduction, and empiricism', *Minnesota Studies in the Philosophy of Science,* ed. Herbert Feigl & Grover Maxwell, vol. III, pp. 28–97. Minneapolis: University of Minnesota Press, 1962.

Firth, Roderick. 'The anatomy of certainty', *Philosophical Review,* **76** (1967), 3–27.

Foster, L. & Swanson, J. W., (eds.). *Experience and Theory.* London: Duckworth & Co., 1971.

Frankfurt, Harry. 'Memory and the Cartesian circle', *Philosophical Review,* **71** (1962), 504–11.

—'Descartes' validation of reason', in *Descartes: A Collection of Critical Essays,* ed. Willis Doney, pp. 209–26. New York: Doubleday & Co., 1967.

—*Demons, Dreamers, and Madmen: The Defense of Reason in Descartes's Meditations.* Indianapolis and New York: Bobbs–Merrill, 1970.

—'Descartes on the creation of the eternal truths', *Philosophical Review,* **86** (1977), 36–57.

238   *List of references*

Gabbey, Alan. 'Force and inertia in seventeenth-century dynamics, I', *Studies in the History and Philosophy of Science,* **2** (1971), 1–67.

Gadoffre, Gilbert. 'Sur la chronologie du *Discours de la méthode*', *Revue d'histoire de la philosophie et d'histoire générale de la civilisation,* **33** (1943), 45–70.

—'Réflexions sur la genèse du *Discours de la méthode*', *Revue de synthèse,* New Series **22** (1958), 11–27.

Gallois, P. 'La méthode de Descartes et la médecine', *Hippocrate,* **6** (1938), 65–77.

Gaukroger, Stephen, (ed.). *Descartes: Philosophy, Mathematics and Physics.* Hassocks, Sussex: Harvester Press, 1980.

George-Berthier, Auguste. 'Le mécanisme cartésien et la physiologie au XVIIe siècle', *Isis,* **2** (1914), 37–89; **3** (1920), 21–58.

Gewirtz, Alan. 'The Cartesian circle', *Philosophical Review,* **50** (1941), 368–95.

—'Experience and the non-mathematical in the Cartesian method', *Journal of the History of Ideas,* **2** (1941), 183–210.

Gewirth, Alan. 'Clearness and distinctness in Descartes', *Philosophy,* **18** (1943), 17–36. Reprinted in *Descartes: A Collection of Critical Essays,* ed. W. Doney, pp. 250–77. New York: Doubleday & Co., 1967.

—'The Cartesian circle reconsidered', *Journal of Philosophy,* **67** (1970), 668–85.

—'Descartes: two disputed questions', *Journal of Philosophy,* **68** (1971), 288–96.

Gilbert, Neal Ward. *Renaissance Concepts of Method.* New York and London: Columbia University Press, 1960.

Gilson, Étienne. *Index scolastico-cartésien.* Paris: 1912. Reprinted by Franklin, Bibliography and Reference Series, No. 57. New York: Franklin, 1963.

—*Discours de la méthode: Texte et commentaire.* 2nd ed. Paris: Vrin, 1947.

—*Études sur le rôle de la pensée médiévale dans la formation du système cartésien,* vol. XIII of *Études de philosophie mediévale.* Paris: Vrin, 1930.

Golliet, P. 'Le problème de la méthode chez Descartes', *Revue des sciences humaines,* **61** (1951), 56–73.

Gouhier, Henri. *Essais sur Descartes.* Paris: Vrin, 1937.

—'Pour une histoire des *Méditations métaphysiques*', *Revue des sciences humaines,* **61** (1951), 5–29.

—*Les Premières Pensées de Descartes.* Paris: Vrin, 1958.

Grünbaum, Adolf. 'Can we ascertain the falsity of a scientific hypothesis?', in *Observation and Theory in Science,* by E. Nagel *et al.,* pp. 69–129. Baltimore: Johns Hopkins University Press, 1971.

Gueroult, Martial. *Descartes selon l'ordre des raisons.* 2 vols. Paris: Aubier, 1953.

—'Métaphysique et physique de la force chez Descartes et chez Malebranche', *Revue de métaphysique et de morale,* **59** (1954), 1–37, 113–34.

Hacking, Ian. *Leibniz and Descartes: Proof and Eternal Truths*, Dawes Hicks Lecture on Philosophy, British Academy. London: Oxford University Press, 1973.

Hall, T. S. 'Microbiomechanics', in *Ideas of Life and Matter*, vol. I, pp. 250–63. Chicago: University of Chicago Press, 1969.

—'Descartes' physiological method: position, principles, examples', *Journal of the History of Biology*, 3 (1970), 53–79.

—*Treatise of Man of René Descartes*. Cambridge, Mass.: Harvard University Press, 1972.

Hanson, Norwood Russell. *Patterns of Discovery*. Cambridge: Cambridge University Press, 1969.

—*Observation and Explanation*. Harper Torchbooks; New York: Harper & Row, 1971.

Hart, Alan. 'Descartes' "notions"', *Philosophy and Phenomenological Research*, 31 (1970–71), 114–22.

Hartland-Swann, John. 'Descartes' "simple natures"', *Philosophy*, 22 (1947), 139–52.

Harvey, William. *Exercitatio Anatomica de Motu Cordis et Sanguinis in Animalibus*, 3rd ed., translated, with annotations, by Chauncey D. Leake. Springfield, Ill.: Charles Thomas, 1941.

—*The Circulation of the Blood; Two Anatomical Essays Together With Nine Letters*, translated from the Latin by Kenneth J. Franklin. Oxford: Blackwell, 1958.

Hatfield, Gary C. 'Force (God) in Descartes' physics', *Studies in History and Philosophy of Science*, 10 (1979), 113–40.

Hempel, Carl G. *Fundamentals of Concept Formation in Empirical Science*, vol. II, No. 7 of *International Encyclopedia of Unified Science*. Chicago: University of Chicago Press, 1952.

Hesse, Mary. *Forces & Fields*. Edinburgh: Nelson, 1961.

—*Models and Analogies in Science*. Notre Dame, Indiana: University of Notre Dame Press, 1966.

Hintikka, J. 'A discourse on Descartes' method', in *Descartes: Critical and Interpretive Essays*, ed. M. Hooker, pp. 74–88. Baltimore: Johns Hopkins University Press, 1978.

—& Remes, U. *The Method of Analysis*. Dordrecht: Reidel, 1974.

Hinton, J. M. *Experiences: An Inquiry into Some Ambiguities*. Oxford: Clarendon Press, 1973.

Hooker, Michael, (ed.). *Descartes: Critical and Interpretive Essays*. Baltimore: Johns Hopkins University Press, 1978.

Hübner, K. 'Descartes' rules of impact and their criticism', *Boston Studies in Philosophy of Science*, vol. 39. ed. R. S. Cohen, *et al.*, pp. 229–310. Dordrecht, Holland: Reidel, 1976

Jammer, Max. *Concepts of Mass in Classical and Modern Physics*. Cambridge, Mass.: Harvard University Press, 1961.

Jardine, Lisa. *Francis Bacon: Discovery and the Art of Discourse*. Cambridge: Cambridge University Press, 1974.

Keeling, S. V. 'Le Réalisme de Descartes et le rôle des natures simples', *Revue de métaphysique et de morale*, **44** (1937), 63–99.

Kemp Smith, Norman. *New Studies in the Philosophy of Descartes*. London: Macmillan, 1966.

Kennington, Richard. 'The "teaching of nature" in Descartes' soul doctrine', *Review of Metaphysics*, **26** (1972), 86–117.

Kenny, Anthony. *Descartes: A Study of his Philosophy*. New York: Random House, 1968.

—'The Cartesian circle and the eternal truths', *Journal of Philosophy*, **67** (1970), 685–700.

—'Descartes on the will', in A. Kenny, *The Anatomy of the Soul*, pp. 81–112. Oxford: Blackwell, 1973.

Knudsen, O. & Pederson, K. M. 'The link between "determination" and conservation of motion in Descartes' dynamics'. *Centaurus*, **13** (1968), 183–6.

Körner, Stephan. *Experience and Theory*. London: Routledge & Kegan Paul; New York: Humanities Press, 1966.

Kordig, Karl R. 'The theory-ladenness of observation', *Review of Metaphysics*, **24** (1971), 448–84.

Korteweg, D. J. 'Descartes et les manuscrits de Snellius', *Revue de métaphysique et de morale*, **4** (1896), 489–501.

Kuhn, Thomas S. *The Copernican Revolution*. New York: Vintage Books, 1959.

—*The Structure of Scientific Revolutions*, 2nd ed. Chicago: University of Chicago Press, 1970.

Lalande, André. *Vocabulaire technique et critique de la philosophie*. 4th ed. Paris: Alcan, 1932.

Laporte, Jean. *Le Rationalisme de Descartes*. Paris: Presses Universitaires de France, 1954.

Laudan, Laurens. 'The clock metaphor and probabilism: the impact of Descartes on English methodological thought, 1650–65', *Annals of Science*, **22** (1966), 73–104.

Lewis, Geneviève. *L'Individualité selon Descartes*. Paris: Vrin, 1950.

Liard, Louis. *Descartes*. Paris: Librairie Ballière, 1882.

Lindsay, Robert Bruce & Margenau, Henry. *Foundations of Physics*, 2nd ed. New York: Dover, 1957.

Machamer, Peter & Turnbull, R. G. (eds.). *Motion and Time, Space and Matter. Interrelations in the History of Philosophy and Science*. Columbus, Ohio: Ohio State University Press, 1976.

McMullin, Ernan. 'Empiricism and the scientific revolution', in *Art, Science and History in the Renaissance*, ed. Charles S. Singleton, pp. 331–69. Baltimore: Johns Hopkins Press, 1968.

—(ed.). *Galileo: Man of Science*. New York: Basic Books, 1967.

—'Philosophies of Nature', *New Scholasticism*, **43** (1968), 29–74.

—'The conception of science in Galileo's work', in *New Perspectives on Galileo*, ed. R. E. Butts & J. C. Pitt, pp. 209–57. Dordrecht: Reidel, 1978.

McRae, Robert. 'Innate ideas', in *Cartesian Studies,* ed. R. J. Butler, pp. 32–54. Oxford: Blackwell, 1972.

Madden, Edward M., (ed.). *Theories of Scientific Method.* Seattle: University of Washington Press, 1960.

Marion, Jean-Luc. *Sur l'ontologie grise de Descartes.* Paris: Vrin, 1975.

—(ed.). *Règles Utiles et claires pour la direction de l'esprit en la recherche de la vérité.* Hague: Nijhoff, 1977.

Martinet, M. 'Science et hypothèses chez Descartes', *Archives internationales d'histoire des sciences,* 24 (1974), 319–39.

—'La théorie de la lumière selon Descartes', *Recherches sur le xviie siècle,* 1 (1976), 92–110.

—'Apologie de la briève description des principaux phénomènes', *Recherches sur le xviie siècle,* 2 (1978), 32–44.

Maull, Nancy. 'Cartesian optics and the geometrization of nature', *Review of Metaphysics,* 32 (1978), 253–73.

Maxwell, N. 'The rationality of scientific discovery', *Philosophy of Science,* 41 (1974), 123–53, 247–95.

Mendelsohn, Everett. 'The changing nature of physiological explanation in the seventeenth century', *L'Aventure de la science,* vol. I of *Mélanges Alexandre Koyré,* ed. F. Braudel, pp. 367–86. Paris: Hermann, 1964.

Mercier, Jeanne. 'Expérience Humaine et philosophie cartésienne', in *Cartesio* (supplement to *Rivista di Filosofia Neo-scolastico*), pp. 581–98. Milan: Vita e Pensiero, 1937.

Mesnard, P. 'L'Esprit de la physiologie cartésienne', *Archives de philosophie,* 13 (1937), 181–220.

Milhaud, Gaston. *Descartes savant.* Paris: Alcan, 1921.

Miller, Leonard G. 'Descartes, mathematics, and God', in *Meta-Meditations: Studies in Descartes,* ed. A. Sesonske & N. Fleming, pp. 37–49. Belmont, California: Wadsworth, 1965.

Morgenbesser, Sidney; Suppes, Patrick & White, Morton, (eds.). *Philosophy, Science and Method, Essays in Honour of Ernest Nagel.* New York: St Martin's Press, 1969.

Morris, John. 'Cartesian certainty', *Australasian Journal of Philosophy,* 47 (1969), 161–8.

—'Descartes and probable knowledge', *Journal of the History of Philosophy,* 8 (1970), 303–12.

—(ed. and trans.). *Descartes Dictionary.* New York: Philosophical Library, 1971.

Mougin, Henri. 'L'Esprit Encyclopédique et la tradition philosophique française', *Pensée,* 5 (1945), 8–18; 6 (1946), 25–38; 7 (1946), 65–74.

Nagel, Ernest. *The Structure of Science.* London: Routledge & Kegan Paul, 1968.

— Bromberger, Sylvain & Grünbaum, Adolf. *Observation and Theory in Science.* Baltimore: Johns Hopkins University Press, 1971.

Nash, Leonard K. *The Nature of the Natural Sciences.* Boston and Toronto: Little, Brown and Co., 1963.

Newton, Isaac. *Philosophiae Naturalis Principia Mathematica*. 3rd ed. London: William & John Innys, 1726. Rpt. Glasgow, 1871.
— *Opticks*. New York: Dover Books, 1952.
Nicot, Jean. *Le grand dictionaire françois–latin*. Paris, 1605.

Ockenden, R. E. 'Marco Antonio de Dominis and his explanation of the rainbow', *Isis*, **26** (1936), 40–49.
Olscamp, Paul J. 'Introduction' to *Descartes: Discourse on Method, Optics, Geometry, and Meteorology*. Indianapolis: Bobbs-Merrill, 1965.

Passmore, J. A. 'William Harvey and the philosophy of science', *Australasian Journal of Philosophy*, **36** (1958), 85–94.
Pirenne, M. H. 'Descartes and the body–mind problem in physiology', *British Journal for the Philosophy of Science*, **1** (1950), 43–59.
Popkin, Richard H. *The History of Scepticism from Erasmus to Descartes*. Revised ed. Assen: Van Gorcum, 1960.
Popper, Karl. *The Logic of Scientific Discovery*. Revised ed. London: Hutchinson, 1968.
Prendergast, Thomas L. 'Descartes and the relativity of motion', *The Modern Schoolman*, **50** (1972), 64–72.
— 'Motions, actions and tendency in Descartes' physics', *Journal of the History of Philosophy*, **13** (1975), 453–62.
Price, H. H. *Thinking and Experience*. 2nd ed. London: Hutchinson, 1969.

Quine, W. V. O. 'Two dogmas of empiricism', in *From a Logical Point of View*. 2nd ed. pp. 20–46. Cambridge, Mass.: Harvard University Press, 1964.
— 'Grades of theoreticity', in *Experience and Theory*, ed. L. Foster & J. W. Swanson, pp. 1–17. London: Duckworth & Co., 1971.

Randall, John Herman, Jr. 'The development of scientific method in the school of Padua', *Journal of the History of Ideas*, **1** (1940), 177–206.
— *The Career of Philosophy*, Vol. I. New York and London: Columbia University Press, 1962.
Régis, Pierre-Sylvain. *L'Usage de la raison et de la foy, ou l'accord de la foy et de la raison*. Paris: Jean Cusson, 1704.
— *Cours entier de philosophie ou systeme generale selon les Principes de M. Descartes contenant la logique, la metaphysique, la physique, et la morale*, final ed., 3 vols. Amsterdam: Huguetan, 1691.
Rescher, Nicholas. 'A new look at the problem of innate ideas', *British Journal for the Philosophy of Science*, **17** (1966–7), 205–18.
Rodis-Lewis, Geneviève. *Descartes et le rationalisme*, 2nd ed. Paris: Presses Universitaires de France, 1970.
Rostand, Jean. 'Descartes et la biologie', *L'Atomisme en biologie*, 11th ed. Paris: Gallimard, 1956.
Roth, Leon. *Descartes' Discourse on Method*. Oxford: Clarendon Press, 1937.

List of references 243

—'The Discourse of Method (1637–1937)', Mind, 46 (1937), 32–43.

Sabra, Abdelhamid I. Theories of Light from Descartes to Newton. London: Oldbourne, 1967.

Salmon, Elizabeth G. 'Mathematical roots of Cartesian metaphysics', New Scholasticism, 39 (1965), 158–69.

Scheffler, Israel. Science and Subjectivity. Indianapolis and New York: Bobbs–Merrill, 1967.

Schmitt, C. B. 'Experimental evidence for and against a void: the sixteenth century arguments', Isis, 58 (1967), 352–66.

—'Experience and experiment: a comparison of Zabarella's view with Galileo's in De Motu', Studies in the Renaissance, 16 (1969), 80–138.

Schouls, Peter A. 'Cartesian certainty and the "natural light"', Australasian Journal of Philosophy, 48 (1970), 116–19.

—'Reason, method and science in the philosophy of Descartes', Australasian Journal of Philosophy, 50 (1972), 30–39.

Schrecker, Paul. 'La méthode cartésienne et la logique', Revue de philosophie de la France et de l'étrangère, 123 (1937), 336–67.

Scott, J. F. The Scientific Work of René Descartes (1596–1650). London: Taylor & Francis, 1952.

Scott, Wilson L. 'The significance of "hard bodies" in the history of scientific thought', Isis, 50 (1959), 199–210.

Sebba, Gregor. Bibliographia Cartesiana. A Critical Guide to the Descartes Literature, 1800–1960. The Hague: Nijhoff, 1964.

Segond, J. La Sagesse cartésienne et la doctrine de la science. Paris: Vrin, 1932.

Sellars, Wilfrid. Philosophical Perspectives. Springfield Ill.: C. Thomas, 1967.

—Science, Perception and Reality. London: Routledge & Kegan Paul; New York, Humanities Press, 1963.

—Science and Metaphysics. London: Routledge & Kegan Paul; New York: Humanities Press, 1968.

Sesonske, A. and Fleming, N. (eds.). Meta-Meditations: Studies in Descartes. Belmont, California: Wadsworth, 1965.

Shea, William R. 'Descartes as critic of Galileo', in New Perspectives on Galileo, ed. R. E. Butts and J. C. Pitt, pp. 139–59. Dordrecht: Reidel, 1978.

Shirley, John W. 'An early experimental determination of Snell's law', American Journal of Physics, 19 (1951), 507–8.

Sirven, J. 'La Déduction cartésienne dans les recherches mathématiques et physiques', Cartesio (supplement to Rivista di Filosofia Neo-scolastico) pp. 747–51. Milan: Vita e Pensiero, 1937.

Sklar, Lawrence. 'Inertia, gravitation and metaphysics', Philosophy of Science, 43 (1976), 1–23.

Spector, Marshall. 'Leibniz vs. the Cartesians on motion and force', Studia Leibnitiana, 7 (1975), 135–44.

Stich, Stephen P. (ed.). Innate Ideas. Los Angeles: University of California Press, 1975.

Stock, Hyman. The Method of Descartes in the Natural Sciences. Jamaica, New York: Marion Press, 1931.

Strong, Edward William. *Procedures and Metaphysics*. Berkeley: University of California Press, 1936.
—'The relationship between metaphysics and scientific method in Galileo's work', in *Galileo: Man of Science*, ed. E. McMullin, pp. 352–64. New York: Basic Books, 1967.

Tannery, Paul. 'Descartes physicien', *Revue de métaphysique et de morale*, **4** (1896), 478–88.

Unger, Peter. *Ignorance: A Case for Scepticism*. Oxford: Clarendon Press, 1975.

Vendler, Zeno. *Res Cogitans: An Essay in Rational Psychology*. Ithaca and London: Cornell University Press, 1972.
Volgraff, J. A. 'Snellius' notes on the reflection and refraction of rays', *Osiris*, **1** (1936), 718–25.
Vuillemin, Jules. *Mathématiques et métaphysique chez Descartes*. Paris: Presses Universitaires de France, 1960.

Wahl, Jean. *Du role de l'idée de l'instant dans la philosophie de Descartes*. Paris: Vrin, 1953.
Wartofsky, Marx W. *Conceptual Foundations of Scientific Thought*. New York: Macmillan; London: Collier-Macmillan, 1968.
Watkins, J. W. N. 'Metaphysics and the advancement of science', *British Journal for the Philosophy of Science*, **26** (1975), 91–121.
Weber, J.-P. 'Sur une certaine "méthodologie officieuse" chez Descartes', *Revue de métaphysique et de morale*, **63** (1958), 246–50.
Westfall, Richard S. *The Construction of Modern Science: Mechanisms and Mechanics*. New York: John Wiley & Sons, 1971.
—*Force in Newton's Physics*. London: Macdonald; New York: American Elsevier, 1971.
Whitteridge, Gweneth. *William Harvey and the Circulation of the Blood*. London: Macdonald; New York: American Elsevier, 1971.
Williams, Bernard. *Descartes: The Project of Pure Inquiry*. Harmondsworth: Penguin, 1978.
Wilson, Margaret D. *Descartes*. London: Routledge & Kegan Paul, 1978.
Wittgenstein, L. *Notebooks 1914–16*, ed. G. H. von Wright & G. E. M. Anscombe. Oxford: Blackwell, 1961.
—*Tractatus Logico-Philosophicus*, trans. D. F. Pears & B. F. McGuinness. London: Routledge & Kegan Paul, 1961.

Index